Daniel Waterland

A Critical History of the Athanasian Creed

Representing the opinions of antients and moderns concerning it

Daniel Waterland

A Critical History of the Athanasian Creed
Representing the opinions of antients and moderns concerning it

ISBN/EAN: 9783744755429

Printed in Europe, USA, Canada, Australia, Japan

Cover: Foto ©ninafisch / pixelio.de

More available books at **www.hansebooks.com**

A CRITICAL HISTORY

OF THE

ATHANASIAN CREED.

BY

DANIEL WATERLAND, D.D.

FORMERLY MASTER OF MAGDALEN COLLEGE, CAMBRIDGE; CANON
OF WINDSOR; AND ARCHDEACON OF MIDDLESEX.

A New Edition,

REVISED AND CORRECTED BY THE

REV. J. R. KING, M.A.

LATE FELLOW AND TUTOR OF MERTON COLLEGE, OXFORD.

Oxford and London:
JAMES PARKER AND CO.
1870.

EDITOR'S PREFACE.

THE "Critical History of the Athanasian Creed" had its origin in Dr. Waterland's controversy with Dr. Clarke, and other Anti-Trinitarians, on the subject of the blessed Trinity. First published in 1723, in the interval between his "Second Vindication of Christ's Divinity," and his "Farther Vindication," both of them directly controversial works, it yet is singularly free from polemics; and it is only in the last chapter that he thinks it well to answer the objections of Dr. Clarke, who "out of his abundant zeal to promote Arianism had taken upon him to disparage this excellent Form of Faith."

After an Introduction, in which the Author explains the scope and method of the work, disclaiming any pretence at originality, and declaring that it professes to be nothing more than a careful digest, in a form convenient for the English reader, of all that he had been able to discover written on the subject, the treatise is divided into eleven chapters, of which eight are concerned with the history of the Creed, and the remaining three with its substance, and its use in the Church of England.

The first chapter sets forth the opinions of the chief modern authorities as to the date and authorship of the Creed, beginning with Gerard Voss, who published his treatise, *De tribus Symbolis*, in 1642, and ending with Casimir Oudin, whose Commentary on the Ecclesiastical Writers appeared in its final form in 1722. The great majority of the thirty-two authors whom he cites are agreed that the Creed is not the work of Athanasius; and most of them would assign to it an origin in the Western Church, not earlier than the fifth century. Eight of them ascribe it to Vigilius Tapsensis, whilst no two are agreed in upholding the claims of any other Latin writer to its authorship. Dr. Clarke is alone in bringing it down to so late a period as the eighth or ninth century, though Voss and Dr. Cave agree with him in supposing it not to have been generally received till about the year 1000.

In the second chapter, Dr. Waterland considers the testimony of more ancient writers to the existence and authority of the Creed. Rejecting the evidence adduced from writers earlier than the seventh century as spurious or irrelevant, he attaches some importance to that afforded by a Canon which is attributed to the Synod of Autun, in 670. The first unquestionable testimony, however, is supplied in certain articles of enquiry, preserved by Rhegino, Abbot of Prom in Germany, and referable to the middle of the eighth century. Thenceforward quotations from the Creed are not uncommon, though the title *Symbolum* is not applied to it by any author before Hincmar, Archbishop of Rheims in the middle of the ninth century, and the appellation was not generally in use for some three centuries more. Dr. Waterland quotes in all thirty-six authorities in this chapter, ending with Johannes Plusiadenus, in 1439. Most of them ascribe the Creed to Athanasius, and none to any other author, though Beleth mentions as a common view the theory that it was written by Anastasius.

The third chapter is taken up with the consideration of the ancient commentators on the Athanasian Creed, beginning with Venantius Fortunatus in the sixth, and ending with Peter d'Osma of Salamanca, in the fifteenth century. The first of these is the most important, proving the existence of the Creed at an earlier period than any other evidence which we possess: insomuch that Muratori erroneously supposed Fortunatus to have been himself the author.

The fourth chapter contains an account of the various manuscripts of the Athanasian Creed which Dr. Waterland could trace. The earliest of these is quoted by Bishop Usher as belonging to the end of the sixth century; but this, as well as the Manuscript of Tréves, referred to the middle of the seventh century, was already lost in the time of Dr. Waterland; so that the earliest manuscript then known to exist was that in the Ambrosian Library at Milan, belonging to the end of the seventh century. Between that time and the end of the eleventh century, twenty-two manuscripts are described, most of them being attached to Psalters, mainly of the Gallican version. This chapter closes with an account of the principal Latin versions of the Psalter, severally known as the Italic, Gallican, Roman, and Hebraic.

The fifth chapter is occupied with a discussion of the ancient versions of the Creed, among which, adopting the view that Latin was its original language, Dr. Waterland includes the Greek manuscripts. The correctness of this opinion is confirmed by the fact that these do not rank early even among the versions; no copy being known of a date previous to the middle of the fourteenth century. The earliest version of which any trace is to be found was in the *Lingua Romana*, prevalent in France in the middle of the ninth century: but the earliest extant is in German, in the Imperial Library at Vienna, and is referred by Dr. Waterland to the year 870. Of the following century there are Anglo-Saxon versions, but none of those in French, properly so called, reach higher than the eleventh century. Of the date of the versions in other languages, Dr. Waterland had no information on which it was possible to form an estimate.

From the foregoing evidence, Dr. Waterland argues, in the sixth chapter, that the Creed was received into the Gallican Church as early as the middle of the sixth century. That it was known in Spain within a century after this is clear, from its being quoted in the Canons of the Fourth Council of Toledo, held in 633; and the general affinity between the French and Spanish Liturgies would lead us to suppose that it probably then formed a recognised element in the Spanish services. In Germany it was certainly received in 787, perhaps some years before: while in England we can trace it as early as 799, when considerable portions of it were quoted in a profession of faith made by Denebert, Bishop of Worcester. The date of its reception in Italy is very doubtful, and though inclined to trace it to the conquest of Lombardy by Charlemagne, yet Dr. Waterland does not venture to insist on an earlier date than 880 for its regular introduction into the Italian Liturgies. The Roman Church was the last to adopt it among the Western Christians; and we cannot prove that it was admitted into any Roman Liturgy earlier than the Psalter of King Athelstan in 930. The fact of its admission into the Greek and Oriental Churches has been questioned altogether, but it appears probable, that, though unknown to the Greek Churches in Africa and Asia, yet that it had, for some little time, been accepted by the main body of the Greeks in Europe, with alterations in the Article concerning the Procession of the Holy Ghost.

From a consideration of all this evidence Dr. Waterland concludes, in the seventh chapter, that the Athanasian Creed was probably composed in Gaul: and as it was in sufficient repute for a Comment to be written on it about the year 570, it may fairly be presumed to be from a century to a century and a-half more ancient than that date. But, from internal evidence, he conceives that we can fix the time of its composition with much greater nicety. It is obviously later than the rise of the heresy of Apollinarius, from the precision with which his tenets are refuted on the subject of the Incarnation; and it is most probably subsequent to the publication of St. Augustine's work, *De Trinitate*, from the use of expressions first worked out in that treatise. This would bring it down to the year 420, nearly fifty years after Athanasius's death. On the other hand, the absence of any direct refutation of Eutyches, and even the admission of equivocal expressions which might be interpreted as favouring his views, would mark the Creed as earlier than his condemnation at Chalcedon in 451. Similarly, its language seems to place it even before the condemnation of Nestorius at Ephesus in 431; so that its composition is brought within the compass of the ten years between 420 and 430; and as we know that St. Augustine, whose writings had manifestly an important influence upon it, was in close communication with the Church in Gaul during the latter half of this decade, we may ultimately fix its date, with great probability, to that time.

After determining the time and place of the composition of the Creed, Dr. Waterland proceeds, in the eighth chapter, to determine the question of its authorship. This he decides in favour of Hilary of Arles, as best fulfilling the requisite conditions of time, place, capacity, and authority in the Church. He is also known to have been an admirer of St. Augustine; and is said to have written an "admirable exposition of the Creed," of which we have no trace, unless we hold it to be the work in question. The style, moreover, and tenor of his other writings, favour the hypothesis, which is not overthrown by the only objections which have been advanced against it.

The ninth chapter consists simply of the Creed itself, in the original Latin text, supported by passages from authorities of the fourth and fifth centuries, mainly from the works of St. Augustine. To this has been added, in the present edition, an Appendix, comprising passages from the earlier Fathers, setting forth the same doctrines that are stated in the Creed.

The tenth chapter contains Dr. Waterland's own commentary on the Creed, in which he briefly shews the origin, scope, and meaning of each several Article. He explains the damnatory clauses in the moderate sense in which they were accepted even by the leading Nonconformist Divines of his own day; and is particularly felicitous in his exposition of that portion of the Creed which declares each Person of the blessed Trinity to be *incomprehensible, eternal, &c.*, and yet the whole to be not *Three*, but *One*.

So far the treatise has been purely didactic, but in the eleventh chapter it assumes a controversial form, being occupied with the refutation of the objections brought by Dr. Clarke to its use in our services. In the course of his reply, Dr. Waterland takes occasion to set forth the necessity of Creeds in general, and especially the need of gradually expanding the confessions of our faith, to meet the errors gradually introduced into the world.

At the end of the whole treatise he reprints the work of Venantius Fortunatus, already referred to as the earliest commentary on the Athanasian Creed.

The present edition is based upon the second, published by the author in 1727. The treatise has been previously reprinted in the several editions of the collected works of Dr. Waterland; and in a separate form in 1850 by the Society for Promoting Christian Knowledge. The references have now, so far as possible, been verified and rendered more complete; and besides the Appendix to the ninth chapter, a list of the editions used for reference is added by the present editor. Obsolete and antiquated modes of spelling have been modernized, but in other respects the work is reproduced as it issued finally from its Author's hands.

St. Peter's-in-the-East, Oxford,
June 24th, 1870.

A CRITICAL HISTORY

OF THE

ATHANASIAN CREED.

REPRESENTING THE OPINIONS OF

ANTIENTS and MODERNS
CONCERNING IT:

With an Account of the MANUSCRIPTS, VERSIONS, *and* COMMENTS, *and such other particulars as are of moment for the determining the* Age, *and* Author, *and* Value *of it, and the Time of its* Reception *in the Christian Churches.*

By *DANIEL WATERLAND*, D.D.

CHANCELLOR *of the* CHURCH *of* YORK, *and Chaplain in Ordinary to His MAJESTY.*

THE SECOND EDITION
Corrected and Improv'd.

CAMBRIDGE:
Printed at the UNIVERSITY-PRESS, for CORN. CROWNFIELD, Printer to the UNIVERSITY: And are to be Sold by J. KNAPTON, and R. KNAPLOCK, Booksellers in *LONDON.* 1728.

TO HIS GRACE

WILLIAM,

LORD ARCHBISHOP OF YORK,

PRIMATE OF ENGLAND AND METROPOLITAN.

My Lord,

I AM desirous of sending these papers abroad under your Grace's name, in confidence you will be a Patron to them, as you have been to the Author. I would make their way short and easy to the publick esteem, by introducing them first into your Grace's acquaintance and good opinion; which, if they have once the honour to obtain, I may then be assured that they will be both useful to the world and acceptable with all good men; the height of my ambition.

The subject, my Lord, is the Athanasian Creed, the most accurate system of the Athanasian, that is, the Christian Faith, of which your Grace is, by your station and character, by duty and office, and, what is more, by inclination and principle, and real services, the watchful guardian and preserver.

The happy fruits of it are visible in the slow and inconsiderable progress that the new heresy has been able to make within your province, where it died, in a manner, as it first arose, and no sooner began to lift up its head but sunk down again in shame and confusion: as if the plenty of good seed sown had left no room for tares, or they could take no root in a soil so well cultivated.

While your Grace is promoting the honour and interests of our Holy Faith, in the eminent way, by the wisdom of your counsels, the authority of your precepts, and the brightness of your high example; I am endeavouring, in such a way as I can, to contribute something to the same common cause, tho' it be but slight and small, tho' it be only reviewing the fences and surveying the outworks; which is the most I pretend to in the history here presented.

What advantage others may reap from the publication will remain in suspence; but I am sure of one to myself (and I lay hold of it with a great deal of pleasure) the opportunity I thereby have of returning my publick thanks to your Grace for your publick favors. Tho' this, my Lord, is but a scanty expression for them, and far short, where the engaging manner and circumstances, known but to few, and not to be understood by many, make so considerable an addition in the whole, and almost double the obligation upon

My LORD,

Your Grace's most obliged, most dutiful,

and most obedient humble Servant,

DANIEL WATERLAND.

CAMBRIDGE, MAGD. COLL.,
Oct. 25, 1723.

THE AUTHOR'S PREFACE.

WHAT I here present the reader with, will not require much Preface. The Introduction intimates the design and use and partition of the Work. The Appendix, which is an additional enlargement beyond my first design, gives account of itself. I subjoin two Indexes for the ease and convenience of such persons as may be disposed, not only to read these sheets, but to study the subject. I should scarce have thought of making Indexes to so small a treatise, had I not found the like in Tentzelius, upon the same subject, and to a smaller tract than this is. His were of considerable use to me, as often as I wanted to review any particular author, or passage, or to compare distant parts relating to the same things, one with another. The benefit, therefore, which I reaped from his labours, I am willing to pay back to the public by mine.

As to the subject of the following sheets, I make no question of its well deserving the thoughts and consideration of every studious reader; having before passed through the hands of many the most learned and most judicious men, and such as would not misemploy their time and pains upon a trifle. As to the present management of it, it must be left to the reader to judge of, as he sees cause.

For the chronology of the several parts, I have consulted the best authors; endeavouring to fix it with as much accuracy as I could. Wherever I could certainly determine the age of any tract, printed or manuscript, to a year, I set down that year: where I could not do it (as in manuscripts one seldom can) I take any probable year within the compass of time when an author is known to have flourished; or for a manuscript, any probable year within such a century or such a king's reign wherein the manuscript is reasonably judged to have been written; and I generally choose a round number, rather than otherwise, in such indefinite cases and instances.

Thus, for example, first in respect of authors: there is a Comment of Venantius Fortunatus, upon the Athanasian Creed, which I reprint in my Appendix. I cannot fix the age of it to a year, no, nor to twenty years. All that is certain is, that it was made between 556, when Fortunatus first went into the Gallican parts, and 599 when he was advanced to the bishopric of Poictiers. Within this wide compass, I choose the year 570. If any one shall rather choose 580, or 590, I shall not dispute it with him, nor doth anything very material depend upon it: but if any good reason can be given for taking some other year rather than 570, I shall immediately acquiesce in it.

As to manuscripts, it is well known there is no fixing them precisely to a year, merely from the hand or character: and there are but few, in comparison, that carry their own certain dates with them. The best judges, therefore, in these matters, will think it sufficient to point out the king's reign, or sometimes the century, wherein a manuscript was written: and in the very ancient ones, above a thousand years old, they will hardly be positive so much as to the century, for want of certain discriminating marks between manuscripts of the fifth, sixth, and seventh centuries.

It may be asked, then, why I pretend to fix the several manuscripts, hereafter to be mentioned, to certain years in the margin; those that carry no certain dates, as well as the others that do? I do it for order and regularity, and for the more distinct perception of things, which is much promoted and assisted by this orderly ranging them according to years. At the same time, the intelligent reader will easily understand where to take a thing as certain, and where to make allowances. It is something like the placing of cities, towns, rivers, &c., in a map or a globe: they have all their certain places there, in such or such precise degrees of longitude and latitude; which perhaps seldom answer to the strict truth of things or to a mathematical exactness. But still it serves the purpose very near as well as if everything had been adjusted with the utmost nicety; and the imagination and memory are mightily relieved by it. Thus much I thought proper to hint in vindication of my method, and to prevent any deception on one hand, or misconstruction on the other. I have, I think, upon the whole, generally gone upon the fairest and most probable presumption, and according to the most correct accounts of knowing and accurate men: but if I have anywhere, through inadvertency, or for want of better information, happened to mistake in any material part, the best way of apologizing for it, will be to correct it the first opportunity after notice of it.

As to mere omissions, they will appear more, or fewer, according to men's different judgments, or opi-

b

nions what to call an omission. I might have enlarged considerably the first chapter, which treats of the learned moderns, though some, perhaps, will think it too large already, and that it might better have been contracted. I have omitted several moderns mentioned by Tentzelius, whose professed design was to take in all; mine is only to take the principal or as many as may suffice to give the reader a full and distinct idea how this matter has stood with the learned moderns for eighty-five years last past.

In this second edition I have considerably shortened my Appendix, by throwing the several parts of it into the book itself, referring them to their proper places. Some few additional observations will be found here and there interspersed, and some corrections, of slight moment as to the main thing (in which I make no alteration) but contributing in some measure to the perfection and accuracy of the Work.

I conclude with professing, as before, that I shall be very glad if what hath been here done may but prove an useful introduction to more and larger discoveries. If anything considerable still remains, either in private hands or public repositories; anything that may be serviceable to clear up some dark part, or to correct any mistake, or to confirm and illustrate any important truth relating to the subject, I shall be very thankful to the person that shall oblige either me with private notice, or the public with new improvements.

CAMBRIDGE, MAGD. COLL.,
Nov. 1, 1727.

CONTENTS.

CHAP.		PAGE
	THE INTRODUCTION, Shewing the Design and Use of this Treatise; with the Method and Partition of it . . .	1
I.	The Opinions of the Learned Moderns concerning the Athanasian Creed . .	5
II.	Ancient Testimonies	20
III.	Ancient Commentators and Paraphrasts upon the Athanasian Creed . . .	43
IV.	Latin Manuscripts of the Athanasian Creed	66
V.	Ancient Versions, Printed or Manuscript .	91
VI.	Of the Reception of the Athanasian Creed in the Christian Churches . . .	109
VII.	Of the Time when, and Place where, the Creed was Composed	138
VIII.	Of the Author of the Creed . . .	162
IX.	The Creed itself in the Original Language, with Parallel Passages from the Fathers	173
	APPENDIX TO CHAPTER IX.—Passages from the Ante-Nicene Fathers, Confirming the Statements of the Athanasian Creed	192
X.	A Commentary on the Athanasian Creed .	208

CHAP.   PAGE

XI. THE CHURCH OF ENGLAND VINDICATED, BOTH AS TO THE RECEIVING AND RETAINING THE ATHANASIAN CREED . . . 231

APPENDIX 248

INDEX OF AUTHORS AND EDITIONS . . . 267

INDEX OF MANUSCRIPTS 278

INDEX OF AUTHORITIES 280

A CRITICAL HISTORY OF

THE ATHANASIAN CREED.

THE INTRODUCTION,

SHEWING THE DESIGN AND USE OF THIS TREATISE;
WITH THE METHOD AND PARTITION OF IT.

MY design is, to enquire into the age, author, and value of that celebrated confession, which goes under the name of *The Athanasian Creed*. The general approbation it hath long met with in the Christian Churches, and the particular regard which hath been, early and late, paid to it in our own, (while it makes a part of our Liturgy, and stands recommended to us in our Articles,) will, I doubt not, be considerations sufficient to justify an undertaking of this kind: provided only, that the performance be answerable, and that it fall not short of its principal aim, or of the just expectations of the ingenuous and candid readers. No one will expect more of me than my present materials, such as I could procure, will furnish me with; nor any greater certainty in an essay of this nature, than things of this kind will admit of. If a reasonable diligence has been used in collecting, and due pains in digesting, and a religious care in building thereupon, (more than which I pretend not to), it may, I hope, be sufficient with all equitable judges.

Many learned and valuable men have been before

employed in the same design; but their treatises are mostly in Latin, and some of them very scarce, and hard to come at. I know not that any one hitherto has attempted a just treatise upon the subject in our own language, however useful it might be to the English readers; and the more so at this time when the controversy about the Trinity is now spread abroad among all ranks and degrees of men with us, and the Athanasian Creed become the subject of common and ordinary conversation. For these reasons, I presumed, an English treatise might be most proper and seasonable: though otherwise, to avoid the unseemly mixture of English and Latin (which will here be necessary), and because of some parts which none but the learned can tolerably judge of, it might be thought more proper rather to have written a Latin treatise, and for the use only of scholars. However, there will be nothing very material but what an English reader may competently understand: and I shall endeavour to lay before him all that has been hitherto usefully observed upon the subject, that he may want nothing which may be conceived of any moment for the enabling him to form a true judgment. What I borrow from others shall be fairly acknowledged as I go along, and referred to its proper author, or authors; it being as much my design to give an historical account of what others have done, as it is to supply what they have left undone, so far as my present materials, leisure, and opportunities may enable me to do it. Now, to present the reader with a sketch of my design, and to shew him how one part is to hang upon another, my method will be as follows:—

I. First, in order to give the clearer idea of what has been already done, and of what may be still wanting, I begin with recounting the several conjectures or discoveries of the learned moderns.

II. Next, to enter upon the matter itself, and the evidence proper to it, I proceed to lay down the direct testimonies of the ancients concerning the age, author, and value of this Creed.

III. To these I subjoin an account of the ancient comments upon the same Creed, being but another kind of ancient testimonies.

IV. After these follows a brief recital of the most ancient, or otherwise most considerable, manuscripts of this Creed, which I have either seen myself, or have had notice of from others.

V. After the manuscripts of the Creed itself, I enquire also into the ancient versions of it, printed, or manuscript; which will be also very serviceable to our main design.

VI. I come in the next place to treat of the ancient reception of this Creed in the Christian Churches; as being a point of great moment, and which may be more certainly determined than the time of its composition, and may give great light into it.

VII. These preliminaries settled, to introduce to what follows, I then fall directly to the darkest part of all, namely, to the enquiry after the age, and author of the Creed; which I despatch in two distinct chapters.

VIII. Next, I lay before the learned reader the Creed itself in its original language, with the most considerable various lections; together with select passages from ancient writers, either parallel to those of the Creed, or explanatory of it. And lest the English reader should appear to be neglected, I subjoin the Creed in English with a running English Commentary, serving much the same purpose with what is intended by the Latin quotations going before.

IX. I conclude all with a brief vindication of our own Church in receiving, and still retaining this excellent formulary of the Christian faith; answering the most material objections which have been made against us on that account; and shewing the expediency, and even necessity of retaining this form, or something equivalent, for the preservation of the Christian faith against heresies. The reader, I hope, will excuse it, if in compliance with custom, and to save myself the trouble of circumlocution, I commonly speak of it under the name of the Athanasian Creed; not designing thereby to intimate, either that it is a creed strictly and properly so called, or that it is of Athanasius's composing: both which points will be discussed in the sequel.

CHAPTER I.

THE OPINIONS OF THE LEARNED MODERNS CONCERNING THE ATHANASIAN CREED.

A.D. 1642. IN reciting the opinions of the learned moderns, I need go no higher than Gerard Vossius, who in his treatise *de Tribus Symbolis*, published in the year 1642, led the way to a more strict and critical enquiry concerning this Creed than had been before attempted. The writers before him, most of them, took it for granted that the Creed was Athanasius's, without troubling themselves with any very particular enquiry into it: and those few who doubted of it, or ascribed it to another, yet entered not closely into the merits of the cause, but went upon loose conjectures rather than upon any just rules of true and solid criticism. It will be sufficient therefore to begin our accounts from Vossius, who, since the time of his writing, has been ever principally mentioned by writers upon the subject, as being the first and most considerable man that has entered deep into it, and treated of it like a critic. He endeavoured to sift the matter thoroughly, as far as he was well able to do from printed books; as to manuscripts he either wanted leisure or opportunity to search for them. The result of his enquiries concluded in the following particulars, some of them dubiously, all of them modestly proposed by him. 1. That the Athanasian Creed is not Athanasius's. 2. That it was originally a Latin composure, and of a Latin author or authors. 3. That it was made in the eighth or ninth century, in the time of Pepin or of Charles the Great, and probably by some French divine. 4. That the first time it was produced under the name of Athanasius, at least, with any assurance and confidence of it being his, was in the year 1233, when Pope Gregory the Ninth's legates pleaded it at Constantinople in favour of the procession against the Greeks. 5. That it scarce ever obtained in any of the Christian Churches before the year 1000. These were his sentiments when he wrote his treatise *de Tribus Symbolis*. But in a posthumous piece of his, having then seen what some other learned men had written upon the subject, he was content to say that the Creed could not be set higher than the year 600[a]. How far Vossius was mistaken in his accounts will appear in the sequel. Thus far must be allowed him, that he managed the argument with great learning and judgment, made a good use of such materials as he was possessed of, and though he was not very happy in determining the age of the Creed, or the time of its reception, yet he produced so many and such cogent arguments against the Creed's being originally Greek, or being made by Athanasius, that they could never be answered.

1644. The learned Petavius, who in the year 1622 (when he published Epiphanius) had fallen in with the common opinion of this Creed's being Athanasius's, did yet afterward in his treatise of the Trinity, pub-

[a] "Neque ante annum fuisse sexcentesimum, fuse ostendimus in libro de tribus Symbolis."—Voss., *Harmonia Evangelica*, bk. ii. c. 13, in vol. vi. p. 215.

lished in the year 1644, speak more doubtfully of it; in the meanwhile positive that it was written in Latin [b].

1647. The next considerable man, and who may be justly called a first writer in this argument as well as Vossius, was our learned Usher. He had a good acquaintance with libraries and manuscripts, and was able from those stores to produce new evidences which Vossius knew not of. In the year 1647 he printed his Latin tract *de Symbolis*, with a prefatory epistle to Vossius. He there appeals to the testimonies of Ratram of Corbey, and Æneas, Bishop of Paris, neither of them at that time made public, as also to Hincmar's of Rheims, (which had been published but had escaped Vossius's observation), to prove that this Creed had been confidently cited under the name of Athanasius almost 400 years before the time of Pope Gregory's legates, the time set by Vossius. And further, by two manuscripts found in the Cotton Library, he thought he might carry up the antiquity of the Creed to the year 703, or even to 600. In short, he scrupled not to set the date of it above the year 447: for he supposes a Council of Spain, held in that year, to have been acquainted with it, and to have borrowed the *Filioque* from it [c]. Thus far he, without any more particular determination about either the age or the author.

[b] Petavius *de Trinitate*, bk. vii. c. 8. § 7, in vol. ii. p. 392.
[c] Usser *de Symbolis*, p. 29 (24). N.B. Usher went upon the supposition that the words, *a patre, filioque procedens*, were genuine, and not foisted into the Confession of that Council; as they now appear to have been, after a more careful view of the MSS. of best note and greatest antiquity.

1647. About the same time Dr. Jeremy Taylor (afterwards Bishop of Down and Connor) published his "Liberty of Prophesying," wherein he expresses his doubts whether the Creed be justly ascribed to Athanasius[d]. But as he had never seen Usher's Treatise, nor indeed Vossius's, nor was at that time furnished with any proper assistances to enable him to make any accurate enquiries into this matter; it may suffice just to have mentioned him, in regard to the deserved name he has since borne in the learned world.

1653. George Ashwell, B.D., published an English treatise, which was printed at Oxford, entitled *Fides Apostolica*, asserting the received authors and authority of the Apostles' Creed. At the end of which treatise he has a pretty long Appendix concerning the Athanasian Creed, which is well written, and contains a good summary of what learned men before him had advanced upon the subject. His judgment of it is, that it was written in Latin, and by Athanasius himself, about the year 340.

1659. Hamon L'Estrange[e], in his "Alliance of Divine Offices," gives his judgment of the Athanasian Creed, that it is not rightly ascribed to Athanasius, but yet ancient and extant about the year 600 after Christ.

1659. Leo Allatius about this year printed his *Syntagma de Symbolo S. Athanasii*, which no doubt must be a very useful piece, especially in relation to the sentiments of the Greek Churches, and the reception of this Creed amongst them; but I have never seen it; only I learn from Tentzelius (who yet could

[d] Taylor, Liberty of Proph., § 2, 36, in vol. v. p. 407.
[e] L'Estrange, Alliance of Divine Offices, c. 4, p. 99.

never get a sight of it) and Fabricius, that such a piece was written by Allatius in modern Greek, in 12mo., published at Rome 1658 or 1659. It appears to be very scarce, since none of the learned who have since written upon this Creed, have either referred to it, or given extracts out of it, so far as I have observed; excepting only something of that kind at Rome, A.D. 1667, by the College *de propaganda Fide* [f].

1663. Cardinal Bona, some years after, in his book *de Divina Psalmodia*, makes frequent mention of this Creed; touches slightly upon the question about its age and author; takes some cursory notice of what Vossius had said, but nevertheless ascribes it to Athanasius, as being composed by him while in the western parts, *Teste Baronio;* resting his faith upon Baronius as his voucher [g].

1669. Our very learned Bishop Pearson, in his Exposition of the Creed, occasionally delivers his opinion that the Athanasian Creed was written in Latin, and by some member of the Latin Church [h], and extant about the year 600; though the last particular he builds only upon an epistle attributed to Isidore of Seville, and since judged to be spurious.

1675. Joh. Lud. Ruelius, in his second volume or tome, *Conciliorum illustratorum*, has a particular dissertation, about thirty pages in quarto, upon this Creed. He follows Vossius's opinion for the most part, repeating the same arguments [i].

[f] Vid. Tentzel, *Judic.* &c., p. 147; Fabricius, *Biblioth. Graeca*, vol. v. p. 410.
[g] Bona, *de Divina Psalmod.*, c. 16, § 18, p. 864.
[h] Pearson on the Creed, Art. 8, p. 569, n. (p. 324, ed. 3); Art. 5, p. 400, n. (p. 226.)
[i] Ruelius, *Concil. Illustrat.*, vol. ii. pp. 639—670.

1675. Our next man of eminent character is Paschasius Quesnel, a celebrated French divine. In the year 1675, he published his famous edition of Pope Leo's works, with several very valuable dissertations of his own. His fourteenth contains, among other matters, a particular enquiry about the author of this Creed. He ascribes it to Vigilius Tapsensis, the African[k]; and so well defends his position, that he has almost drawn the learned world after him. He is looked upon as the father of that opinion, because he has so learnedly and handsomely supported it; but he is not the first that espoused it, for Labbe, about fifteen years before, had taken notice of some that had ascribed this Creed to Vigilius, at the same time signifying his dissent from them[l].

1676. The year after Quesnel, Sandius, the famous Arian, printed a second edition of his *Nucleus*, &c., with an Appendix; wherein he corrects his former judgment[m] of this Creed, taken implicitly from Vossius; and allows, nay, contends and insists upon it, that this Creed was not only known, but known under the name of Athanasius, as high at least as the year 770[n]. He ascribes it, upon conjecture, to one Athanasius, Bishop of Spire in Germany, who died in the year 642.

1678. I ought not to pass over our very learned Cudworth, though he has entered very little into the point before us. He gives his judgment, in passing,

[k] Quesnel, Dissert. xiv. p. 729, &c.
[l] Labbe, *Dissert. de Script. Eccles.*, vol. ii. p. 477.
[m] Sandius, *Nucl. Histor. Eccles.*, p. 256.
[n] Sandius, Appendix, p. 35.

of the Creed commonly called Athanasian, that it was written a long time after Athanasius, by some other hand °.

1680. Henricus Heideggerus, in his second volume of select dissertations (published at Zurich), has one whole dissertation, which is the eighteenth, containing near forty pages in quarto. This author takes his account of the Creed mostly from Vossius; does not allow it to be Athanasius's, only called by his name as containing the Athanasian faith: and he defends the doctrine of the Creed at large against the objections of Dudithius and other Antitrinitarians; and concludes with a running comment upon the whole.

1681. Wolfgang Gundling, a German writer, the year after, published a small tract, containing notes upon a little piece relating to the religion of the Greek Churches, written by Eustratius Johannides Zialowski. What is chiefly valuable in Gundling, is his account of the Greek copies of this Creed, (printed ones I mean,) giving us six of them together. He occasionally expresses his doubts whether the Creed be Athanasius's, or of some later writer [p].

1683. I may next mention our celebrated ecclesiastical historian, Dr. Cave, who about this time published his Lives of the Fathers, and particularly of Athanasius. His account of this Creed is, that it was never heard of in the world till above 600 years after Athanasius was dead; but barely mentioned then, and not urged with any confidence till above 200 years after, when the legates of Pope Gregory IX. produced

---

° Cudworth, Intellect. Syst., bk. i. c. 4. p. 620.
[p] Gundling, Notes on Zialowski, p. 68, &c.

and pleaded it at Constantinople [q]. The learned doctor, it is plain, took this account from Vossius, and had never seen Usher's treatise, which one may justly wonder at. Five years after, in his *Historia Literaria*, he allows that this Creed had been spoken of by Theodulphus, which was within 436 years of Athanasius; but not a word yet of any elder testimony or manuscript, though both had been discovered and publicly taken notice of before this time. He still contends that the Creed obtained not in the Christian Churches before 1000, nor became famous everywhere before 1233; but inclines nevertheless to ascribe it to Vigilius Tapsensis, who flourished about the year 484 [r].

1684. Dr. Comber, in his book entitled "A Companion to the Temple," closes in with the old tradition of the Creed being Athanasius's, repeating the most considerable arguments usually pleaded for that persuasion [s].

1684. To him I may subjoin Bishop Beveridge, who perhaps about this time might write his thoughts on the Creed, in his Exposition of our Articles, published after his death. He was so diligent and knowing a man, that had he been to consider this matter in his later years, he would certainly have given a more particular and accurate account than that which now appears. He ascribes the Creed to Athanasius, but with some diffidence, and thinks it might have been originally a Greek composition, but that the old Greek

---
[q] Cave, Life of Athanasius, § 6, Art. 10, in vol. ii. p. 106.
[r] Cave, *Histor. Literar.*, vol. i. pp. 146, 371.
[s] Comber, Companion to the Temple, p. 144.

copies have been lost, and that the only remaining ones are Versions from the Latin [t].

1685. Cabassutius, in his *Notitia Ecclesiastica*, hath a short dissertation about the author of this Creed [u]. He contents himself with repeating Quesnel's Arguments, to prove that Athanasius was not the author of it, determining nothing farther, save only that it was originally a Latin composure, known and cited by the Council of Autun, about the year 670.

1687. The celebrated Dupin, in his Ecclesiastical History, sums up the reasons usually urged to prove the Creed is none of Athanasius's, and assents to them. He determines with confidence that it was originally a Latin composition, and not known till the fifth century; repeats Father Quesnel's reasons for ascribing it to Vigilius Tapsensis, and acquiesces in them as having nothing more certain in this matter [v].

1687. About the same time, Tentzelius, a learned Lutheran, published a little treatise upon the subject, setting forth the several opinions of learned men concerning this Creed. He is very full and accurate in his collection, omitting nothing of moment that had been said before him by any of the learned moderns, but bringing in some further materials from his own searches to add new light to the subject. He determines nothing, but leaves it to the reader to make a judgment as he sees cause from a full view of the pleadings.

1688. I may place here the learned Pagi, who in

---

[t] Beveridge, on Art. 8, (p. 162), in vol. ix. p. 277.
[u] Cabassutius, *Notit. Eccles.*, Dissert. xix. p. 54.
[v] Dupin, Eccles. Histor., vol. ii. p. 35.

his critic upon Baronius passes his judgment of this Creed [x]: which being the same with Quesnel's, and little more than repetition from him, I need not be more particular about him.

1693. Joseph Antelmi, a learned Paris divine, first began directly to attack Quesnel's opinion, and to sap the reasons on which it was founded. He published a particular dissertation to that purpose, consisting of eighty-five pages in octavo. He ascribes the Creed to Vincentius Lirinensis, who flourished in the year 434.

1695. The famous Tillemont wrote after Antelmius, for he makes mention of his treatise, and examines his hypothesis, and yet it could not be long after, for he died in the year 1697. He commends Mr. Antelmi's performance as a considerable work, but inclines still rather to Quesnel's opinion. All that he pronounces certain is, that the Creed is none of Athanasius's, but yet as old as the sixth century or older [y].

1698. In the year 1698 Montfaucon published his new and accurate edition of Athanasius's works. In the second tome he has an excellent dissertation upon this Creed, the best that is extant, either for order and method, or for plenty of useful matter. The sum of his judgment is, that the Creed is certainly none of Athanasius's, nor yet Vigilius Tapsensis's, nor sufficiently proved to belong to Vincentius Lirinensis; but probably enough composed about the time of Vincentius, and by a Gallican writer or writers [z].

---

[x] Pagi, *Critic. in Baron. Ann.* 340, §§ 6—8, pp. 120, 121 (p. 440).
[y] Tillemont, *Mémoires*, note xxxiv. vol. viii. p. 282 (p. 667).
[z] "Symbolum 'Quicunque' Athanasio incunctanter abjudicandum arbitramur.—Afro itaque Vigilio nihil est quod symbolum 'Quicunque' tribuatur.—non ægre quidem concesserim Vincentii ætate

1698. In the same year, Ludovicus Antonius Muratorius, an Italian writer, published a second tome of *Anecdota* out of the Ambrosian library at Milan. Among other manuscripts there, he had met with an ancient comment upon this Creed, ascribed to Venantius Fortunatus, who was Bishop of Poictiers in France in the sixth century. He publishes the comment, together with a dissertation of his own concerning the author of the Creed, concluding, at length, that Venantius Fortunatus, the certain author of the Comment, might possibly be the author of the Creed too. He entirely rejects the opinion of those that would ascribe it to Athanasius, and disapproves of Quesnel's persuasion about Vigilius Tapsensis, but speaks favourably of Antelmi's, as coming nearest to the truth [a].

1712. Fabricius, in his *Bibliotheca Græca* [b] (highly valued by all men of letters), gives a summary account of the sentiments of the learned relating to this Creed. His conclusion from all is, that thus far may be depended on as certain: that the Creed was not composed by Athanasius, but long after in the fifth century, written originally in Latin, and afterwards translated into Greek.

1712. In the same year, the learned Le Quien published a new edition of Damascen, with previous dissertations to it. In the first of these he has several

editam fuisse illam fidei professionem.—Haud abs re conjectant Viri eruditi in Galliis illud (symbolum) fuisse elucubratum."— Montf., *Diatrib. in Symb.*, pp. 723, 724, 726.

[a] " Hæc et similia pluribus pertractavit eruditissimus Antelmius, cujus opinioni quorumnam eruditorum suffragia accesserint me penitus fugit: fateor tamen ad veritatem omnium maxime illam accedere."—Muratori, *Anecd.*, vol. ii. p. 222.

[b] Fabricius, *Biblioth. Græca*, bk. v. c. 2, § 88, in vol. v. p. 315.

very considerable remarks concerning the age and author of the Athanasian Creed. He appears inclinable to ascribe it to Pope Anastasius I. (who entered upon the pontificate in the year 398) because of some ancient testimonies, as well as manuscripts, carrying the name of Anastasius in the title of the Creed; but he is positive that the Creed must be set as high as the age of St. Austin, Vincentius, and Vigilius[e]. And, as Antelmius before had made light of the supposition that the internal characters of the Creed shew it to be later than Eutyches, he makes as light of the other supposition of the internal characters setting it later than Nestorius.

1714. Natalis Alexander's new edition of his Ecclesiastical History bears date A.D. 1714. He had examined into our present question some years before (about 1676, when his first edition came abroad), subscribing to the opinion of Quesnel, and he does not appear to have altered his mind since. He takes notice of Antelmi's opinion, and speaks respectfully of it, as also of the author, but prefers the other hypothesis[d].

1715. I ought not here to omit the late learned Mr. Bingham, to whom the public has been highly indebted for his *Origines Ecclesiasticæ*, collected with great judgment, and digested into a clear method. He had a proper occasion to say something of the Athanasian Creed in passing, and very briefly. He observes that it was not composed by Athanasius, but

[e] "Omnino fateri cogor Augustini, Vincentii, et Vigilii ætate extitisse expositionem Latinam Fidei, quæ postmodum Athanasio magno attribui meruerit."—Le Quien, *Dissert. Damasc.*, i. p. 9.
[d] Natal. Alexand., Eccl. Hist., vol. iv. p. 111.

by a later and a Latin writer, and particularly Vigilius Tapsensis; referring to such learned moderns as I have above mentioned, for the proof of it, and giving no more than short hints of their reasons [e].

1719. Dr. Clarke of St. James's, in his second edition of his Scripture Doctrine [f], gives us his last thoughts in relation to this Creed. Referring to Dr. Cave he informs us, that this Creed was never seen till about the year 800, near 400 years after the death of Athanasius (they are his own words), nor was received in the Church till so very late as about the year 1000. Yet Cave does not say, "was never seen" (for he himself ascribes it to Vigilius Tapsensis of the fifth century), but only that it was not quoted before the year 800, or nearly, which yet is a very great mistake. What the learned Doctor intended by saying "about the year 800," and yet only "near 400 years after the death of Athanasius," or, as he elsewhere [g] expresses it, "above 300 years after the death of Athanasius," I do not understand, but must leave to those that can compute the distance between 373 (the latest year that Athanasius is ever supposed to have lived) and the year 800. I am persuaded the Doctor was thinking, that if Athanasius had lived to the year 400, then the distance had been just 400 years; but as he died twenty-seven years before, the distance must be so much the less, when it is quite the contrary.

1722. The last man that has given his sentiments in

[e] Bingham, *Orig. Eccles.*, bk. x. c. 4, § 18, in vol. iii. p. 92, &c. (vol. iv. p. 112, &c.)
[f] Clarke's Script. Doctr., pt. iii. c. 2, in vol. iii. p. 205, (p. 379, 2nd edit.)
[g] Ibid., p. 447, 1st ed.

relation to this Creed is Casimirus Oudinus, in his new edition of his Supplement (now called a Commentary) to the Ecclesiastical Writers. I need say no more than that he does not seem to have spent much pains in re-examining this subject, but rests content with his first thoughts, ascribing the Creed, with Quesnel, to Vigilius Tapsensis [h].

These are the principal moderns that have fallen within my notice, and of these the most considerable are Vossius, Usher, Quesnel, Tentzelius, Antelmius, Tillemont, Montfaucon, Muratorius, and Le Quien; as having particularly studied the subject, and struck new light into it, either furnishing fresh materials, or improving the old by new observations. Some, perhaps, may wish to have the several opinions of the moderns thrown into a narrower compass: for which reason I have thought it not improper to subjoin the following table, which will represent all in one view, for the ease and conveniency of every common reader.

[h] Oudin., *Comment. de Scriptor. Eccles.*, vol. i. pp. 345, 1248, 1322.

THE OPINIONS OF THE LEARNED MODERNS.

A.D.	Writers.	Author of the Creed.	What Century composed in.	What Year composed.	When received
1642	Vossius.	A Latin author.		Not bef. 600	A.D. 1000
1644	Petavius.	Doubtful.			
1647	Bishop Usher.		Fifth.	Before 447	Before 852
1647	Bishop Taylor.	Not Athanasius.			
1653	G. Ashwell.	Athanasius.	Fourth.	340	
1659	L'Estrange.	Not Athanasius.		Before 600	
1659	Leo Allatius.	Athanasius.	Fourth.	340	
1663	Card. Bona.	Athanasius Alex.	Fourth.	340	
1669	Bishop Pearson.	A Latin author.		About 600	
1675	Ruelius.	Not Athanasius.			
1675	Paschas. Quesnel.	Vigilius Tapsensis.	Fifth.	484	Before 670
1676	Sandius.	Athanasius of Spire.	Seventh.	Before 642	Before 770
1678	Dr. Cudworth.	Not Athanasius.	After the Fourth.		
1680	Heideggerus.	Vigilius Tapsensis.	Fifth.	484	
1681	Wolf. Gundling.	Doubtful.			
1683	Dr. Cave.	Vigilius Tapsensis.	Fifth.	484	1000
1684	Dr. Comber.	Athanasius Alex.	Fourth.	333	
1684	Bp. Beveridge.	Athanasius Alex.	Fourth.		Before 850
1685	Cabassutius.	A Latin author.			Before 670
1687	Dupin.	Vigilius Tapsensis.	Fifth.	484	
1687	Tentzelius.	Doubtful.			
1688	Pagi.	Vigilius Tapsensis.	Fifth.	484	570
1693	Antelmius.	Vincentius Lirinens.	Fifth.	Before 450	
1695	Tillemont.	Not Athanasius.	Sixth, or sooner.		
1698	Montfaucon.	A Gallican writer.	Fifth.		Before 670
1698	Ant. Muratorius.	Venant. Fortunatus.	Sixth.	570	800
1712	Fabricius.	A Latin author.	Fifth.		663
1712	Le Quien.	Anastasius I.	Fourth or Fifth.	Before 401	500
1714	Natal. Alexander.	Vigilius Tapsensis.	Fifth.	484	
1715	Mr. Bingham.	Vigilius Tapsensis.	Fifth.		670
1719	Dr. Clarke.	Doubtful.	Seventh or Eighth.		1000
1722	Oudin.	Vigilius Tapsensis.	Fifth.	484	

CHAPTER II.

ANCIENT TESTIMONIES.

HAVING taken a view of the moderns in relation to the Creed, we may now enter upon a detail of the ancients and their testimonies, by which the moderns must be tried. My design is to lay before the reader all the original evidence I can meet with, to give any light either into the age or author of the Creed, or its reception in the Christian Churches, that so the reader may be able to judge for himself concerning the three particulars now mentioned, which are what I constantly bear in my eye, producing nothing but with a view to one or more of them.

Ancient testimonies have been pretended from Gregory Nazianzen, Gaudentius Brixiensis, St. Austin, and Isidorus Hispalensis, of the fourth, fifth, and sixth centuries[a]; but they have been since generally and justly exploded by the learned as being either spurious or foreign to the point; and therefore I conceive it very needless to take any further notice of them. As to quotations from our Creed, or comments upon it, falling within the compass of the centuries now mentioned, if there be any such, they shall be considered under other heads, distinct from that of ancient testimonies, properly so called, to be treated of in this chapter.

[a] These testimonies are collected and discussed by Montfaucon, (*Diatrib. in Symb.*, pp. 719, 720); from whom Dr. Waterland appears to have obtained most of the passages quoted in this chapter.

670. The oldest of this kind hitherto discovered or observed, is that of the Council of Autun in France, under Leodegarius, or St. Leger, the Bishop of the place in the seventh century. There is some dispute about the year when the Council was held, whether in 663, or 666, or 670. The last is most probable, and most generally embraced by learned men. The words of this Council in English, run thus:—"If any presbyter, deacon, sub-deacon, or clerk, doth not unreprovably recite the Creed which the Apostles delivered by inspiration of the Holy Ghost, and also the faith of the holy prelate Athanasius, let him be censured by the Bishop [b]." By the faith of Athanasius is here meant what we now call the Athanasian Creed, as may be reasonably pleaded from the titles which this Creed bore in the earlier times before it came to have the name of a Creed; which titles shall be exhibited both from manuscripts and written evidences in the sequel. Yet it must not be dissembled that Papebrochius, a learned man, and whom I find cited with approbation by Muratorius [c], is of opinion that the faith of Athanasius here mentioned, means the Nicene

[b] "Si quis presbyter, diaconus, sub-diaconus, vel clericus, symbolum quod Sancto inspirante Spiritu Apostoli tradiderunt et fidem Sancti Athanasii præsulis irreprehensibiliter non recensuerit; ab episcopo condemnetur."—Augustodun. Synod., in Harduin, vol. iii. p. 1016.

[c] "Atqui, ut eruditissime adnotavit clarissimus P. Papebrochius, in Respons. ad exhibitionem Errorum par. ii. Art. 13. n. 36, verbis illis fidem S. Athanasii, minime symbolum Athanasianum designatur, sed quidem Nicænum, in quo elaborando plurimum insudasse Athanasium verisimile est. Etenim cur Apostolico symbolo commendato Nicænum prætermisissent Augustodunenses Patres ? Cur Athanasiani symboli, cujus tunc nullus erat usus in sacris, cognitionem exegissent, Nicænumque ne uno quidem verbo commemorassent?"—Murator., *Anecdot.*, vol. ii. p. 223.

Creed, which Athanasius had some hand in, and whereof he was the great defender. I can by no means come into his opinion, or allow any force to his reasonings. He asks, Why should the Nicene Creed be omitted and not mentioned with the Apostles'? and, why should the Athanasian not then used in the sacred offices, be recommended so carefully without a word of the Nicene? I answer, because it does not appear that the Nicene Creed was so much taken notice of at that time in the Gallican Churches, while the Apostolical or Roman Creed made use of in baptism in the Western Churches instead of the Nicene, (which prevailed in the East,) in a manner superseded it; which no one can wonder at who considers how prevailing and universal the tradition had been in the Latin Church, down from the fifth century at least, that the Apostolical Creed was composed by the twelve Apostles, and therefore as sacred and of as great authority as the inspired writings themselves. Besides that, it appears from Hincmar, who will be cited in his place, that it was no strange thing even so low as his time, about 850, to recommend the Athanasian Creed along with the Apostles', without a word of the Nicene. And why should it be thought any objection against the Athanasian Creed that it was not at that time received into the sacred offices, (supposing it really was not, which may be questioned,) when it is certain that the Nicene was not yet received into the sacred offices in France, nor till many years after, about the time of Pepin or of Charles the Great? There is therefore no force at all in the argument of Papebrochius; but there is this strong prejudice against it, that the title there given is a very common title for the Athanasian Creed and not for the Nicene. Nor would the Fathers of that Council have been so extravagantly fond of the name of Athanasius, as to think it a greater commendation of the Creed of Nice to call it after him than to call it the Nicene. There is, then, no reasonable doubt to be made but that the Council of Autun in the Canon intended the Athanasian Creed, as the best critics and the generality of the learned have hitherto believed.

But there are other objections of real weight against the evidence built upon this canon. 1. Oudin makes it a question whether there was ever any Council held under Leodegarius, a suffragan bishop under the Archbishop of Lyons, having no metropolitical authority [d]. But it may suffice if the Council was held at Autun, while he was bishop of the place, a good reason why he should be particularly mentioned; especially considering the worth and fame of the man, to say nothing of the dignity of his see, which from the time of Gregory the Great, had been the second or next in dignity to the metropolitical see of Lyons. Nor do I perceive any force in Oudin's objection against St. Leger's holding a diocesan synod (for a provincial synod is not pretended), though he was no metropolitan. 2. A stronger objection is that the canon we are concerned with, cannot be proved to belong to the council held under Leodegarius. It is not found among the canons of that council published by Sirmondus, from the manuscripts of the Library of the Church of Angers, but it is from another collection out of the library of the

[d] Oudin, *Comment. de Scriptor. Eccles.*, vol. i. p. 348.

monastery of St. Benignus, of Dijon, with this title only, *Canones Augustodunenses;* so that one cannot be certain whether it belongs to the synod under St. Leger, or to some other synod of Autun much later. It must be owned that the evidence can amount to no more than probable presumption or conjecture; wherefore Dupin [e], Teutzelius [f], Muratorius [g], and Oudin [h], do not scruple to throw it aside as of too suspected credit to build anything certain upon: and even Quesnel [i] expresses some dissatisfaction about it; only in respect to some great names, such as Sirmondus, Peter le Lande, Godfr. Hermantius, &c., he is willing to acquiesce in it. To whom we may add, Labbe [j], Le Coint [k], Cabassutius [l], Pagi [m], Tillemont [n], Montfaucon [o], Fabricius [p], Harduin [q], and our learned antiquary Mr. Bingham [r], who all accept it as genuine, but upon probable persuasion rather than certain conviction. Neither do I pretend to propose it as clear and undoubted evidence, but probable only, and such as will be much confirmed by other evidences to be mentioned hereafter.

760. Regino, Abbot of Prom in Germany, an author

[e] Dupin, Eccl. Hist., vol. ii. p. 35.
[f] Teutzel., *Judic. Erud.*, p. 61, &c.
[g] Murator., *Anecdot.*, vol. ii. p. 223.
[h] Oudin, *Comment. de Scriptor. Eccles.*, vol. i. p. 348.
[i] Quesnel, *Dissert.* xiv. p. 731.
[j] Labbe, *Dissert. de Scriptor. Eccles.*, vol. ii. p. 478.
[k] Le Cointe, *Annal. Franc. ad Ann.* 663, n. 22.
[l] Cabassut., *Notit. Eccl. Dissert.* xix. p. 54.
[m] Pagi, *Crit. in Baron. Ann.* 340, § 6. p. 120.
[n] Tillemont, *Mémoires*, vol. viii. p. 283, (vol. viii. p. 668.)
[o] Montfauc., *Diatrib. in Symb.*, p. 720.
[p] Fabric., *Bibl. Græc.*, lib. v. c. 2, § 88, in vol. v. p. 316.
[q] Harduin, *Concil.*, vol. iii. p. 1016.
[r] Bingham, *Orig. Eccles.*, bk. x. c. 4, § 18, in vol. iii. p. 94, (vol. iv. p. 120.

of the ninth and tenth centuries, has among other collections, some Articles of Inquiry, supposed by Baluzius the editor to be as old, or very nearly, as the age of Boniface, Bishop of Mentz, who died in the year 754. In those articles, there is one to this purpose: "Whether the clergy have by heart Athanasius's tract upon the faith of the Trinity, beginning with Whosoever will be saved [s]," &c. This testimony I may venture to place about 760, a little after the death of Boniface.

794. The Council of Frankfort, in Germany, in their 33rd Canon, give orders that "The Catholic faith of the holy Trinity, and Lord's Prayer, and Creed, be set forth and delivered to all [t]."

Vossius [u] understands the canon of the two Creeds Nicene and Apostolical; but I know not why the Apostolical or Roman Creed should be emphatically called *Symbolum Fidei*, the Creed, in opposition to the Nicene, nor why the Nicene should not be called a Creed as well as the other, after the usual way. Besides that *Fides Catholica*, &c., has been more peculiarly the title of the Athanasian Creed; and it was no uncommon thing, either before or after this time, to recommend it in this manner together with the Lord's Prayer, and Apostles' Creed, just as we find here. And nothing could be at that time of greater service against the heresy of Felix and Elipandus, (which occasioned the

---

[s] "Si sermonem Athanasii episcopi de Fide Sanctæ Trinitatis, cujus initium est, ' Quicunque vult Salvus esse,' memoriter teneat." —Regin. *de Discipl. Eccles.*, lib. i. c. 1, § 85.

[t] "Ut fides Catholica sanctæ Trinitatis, et Oratio Dominica, atque Symbolum Fidei omnibus prædicetur, et tradatur."—Concil. Francf., Can. 33, in Harduin, vol. iv. p. 908.

[u] Vossius *de tribus Symb. Dissert.* iii. c. 26, p. 528.

calling of the Council,) than the Athanasian Creed; for which reasons, till I see better reasons to the contrary, I must be of opinion that the Council of Frankfort in their 33rd Canon intended the Athanasian Creed, which Charles the Great had a particular respect for, and had presented in form to Pope Adrian I., above twenty years before, as we shall see in another chapter.

809. Theodulphus, Bishop of Orleans in France, has a Treatise of the Holy Ghost, with a preface to Charles the Great, written at a time when the dispute about the procession began to make disturbance. He brings several testimonies in favour of the procession from the Son out of Athanasius; and, among others, a pretty large part of the Athanasian Creed, from the words, "The Father is made of none," &c.. to, "He therefore that will be saved must think of the Trinity *," inclusive.

809. An anonymous writer of the same time, and in the same cause, and directing himself to the same prince, makes the like use of the Athanasian Creed, in the following words: "St. Athanasius, in the Exposition of the Catholic faith, which that great master wrote himself, and which the Universal Church professes, declares the procession of the Holy Ghost from the Father and Son, thus saying, 'The Father is made of none *,' " &c. This I cite upon the credit of Sirmondus in his Notes to Theodulphus.

---

* "Item idem .... 'Pater a nullo est factus,' &c., usque ad 'Qui vult ergo Salvus esse,'" &c.—Theodulph. *de Spiritu Sancto*, in Sirmond. Oper., vol. ii. p. 978.

* "Incertus Autor quem diximus, hoc ipso utens testimonio, Beatus, inquit, Athanasius, in expositione Catholicæ fidei, quam

809. It was in the same year that the Latin Monks of Mount Olivet wrote their apologetical letter to Pope Leo III., justifying their doctrine of the procession from the Son, against one John of Jerusalem, a monk too, of another monastery, and of an opposite persuasion. Among other authorities they appeal to the faith of Athanasius, that is, to the Creed, as we now call it. This I have from Le Quien, the learned editor of Damascen, who had the copy of that letter from Baluzius, as he there signifies [x].

820. Not long after, Hatto, otherwise called Hetto and Ahyto, Bishop of Basil in France, composed his Capitular, or Book of Constitutions, for the regulation of the clergy of his diocese. Amongst other good rules, this makes the fourth: "That they should have the Faith of Athanasius by heart, and recite it at the Prime (that is, at seven o'clock in the morning) every Lord's Day [y]."

820. Agobardus of the same time, Archbishop of Lyons, wrote against Felix Orgelitanus, where he occasionally cites part of the Athanasian Creed. His words are: "St. Athanasius says, that except a man doth

---

ipse egregius doctor conscripsit, et quam universalis confitetur ecclesia, processionem Spiritus Sancti a Patre et Filio declarat, ita dicens: 'Pater a nullo est factus,'" &c.—Sirmond. Oper., vol. ii. p. 978; cf. p. 967.

[x] "In Regula Sancti Benedicti quam nobis dedit Filius voster Domnus Karolus, quæ habet fidem scriptam de Sancta et inseparabili Trinitate; 'Credo Spiritum Sanctum Deum verum ex patre procedentem et filio:' et in Dialogo quem nobis vestra Sanctitas dare dignata est similiter dicit. Et in Fide S. Athanasii eodem modo dicit."—*Monachi de Monte Oliv.*, in Le Quien, *Dissert. Damasc.*, p. 7.

[y] "Quarto, ut fides Sancti Athanasii a sacerdotibus discatur, et ex corde Die Dominico ad Primam recitetur."—Basil., *Capitul.*, in Harduin., vol. iv. p. 1241.

keep the Catholic faith whole and undefiled, without doubt he shall perish everlastingly[z]."

852. In the same age flourished the famous Hincmar, Archbishop of Rheims, who so often cites or refers to the Creed we are speaking of, as a standing rule of faith, that it may be needless to produce the particular passages. I shall content myself with one only, more considerable than the rest for the use that is to be made of it hereafter. He directs his Presbyters "to learn Athanasius's Treatise of Faith (beginning with 'Whosoever will be saved'), to commit it to memory, to understand its meaning, and to be able to give it in common words[a];" that is, I suppose, in the vulgar tongue. He at the same time recommends the Lord's Prayer and (Apostles') Creed[b], as I take it, without mentioning the Nicene; which I particularly remark for a reason to be seen above. It is farther observable that though Hincmar here gives the Athanasian formulary the name of a Treatise of Faith, yet he elsewhere[c] scruples not to call it (*Symbolum*) a Creed; and he is, probably, as Sirmondus observes[d], the first

---

[z] "Beatus Athanasius ait ; Fidem Catholicam nisi quis integram, inviolatamque servaverit, absque dubio in æternum peribit."— Agobard., *adv. dogma Felicis*, c. 3, in vol. i. p. 5.

[a] "Unusquisque presbyterorum expositionem symboli atque Orationis dominicæ juxta Traditionem Orthodoxorum Patrum plenius discat ... Psalmorum etiam verba, et distinctiones regulariter, et ex corde, cum Canticis consuetudinariis pronuntiare sciat. Necnon et sermonem Athanasii de fide, cujus initium est, 'Quicunque vult Salvus esse,' memoriæ quisque commendet, sensum illius intelligat, et verbis communibus enuntiare queat."—Hincm., *Capitula ad presbyteros*, i. 1, in vol. i. p. 710.

[b] Vid. Hincm., *Opusc. ad Hincmar. Laudunensem*, c. 24, in vol. ii. p. 474.

[c] "Athanasius in Symbolo dicens," &c.; id., *de Prædestin.*, vol. i. p. 309.

[d] Sirmond., *Not. in Theodulph.*, vol. ii. p. 978.

writer who gave it the name it bears at this day. Which I suppose may have led Oudin into his mistake, that no writer before Hincmar ever made mention of this Creed [e]; a mistake, which, though taken notice of by Tentzelius [f] in the year 1687, he has nevertheless again and again repeated in his last edition.

865. In the same age lived Anscharius, monk also of Corbey, and afterwards Archbishop of Hamburg and Bremen in Germany. Among his dying instructions to his clergy, he left this for one; that they should be careful to recite the Catholic faith composed by Athanasius [g]. This is reported by Rembertus, the writer of his life, and successor to him in the same see, who had been likewise monk of Corbey: so that we have here two considerable testimonies in one.

868. Contemporary with these was Æneas Bishop of Paris, who, in his Treatise against the Greeks, quotes the Athanasian Creed under the name of *Fides Catholica* [h], Catholic faith, producing the same paragraph of it which Theodulphus had done sixty years before.

868. About the same time, and in the same cause, Ratram or Bertram, monk of Corbey in France, made the like use of this Creed, calling it, A Treatise of the Faith [i].

[e] Oudin, *Comment. de Scriptor. Eccl.*, vol. i. pp. 345, 1322.
[f] Tentzel., *Judic. Erud.*, p. 144.
[g] "Fratres.... admonuit ipse.... ut canerent Fidem Catholicam a Beato Athanasio compositam."—Rembert., *Vit. Anschar.*, p. 237.
[h] "Sanctus Athanasius, Alexandrinæ sedis Episcopus, &c....Item idem in Fide Catholica: quod Spiritus Sanctus a Patre procedat, et Filio. Pater a nullo est factus," &c.—Æneas Paris., *adv. Græc.*, c. 19.
[i] "Beatus Athanasius, Alexandrinus episcopus, in Libello de fide quem edidit, et omnibus Catholicis tenendum proposuit inter cætera sic ait; Pater a nullo est factus, nec creatus, nec genitus," &c.—Ratr., *contra Græcor. oppos.*, lib. ii. c. 3.

871. Adalbertus of this time, upon his nomination to a Bishopric in the province of Rheims, was obliged to give in a profession of his Faith to Archbishop Hincmar. Among other things, he professes his great regard to the Athanasian Creed (*Sermo Athanasii*), as a Creed received with great veneration by the Catholic Church, or being of customary and venerable use in it[k]. This testimony is considerable in regard to the reception of this Creed; and not before taken notice of, so far as I know, by those that have treated of this argument.

889. This Creed is again mentioned in the same age by Riculphus, Bishop of Soissons in France, in his pastoral Charge to the Clergy of his diocese. He calls it a Treatise (or Discourse) of Catholic Faith[l]. This I take from Father Harduin's Councils, as also the former, with the dates of both.

960. Ratherius, Bishop of Verona in Italy in the year 928, and afterwards of Liege in Germany in the year 953, and restored to his See of Verona in the year 955, did after this time write instructions to his clergy of Verona; in which he makes mention of all the three Creeds, Apostolical, Nicene, and Athanasian; obliging his clergy to have them all by heart; which

---

[k] "In Sermone Beati Athanasii, quem Ecclesia Catholica venerando usu frequentare consuevit, qui ita incipit; 'Quicunque vult Salvus esse, ante omnia opus est ut teneat Catholicam Fidem.' Professio Adalberti episcopi Morinensis futuri."—Harduin., *Concil.*, vol. v. p. 1445.
[l] "Item monemus, ut unusquisque vestrum Psalmos, et sermonem fidei Catholicæ, cujus initium, 'Quicunque vult Salvus esse,' et canonem missæ, et cantum, vel compotum, memoriter, et veraciter et correcte tenere studeat."—Riculf., Constitution 5, in Harduin, vol. vi. p. 415.

shews that they were all of standing use in his time, in his diocese at least [m].

997. Near the close of this century lived Abbo, or Albo, Abbot of Fleury, or St. Benedict upon the Loire in France. Upon some difference he had with Arnulphus, Bishop of Orleans, he wrote an apology which he addressed to the two kings of France, Hugh and Robert. In that apology he has a passage relating to our purpose running thus: "I thought proper, in the first place, to speak concerning the Faith, which I have heard variously sung in alternate choirs, both in France and in the Church of England. For some, I think, say in the Athanasian form, 'The Holy Ghost is of the Father and of the Son, neither made, nor created, but proceeding:' who while they leave out 'nor begotten,' are persuaded that they are the more conformable to Gregory's Synodical Epistle, wherein it is written that the 'Holy Ghost is neither unbegotten, nor begotten, but proceeding[n].'" I have taken the liberty of throwing in a word or two to make the sentence run the clearer. What the author intends is, that some scrupulous persons both in France and Eng-

[m] "Ipsam fidem, id est credulitatem Dei, trifarie parare memoriter festinetis: Hoc est, secundum Symbolum id est collationem Apostolorum, sicut in Psalteriis correctis invenitur; et illam quæ ad missam canitur; et illam Sancti Athanasii quæ ita incipit; 'Quicunque vult Salvus esse'... Sermonem, ut superius dixi, Athanasii Episcopi de fide Trinitatis, cujus initium est, 'Quicunque vult, memoriter teneat."—Ratherii, *Synod. Epist.*, in Harduin, vol. vi. p. 791.

[n] "Primitus de Fide dicendum credidi; quam alternantibus choris et in Francia, et apud Anglorum Ecclesiam variari audivi. Alii enim dicunt, ut arbitror, secundum Athanasium, 'Spiritus Sanctus a Patre et Filio non factus, non creatus, sed procedens:' qui dum id quod est nec genitus subtrahunt, Synodicam Domni Gregorii se sequi credunt, ubi ita est scriptum; 'Spiritus Sanctus nec ingenitus est, nec genitus, sed procedens.'"—Abbo Floriacens., *Apol. ad Francor. Reges*, c. 15.

land, recited the Athanasian Creed with some alteration, leaving out two words to make it agree the better, as they imagined, with Gregory's synodical instructions. As to their scruple herein, and the ground of it, I shall say more of it in a proper place. All I am to observe at present is, that this testimony is full for the custom of alternate singing the Athanasian Creed at this time in the French and English Churches. And indeed we shall meet with other as full, and withal earlier evidence of the same custom, when we come to treat of manuscripts in the following chapters. To proceed with our ancient testimonies.

1047. In the next century we meet with Gualdo, a monk of Corbey, who likewise wrote the Life of Anscharius, but in verse, as Rembertus had before done in prose. He also takes some notice of our Creed, ascribing it to Athanasius[o].

1130. In the century following, Honorius, a scholastic divine of the Church of Autun, in his book entitled "The Pearl of the Soul" (which treats of the sacred or Liturgic offices), reckons up the several Creeds of the Church, making in all four: namely, the Apostolical, the Nicene, the Constantinopolitan, and the Athanasian. Of the last he observes, that it was daily repeated at the Prime[p]. He ascribes it to Athanasius of Alexandria, in the time of Theodosius, where he is undoubtedly mistaken in his chronology. For if he means the first Athanasius of Alex-

[o] "Catolicamque Fidem quam composuisse beatus
Fertur Athanasius."—Gualdo, *Vit. Ansch.*, c. 107, p. 322.

[p] "Quarto, fidem 'Quicunque vult,' quotidie ad Primam iterat, quam Athanasius Alexandrinus Episcopus, rogatu Theodosii Imperatoris edidit."—Honor., *Gemm. Animæ*, lib. ii. c. 59, p. 1086.

andria, he is too early for either of the Theodosiuses: and if he means it of the second, he is as much too late. But a slip in chronology might be pardonable in that age, nor does it at all affect the truth of what he attests of his own times.

1146. Otho, Bishop of Frisinghen in Bavaria, may here be taken notice of, as being the first we have met with who pretends to name the place where Athanasius is supposed to have made this Creed, Triers, or Treves, in Germany ^q. It is no improbable conjecture of M. Antelmi ^r, that the copy of the Creed found at Treves being very ancient, or the most ancient of any, and from which many others were taken, might first occasion the story of the Creed's being made at Treves, and by Athanasius himself, who by his exile thither might render that place famous for his name to all after ages.

1171. Arnoldus, in his Chronicle, informs us of an Abbot of Brunswick, who attending the Duke of Brunswick at this time in his journey into the East, had some disputes with the Greeks at Constantinople upon the Article of Procession, and pleaded the usual passage out of this Creed, whose words are to be seen in the margin ^s. What is most to be noted is the title of *Symbolum Fidei*, which now began to be common to this form, as to the other Creeds.

---

^q "Ibidem manens in Ecclesia Treverorum sub Maximino ejusdem Ecclesiæ Episcopo, 'Quicunque vult,' &c., a quibusdam dicitur edidisse."—Otto Frising., *Chronic.*, lib. iv. cap. 7, p. 44 (al. p. 75).
^r Antelm. *de Symb. Athan.*, p. 27.
^s "Unde Athanasius in Symbolo Fidei: Spiritus Sanctus a Patre et Filio non factus, nec creatus, nec genitus, sed procedens. Ecce Spiritum Sanctum a Patre dicit procedere et a Filio."—Henric. Abb. apud Arnold., *Chron. Slavor.*, lib. iii. c. 5, p. 248.

1178. Robertus Paululus, Presbyter of Amiens, in the diocese of Rheims, speaking of the offices recited at the Prime, observes that the piety of good Christians had thereunto added the *Quicunque vult*, that the articles necessary to salvation might never be forgotten any hour of the day[t].

1190. Beleth, a celebrated Paris divine, is the oldest writer that takes notice of this Creed being commonly ascribed to Anastasius, though he himself ascribes it to Athanasius[u]. Tentzelius[v] marks some differences between the prints and the manuscripts of this author, and betwixt one manuscript and another. But as the difference, though in words considerable, is yet very little in the sense, it is not material to our present purpose to be more particular about it.

1200. I must not omit Nicolaus Hydruntinus, a native of Otranto in Italy, who sided with the Greeks, and wrote in Greek against the Latins. He understood both languages, and was often interpreter between the Greeks and Latins in their disputes at Constantinople, Athens, and Thessalonica[x]. He wrote several tracts, out of which Leo Allatius has published some fragments. There is one relating to the Athanasian Creed,

[t] "His addidit fidelium devotio, 'Quicunque vult Salvus esse,' ut Articulorum Fidei qui sunt necessarii ad salutem, nulla diei hora obliviscamur."—Rob. Paulul., in Hugo de S. Victor. *de Offic. Eccl.*, lib. ii. c. 1, vol. iii. p. 223 (p. 265).

[u] "Notandum est quatuor esse Symbola ; minimum quod a cunctis communiter in quotidiana oratione dicitur, quod Apostoli simul composuerunt. Secundum est quod in Prima recitatur, 'Quicunque vult Salvus esse :' quod ab Athanasio Patriarcha Alexandrino contra Arrianos hæreticos compositum est, licet plerique eum Anastasium fuisse falso arbitrentur."—Beleth *de Divin. Offic.*, c. 40, (p. 334, ed. Venet.).

[v] Teutzel., *Judic. Erud.*, p. 91.

[x] Fabric., *Bibl. Græc.*, lib. v. c. 42, § 12, in vol. x. p. 293.

which must here be taken notice of; being of use for the certifying us that this Creed was extant in Greek at and before his time. It is this: "They (the Greeks) do not know who made the addition to the Faith of Athanasius, styled Catholic; since the words, 'and of the Son,' are not in the Greek (Form) nor in the Creed (of Constantinople ᵞ)."

From this passage we may learn that there was a Greek copy of the Athanasian Creed at this time; that it wanted the words "of the Son," that it was looked upon as Athanasius's, and that the title was, "The Catholic Faith of St. Athanasius," which is its most usual title in the Latin copies. I may just hint to the reader, that though both πίστις in the Greek and *fides* in the Latin might justly be rendered Creed in English, rather than faith, whenever it stands for a formulary or confession of faith as it does here; yet because I should otherwise want another English word for σύμβολον in the Greek, and *Symbolum* in the Latin, I therefore reserve the word Creed in this case for distinction sake, to be the rendering of *Symbolum*, or σύμβολον, and nothing else. But to proceed.

1230. Alexander of Hales, in Gloucestershire, may here deserve to be mentioned as shewing what Creeds were then received in England. He reckons up three only, not four, (as those that make the Nicene and Constantinopolitan to be two,) namely, The Apostles', the Nicene or Constantinopolitan, and the Athana-

---

ᵞ "Ὅτι καὶ αὐτοὶ ἀγνοοῦσι, τίς ὁ προσθήσας ἐν τῇ πίστει τοῦ ἁγίου Ἀθανασίου, τῇ καθολικῇ λεγομένῃ, ὡς ἐν τῷ ἑλληνικῷ οὐχὶ τοῦτο, ὅπερ ἐστὶ καὶ ἐκ τοῦ υἱοῦ, περίεχεται, οὔτε ἐν τῷ συμβόλῳ.—Leo Allat. *de Consens. Eccl. Occident.*, &c., lib. iii. c. 1, § 5, p. 587.

sian[z], where we may observe that the Athanasian has the name of a Creed, which yet was not its most usual or common title in those times, only the schoolmen for order and method sake chose to throw it under the head of Creeds.

1233. I am next to take notice of the famed legates of Pope Gregory IX., (Haymo, Rudolphus, Petrus, and Hugo,) who produced this Creed in their conferences with the Greeks at Constantinople. They asserted it to be Athanasius's, and made by him while an exile in the Western parts, and penned in the Latin tongue [a]. They had not assurance enough to pretend that it was a Greek composition; there were too many and too plain reasons to the contrary.

1240. In this age, Walter de Cantilupe, Bishop of Worcester, in his Synodical Constitutions, exhorts his clergy to make themselves competent masters of the Psalm called *Quicunque vult*, and of the greater and smaller Creed, (that is, Nicene and Apostolical,) that they might be able to instruct their people [b]; from whence we may observe that at this time the Athanasian formulary was distinguished here amongst us from the Creeds properly so called, being named a Psalm,

---

[z] "Notandum quod cum sint tria Symbola: primum Apostolorum, secundum patrum quod canitur in Missa, tertium Athanasii, quod canitur in Prima."—*Alex. Ales.*, Pars iii. q. 82, § 5, in vol. i. fol. 280.

[a] Ὁ ἅγιος Ἀθανάσιος ὅταν ἐν τοῖς μέρεσι τοῖς δυτικοῖς ἐξόριστος ἦν, ἐν τῇ ἐκθέσει τῆς πίστεως. ἣν τοῖς λατινικοῖς ῥήμασι διεσάφησεν, οὕτως ἔφη. Ὁ πατὴρ ἀπ' οὐδενός ἐστι, &c.—*Definitio Apocrisariorum Greg. IX.*, in Harduin, vol. vii. p. 157.

[b] "Habeat etiam saltem quilibet eorum simplicem intellectum, secundum quod continetur in Psalmo qui dicitur, Quicunque vult, et tam in majori quam in minori Symbolo, ut in his plebem sibi commissam noverint informare."—Spelm., *Conc.*, vol. ii. p. 246.

and sometimes a hymn, (as we shall see from other evidences to be produced hereafter,) suitably to the place it held in the Psalters among the other Hymns, Psalms, and Canticles of the Church, being also sung alternately in churches like the other.

1250. We may here also take notice of a just remark made by Thomas Aquinas of this century: that Athanasius whom he supposes the author of this formulary, did not draw it up in the way of a Creed, but in a doctrinal form, which however was admitted by the authority of the Roman see as containing a complete system of Christian faith [c].

1255. Walter de Kirkham, Bishop of Durham, in his Constitutions, about this time, makes much the same order that Walter Cantilupe had before done, styling the Creed a Psalm also as usual [d].

1286. Johannes Januensis, sometimes styled Johannes Balbus, makes mention of this Creed in his Dictionary or *Catholicon*, under the word *Symbolum*. He reckons up three Creeds, and in this order, Apostles', Nicene, and Athanasian. The name he gives to the last is *Symbolum Athanasii*, thrice repeated [e].

[c] "Athanasius non composuit manifestationem Fidei per modum Symboli, sed magis per modum cujusdam doctrinæ: sed quia integram Fidei veritatem ejus doctrina breviter continebat, authoritate summi Pontificis est recepta, ut quasi regula Fidei habeatur."—Aquinas, *Secunda Secundæ*, q. 1. Art. 10, § 3, in vol. xi. part 2, p. 8.

[d] "Habeat quoque unusquisque eorum simplicem intellectum Fidei, sicut in Symbolo tam majori quam minori; quod est in Psalmo, 'Quicunque vult,' et etiam 'Credo in Deum,' expressius continentur."—Spelm., *Conc.*, vol. ii. p. 294.

[e] "Tria sunt Symbola; scilicet Apostolorum, quod dicitur in Matutinis, in Prima, et in Completorio: item Nicenum, quod dicitur in diebus dominicis post Evangelium: item Athanasii, quod dicitur in Prima in dominicis diebus alta voce. . . . Symbolum autem Athanasii quod contra Hereticos editum est, in Prima dicitur, quasi jam pulsis Hereticorum tenebris. . . . Ad id editum est Sym-

1287. In a synod of Exeter, in this century also, we have mention again made of the Athanasian Creed under the name of a Psalm, and as such distinguished from the two Creeds [f] properly so called; though the name of Psalm was also sometimes given to the Creeds, and to the Lord's Prayer [g] likewise, since those also were sung in the church.

1286. William Durants, or Durandus, the elder, Bishop of Menda, in France, recounting the Creeds, makes their number three, mentioning the Athanasian in the second place between the Apostles' and Nicene. He follows the same tradition which Otho Frisingensis did before, that this Creed was made at Triers or Treves [h]. It is scarce worth noting that some copies here read Anastasius, since the circumstances plainly shew that Athanasius is the man intended, and that Anastasius can be nothing else but a corrupt reading.

1330. Ludolphus Saxo, the Carthusian, numbers three Creeds, with very brief but good hints of their uses respectively: the Apostles' useful for a short compendious instruction in the faith; the Nicene, for

bolum Athanasii qui specialiter contra Hereticos se opposuit."— Johan. Januens., *in core Symbolum*.

[f] "Articulorum Fidei Christianorum saltem simplicem habeant intellectum, prout in Psalmo, Quicunque vult, et in utroque Symbolo continentur."—Spelm., *Conc.*, vol. ii. p. 370.

[g] In a MS. of Trinity College, (called Rythmus Anglicus), written about 1180, is a copy of the Apostles' Creed, and another of the Lord's Prayer, with these titles: 'The Salm the Me Clepeth Credo; The Salm that is cleped pr. nr.' This manner of speaking seems to have been borrowed from the Germans; for Otfridus, as is observed by Lambecius, gives the name of a Psalm to the Apostles' Creed.—Lambec., *Catal.*, vol. ii. p. 760.

[h] "Nota, quod triplex est Symbolum. Primum est Symbolum Apostolorum, quod vocatur Symbolum minus.... Secundum Symbolum est, 'Quicunque vult Salvus esse,' &c., ab Athanasio, patriarcha Alexandrino, in civitate Treviri compositum.... Tertium est Nicænum quod.... vocatur Symbolum majus."—Gul. Durant., *Rational. Divin. Offic.*, lib. iv. c. 25, §§ 6—9, p. 133.

fuller explication; and the Athanasian, for guard or defence[i] against heresies.

1337. William of Baldensal or Boldesale, a German Knight, ought here to be mentioned as being the first writer extant that ascribes the Creed to Eusebius, (of Verceil, in Piedmont,) along with Athanasius. The reason, I presume, was the better to account for the Creed's being originally Latin. Baldensal's treatise, being the History of Piedmont, wherein he makes the remark, is not yet published I suppose; but Cardinal Bona informs us that the manuscript was in his time in the library of the Duke of Savoy, at Turin[k].

1360. Manuel Caleca, a latinizing Greek, wrote a treatise upon the Principles of the Catholic Faith, published by Combefis, in his new *Auctarium* to the *Bibliotheca Patrum*, tome the 2nd, where we find some passages to our present purpose; particularly this, that Caleca ascribes the Creed to Athanasius, and supposes it to have been presented by him to Pope Julius[l]. I know not whether he be not the first writer that mentions that circumstance, nor whether he reports it from others, or from his own invention.

1360. About the same time Johannes Cyparissiota,

---

[i] "Tria sunt Symbola: primum Apostolorum; secundum, Niceni Concilii: tertium, Athanasii. Primum factum est ad Fidei Instructionem. Secundum, ad Fidei explanationem. Tertium, ad Fidei defensionem."—Ludolph. Sax. *de Vit. Christi*, c. 83, p. 732.

[k] "In hoc autem Symbolo, sive componendo, sive e Graeco in Latinum traducendo Adjutorem fuisse Athanasio Eusebium, Vercellensem episcopum, refert Gulielmus Baldesanus in Historia Pedemontana, quae manuscripta Taurini asservatur in Bibliotheca Ducis Sabaudiae, ex Tabulario Vercellensis Ecclesiae."—Bona *de Divin. Psalm.*, c. 16, § 18, p. 864.

[l] Ταύτην γὰρ ἐὰν μή τις πιστῶς πιστεύσῃ, σωθῆναι οὐ δύναται, ὡς ὁ μέγας Ἀθανάσιος ἐν τῇ πρὸς Ἰούλιον πάπαν Ῥώμης τῆς πίστεως ὁμολογίᾳ προσέθηκεν.—Manuel Calec., *de Fid.*, c. 10, p. 284. Cf. Calec., *Contr. Graec.*, lib. ii. c. 20, p. 416.

surnamed "the Wise," wrote his Decads, which are published in Latin in the *Bibliothèques* of Turrianus's version. What we are to observe from him is, that he cites this Creed in the name of Athanasius, and as if it were made at the Council of Nice [m]. It seems, after it once passed current that Athanasius was the author, there was great variety of conjectures about the place where, and the time when, he composed or presented this Creed.

1439. I shall mention but one more, as late as the Council of Florence, or a little later, and that is Johannes (afterwards Josephus) Plusiadenus, a latinizing Greek, who wrote a dialogue in defence of the Latins. What is observable in him is, that he makes the Creed to have been presented by Athanasius to Pope Liberius, instead of Julius [n].

I have now come low enough with the Ancient Testimonies, if I may be allowed so to call those of the later times. A few of the first and earliest might have sufficed, had I no other point in view but the mere antiquity of the Creed: but as my design is to treat of its reception also in various places and at various times, and to lay together several kind of evidences which will require others, both early and late, to clear up and explain them, it was, in a manner, necessary for me to bring my accounts as low as I have here done. Besides that several inferior incidental ques-

[m] "Magnus Athanasius in expositione Fidei, in prima Synodo, ait," &c.—Joan. Cypariss., Decad. ix. c. 3.

[n] 'Ο θεῖος τῷ ὄντι καὶ ἱερὸς 'Αθανάσιος, ἐν τῇ ὁμολογίᾳ τῆς ἑαυτοῦ πίστεως, ἥν ἐξέθετο πρὸς Λιβέριον Πάπαν, ἧς ἡ ἀρχὴ, ὅστις ἂν βούληται σωθῆναι, τὸ πνεῦμα τὸ ἅγιόν φησιν, ἀπὸ τοῦ πατρὸς καὶ τοῦ υἱοῦ, οὐ ποιητὸν, οὐ κτιστὸν, οὐδὲ γεννητὸν. ἀλλ' ἐκπορευτόν.— Plusiad., p. 628 (in Combef. *not. in Calec.*, p. 297).

tions will fall in our way, for the resolving of which most of the testimonies I have here cited will be serviceable in their turn, as will appear more fully in the sequel. I have omitted several testimonies of the later centuries, such as I thought might conveniently be spared, either as containing nothing but what we had before from others more ancient, or as being of no use for the clearing up any that we have, or for the settling any point which will come to be discussed in the following sheets. The rule I have set myself in making the collection, and which I have been most careful to observe, was to take in all those, and none but those, which are either valuable for their antiquity, or have something new and particular upon the subject, or may strike some light into any doubtful question thereunto relating.

I shall shut up this chapter, as I did the former, with a Table, representing in one view the sum and substance of what has been done in it. The several columns will contain the year of our Lord, the authors here recited, the country where they lived, and the title or titles by them given to the Creed. The titles ought to appear in their original language wherein they were written, which my English reader may the more easily excuse, since they have most of them been given in English above, where it was more proper to do it. The use of such a Table will be seen as often as a reader has a mind to look back to this chapter, or to compare several evidences of different kinds, proving the same thing one with another.

A TABLE OF THE ANCIENT TESTIMONIES.

A.D.	Authors.	Country.	Title of the Creed.
670	Council of Autun.	France.	Fides Sancti Athanasii Præsulis.
760	Articles Inqu. Regino.	Germany.	Sermo Athanasii Episcopi de Fide.
794	Conne. Franckfort.	Germany.	Fides Catholica Sanctæ Trinitatis.
809	Theodulphus.	France.	
809	Anonymous.	France.	Expositio Catholicæ Fidei, Athanasii.
809	Monks of M. Olivet.	Judæa.	Fides Sancti Athanasii.
820	Hatto, or Hetto.	France.	Fides Sancti Athanasii.
820	Agobardus.	France.	
852	Hincmar.	France.	Sermo Athanasii de Fide.
			Athanasii Symbolum.
865	Anscharius.	Germany.	Athanasii Fides Catholica.
868	Bertram.	France.	Libellus Athanasii de Fide.
868	Æneas Paris.	France.	Athanasii Fides Catholica.
871	Adalbertus.	France.	Sermo Beati Athanasii.
889	Riculphus.	France.	Sermo Fidei Catholicæ.
960	Ratherius.	Italy.	SermoAthanasii Episc.de Fide Trinitatis.
997	Abbo, or Albo.	France.	Fides secundum Athanasium.
1047	Gualdo.	France.	Fides Catholica Athanasio adscripta.
1130	Honorius.	France.	Fides *Quicunque vult*.
1146	Otho.	Bavaria.	Quicunque vult, &c.
1171	Duke of Brunswick.	Germany.	Athanasii Symbolum Fidei.
1178	Robertus Paululus.	France.	Quicunque vult, &c.
1190	Beleth.	France.	Athanasii Symbolum.
1200	Nic. Hydruntinus.	Italy.	Τοῦ ἁγίου Ἀθανασίου πίστις ἡ Καθολική.
1230	Alexander Alens.	England.	Athanasii Symbolum.
1233	P. Gregory's Legates.		Ἔκθεσις τῆς πίστεως.
1240	Walter Cantilupe.	England.	Psalmus *Quicunque*, &c.
1250	Thom. Aquinas.	Italy.	Athanasii Manifestatio Fidei.
1255	Walter Kirkham.	England.	Psalmus *Quicunque*, &c.
1286	John Januensis.	Italy.	Symbolum Athanasii.
1286	Durandus.	France.	Athanasii Symbolum.
1287	Exon. Synod.	England.	Psalmus *Quicunque*.
1330	Ludolphus.	Saxony.	Athanasii Symbolum.
1337	Baldensal.	Germany.	Athanasii Symbolum.
1360	Man. Calcca.	Greece.	Ἡ τῆς πίστεως ὁμολογία τοῦ Ἀθανασίου.
1360	Joan. Cyparissiota.	Greece.	Athanasii Expositio Fidei.
1439	Joan. Plusiadenus.	Greece.	Ἡ τῆς πίστεως ὁμολογία τοῦ Ἀθανασίου.

CHAPTER III.

ANCIENT COMMENTATORS AND PARAPHRASTS UPON THE ATHANASIAN CREED.

ANCIENT Comments, or Paraphrases, may be properly mentioned after Ancient Testimonies, being near akin to them, and almost the same thing with them. I call none ancient but such as were made before the year 1500, and therefore shall carry my accounts no lower, nor quite so low as that time.

A.D. 570. The first comment to be met with on this Creed is one of the sixth century, composed by Venantius Fortunatus, an Italian by birth, but one that travelled into France and Germany, became acquainted with the most eminent scholars and prelates all over the West, and was at length made Bishop of Poictiers in France. His comment on this Creed has been published from a manuscript about 600 years old[a], out of the Ambrosian Library at Milan, by Muratorius, in his second tome of *Anecdota*, in the year 1698. There can be no reasonable doubt but that the comment really belongs to the man whose name it bears. 1. Be-

---

[a] "Est porro nobis in Ambrosiana Bibliotheca Membranaceus Codex annos abhinc ferme sexcentos manu descriptus; ut ex characterum forma, aliisque conjecturis affirmari posse mihi videtur. Heic, præter alia opuscula multa, Tres Symboli expositiones habentur, quarum unam tantum nunc publici juris facio.

"Prima ita inscribitur, Expositio Fidei Catholicæ. Alteri nullus titulus præfixus est. Postrema vero hunc præ se fert; Expositio Fidei Catholicæ Fortunati. . . . Fortunatus autem, hoic memoratus, alius a Venantio Fortunato non est, quem Insulæ Pictaviensis Ecclesiæ, quem Christianæ poetices ornamenta æternitate donarunt."
—Murator., *Anecdot.*, vol. ii. p. 228.

cause in the same book there is also a comment upon the Apostles' Creed [b] ascribed to Fortunatus, and which is known to belong to Venantius Fortunatus, and has been before printed among his other works. 2. Because it appears highly probable, from what Venantius Fortunatus has occasionally dropped in his other undoubted works [c], that he was really acquainted with the Athanasian Creed, and borrowed expressions from it. 3. Because in the expositions of the Apostles' and Athanasian Creeds, there is great similitude of style, thoughts, and expressions, which shews that both are of the same hand, and indeed, the other circumstances considered, abundantly proves it. It would burden my margin too much, otherwise it were easy to give at least half-a-dozen plain specimens, where either the expressions, or turn of thought, or both, are exactly

---

[b] "Expositionem quoque continet (Codex Ambrosianus) Apostolici Symboli, cum hac inscriptione: Incipit expositio a Fortunato Presbytero conscripta. Eadem vero est ac edita inter Fortunati Opera. Tum sequuntur geminæ ejusdem Symboli explicationes, tres Orationis Dominicæ, et duæ Athanasiani Symboli expositiones incertis auctoribus scriptæ, tandem, ut diximus, Expositio Fidei Catholicæ Fortunati legitur. Quocirco quin ad Venantium quoque Fortunatum opusculum hoc sit referendum, nullus dubito."—Murator., *Anecdot.*, vol. ii. p. 331.

[c] "Præclarum in primordio ponitur cœlestis testimonii fundamentum, quia Salvus esse non poterit, qui recte de Salute non crediderit."—Fortunat., *Expos. Symb. Apost.* in Bibl. Max. PP., vol. x. p. 592.

"Non Deus in carnem est versus, Deus accipit artus:
Non se permutans, sed sibi membra levans.
. . . . . .
Unus in ambabus naturis, verus in ipsis
Æqualis matri hinc, par Deitate Patri.
Non sua confundens, sibi nostra sed omnia nectens.
. . . . . .
De patre natus habens divina, humananaque matris,
De patre sublimis, de genetrice humilis."
Fortunat., lib. viii. Carm. v., vv. 33, &c.; in Bibl. Max. PP., vol. x. p. 574.

parallel. Such as think it of moment to examine, may easily be satisfied by comparing the comment on the Apostles' Creed, in the tenth tome of the last *Bibliothèque*, with the comment on the Athanasian in Muratorius. 4. I may add, that the tenour of the whole comment, and the simplicity of the style and thoughts, are very suitable to that age, and more so than to the centuries following. These reasons convince me that this comment belongs to Venantius Fortunatus, composed by him after his going into France, and before he was Bishop of Poictiers, and so we may probably fix the date of it about the year 570, or perhaps higher. There is an older manuscript copy of this comment (as I find by comparing) in the Museum at Oxford, among Junius's manuscripts, number 25 [d]. I am obliged to the very worthy and learned Dr. Haywood, for sending me a transcript of it, with a specimen of the character. It is reasonably judged to be about 800 years old. It wants in the beginning about ten or a dozen lines: in the other parts it agrees with Muratorius's copy, saving only some slight insertions and such various lections as are to be expected in different manuscripts not copied one from the other. From the two copies compared may be drawn out a much more correct comment than that which Muratorius has given us from one, as will be shewn at the end of this work.

I intimated above, that Muratorius supposes this Venantius Fortunatus to be the author not of the comment only, but Creed also. But his reasons which plead strongly for the former are of no force at all in

[d] The title, *Expositio in Fide Catholica*.

respect of the latter, which he is so sensible of himself, that while he speaks with great assurance of the one, he is very diffident of the other[e]. And indeed, not to mention several other considerations standing in the way of his conjecture, who can imagine Venantius Fortunatus to have been so vain as, after commenting on the Lord's Prayer and Apostles' Creed, to fall to commenting upon a composition of his own?

This comment of Fortunatus is a great confirmation of what hath been above cited from the Council of Autun; for if the Creed was noted enough to deserve a comment upon it so early as the year 570, no wonder if we find it strongly recommended by that Council in the year 670, a hundred years after. And it is observable that as that Council recommends the Apostolical and Athanasian Creeds, without saying a word of the Nicene; so Fortunatus, before them, comments upon those two only, taking no notice of the third.

I cannot take leave of this comment without observing to the reader, that in Pareus's Notes on this Creed, I have met with a passage which I am not well able to account for. He cites a comment upon this Creed under the name of Euphronius Presbyter[f]; does not say whether from a print or a manuscript; but

---

[e] "Hujus Symboli auctor esse potuit Venantius Fortunatus: saltem fuit is hujus Expositionis auctor."—Murator., *Anecdot.*, vol. ii. p. 217.
"Non ita meis conjecturis plaudo, ut facilius non arbitrer Expositionem potius quam Symbolum huic auctori tribuendam."— *Id.*, p. 231.

[f] "Euphronius presbyter in expositione hujus Symboli Athanasii, Fides, inquit, Catholica, seu universalis, dicitur: hoc est, recta, quam Ecclesia universa tenere debet." — David. Parei *not. ad Symb. Athan.*, p. 118. Edit. An. 1635. The words are not in the edition of 1627.

the words he produces are in this very comment of Fortunatus. Who this Euphronius is I can nowhere find; nor whether an ancient or modern writer. There was an Euphronius Presbyter (mentioned by Gregory of Tours), who lived in the fifth century, and was at length Bishop of Autun; but I never heard of any writings of his more than an epistle ascribed to him and Lupus of Troyes. There was another Euphronius, who was Bishop of Tours, with whom Fortunatus had some intimacy: whether his name appearing in any MS. copy of Fortunatus's tracts, might occasion the mistake, I know not. Bruno's comment has the very same passage which Pareus cites, only in a different order of the words; but neither will this help us to account for its being quoted under the name of Euphronius Presbyter, which has no similitude with the name of Bruno, Bishop of Wurtzburgh. I would not, however, omit the mentioning this note of Pareus, because a hint may sometimes lead to useful discoveries, and others may be able to resolve the doubt though I am no t.

852. Our next commentator, or rather paraphrast, is Hincmar of Rheims: not upon the whole Creed, but upon such parts only as he had occasion to cite; for his way is to throw in several words of his own, as explanatory notes, so far as he quotes the Creed[g]. And he sometimes does it more than he ought to have done to serve a cause against Gothescalcus, which I may hint in passing; to say more of it would be foreign to our present purpose.

[g] Hincm. *de non Trin. Deit.*, cc. 2, 4, 18, in vol. i. pp. 452, 464, 469, 552, 553.

1033. S. Bruno, Bishop of Wurtzburgh in Germany, has a formal comment, and much larger than Fortunatus's, upon the Athanasian Creed. It is at the end of his Psalter, and has been several times printed with it. Father Le Long reckons up six editions [h] in this order:—1. At Nuremberg, in folio, A.D. 1494. 2. By Antonius Koburger, in quarto, A.D. 1497. 3. By Cochleus, at Wurtzburgh, in quarto, A.D. 1531. 4. At Leipsic, in quarto, 1533. 5. In the Cologne *Bibliothèque*, A.D. 1618, tom. xi.[i] 6. In the Lyons *Bibl. PP.*, A.D. 1677, tom. xviii. The old editions are scarce and not easy to be met with. I have seen two of them in our Public Library at Cambridge, those of 1494 and 1533. There is an elegant one of the former (as I conceive by the description sent me by a learned gentleman), in the Bodleian, at Oxford: it is in vellum, in a black and red letter, reserved among the manuscripts, and marked Laud E. 81. The title at the beginning, *Fides Anastasii* [j]; at the end, *Fides Athanasii*. The two editions of 1497 and 1531 I never saw. I have seen one by Antonius Koberger, in quarto, bearing date A.D. 1494 [k], in the Bodleian, marked

[h] "Commentarii in totum Psalterium et in Cantica Vet. et N. Testamenti, in fol. Norembergae, 1494. In quarto, per Antonium Koburger, 1497. Idem a Joan. Cochleo restitutum in quarto, Herbipoli, 1531. Lipsiae, 1533, Bibl. PP. Coloniensis et Lugdunensis."—Le Long, *Bibl. Sacr.*, vol. ii. p. 674.
[i] *Bibliotheca Magna Veterum Patrum*, 15 vols. fol. Col. 1618.
[j] 'Anastasii' is evidently a mere misprint, as in the body of the comment the name of Athanasius occurs throughout. The only copy of this edition now in the Bodleian, so exactly corresponds with the details given by Dr. Waterland of the two which he describes as distinct, that it seems probable that he is mistaken on this point. It is now marked Auct. Q. 1, 5. 19. The edition of 1497 is also in the Bodleian.
[k] "Per Antonium Koberger impressum Anno incarnationis Deitatis millesimo quadringentesimo, nonagesimo quarto, finit feliciter."

F. 40. Bishop Usher makes mention of an edition in 1531[1], and seems to have known of none older. I should have suspected 1531 to be a false print for 1533, had not Le Long confirmed it that there is such an edition as 1531, and named the place where it was printed; though I cannot but observe that he makes a folio of it in his first tome[m], and a quarto in the second, which is to me an argument that he had never seen it, but perhaps took the hint from Usher. But leaving the printed editions of this comment of Bruno's, let us next say something of the manuscripts of it, and their differences from the prints, or from each other. There are many manuscript copies which I shall mention in order.

1. The first and most valuable manuscript is in the Library of Wurtzburgh, as old as the author, left by him as a legacy to that Church. The first printed edition (if I mistake not), was taken from that very original manuscript[n], which at the lowest computation must

---

[1] "Psalterii editio vulgata Latina, obelis et asteriscis distincta, cum Brunonis Herbipolensis Episcopi commentariis, Anno 1531, a Johanne Cochlæo in lucem est emissa."—Usser *de Editione LXX. Interpr.*, p. 104.

[m] "Psalterium vetus obelis et asteriscis distinctum, cum Commentariis S. Brunonis, studio Johannis Cochlæi editum, in fol. Herbipoli, 1531, in quarto Lipsiæ 1533." — Le Long, *Bibl. Sacr.*, vol. i. p. 274.

[n] "Posteris Filiis suis (S. Bruno) memorabilem et sanctum Psalmorum Librum, ex quo ille impressus est, sumptuose scriptum, quasi hæreditatis spiritualis non minimam portionem reliquit."—Prolog. ad Editionem Anni 1494.

"Preciosum istum pietatis Thesaurum posteritati post se reliquit, et quidem insigni scriptura sumptuose descriptum ... extat Donum illud memorabile et conspicuum in locuplete antiquorum voluminum Bibliotheca Ecclesiæ Herbipolensis: quod sane religiosa pietate, velut Hæreditas quædam hujus Sancti Patris Custoditur." —Joan. Cochl., *Prolog. ad Edit. Ann.* 1533, in Bibl. Max. PP., vol. xviii. p. 65.

E

be 680 years old. The title of the Creed, *Fides Catholica S. Athanasii Episcopi.*

2. There is a second which I have seen in Trinity College, in Cambridge, annexed to a Psalter described at large by the learned Mr. Wanley in his catalogue[o], and judged by him to have been written about the time of King Stephen; so that this is about a hundred years later than the former, or about 580 years old. No title to the Creed.

3. There is a third of much the same age with the former, or some years older, in the Bodleian, at Oxford, marked Laud, H. 61. Catal. No. 1324. The title of the Creed, *Fides Catholica Sancti Athanasii Episcopi* [p].

4. In the Bodleian also is another, (Laud. E. 71. Catal. No. 994[q].) *Athanasii Symbolum cum Glossis.* This, as I am certified by a learned gentleman, is Bruno's comment. The title of the Creed, *Fides Sancti Athanasii Episcopi.*

5. In Merton College is another, an ancient copy of Bruno's comment, Catal. No. 675—208, (P. 1, 5 [r].)

6. In St. John Baptist's College, Oxon. (Catal. No. 1874, G. 42 [s].) *Commentarius in Symbolum Athanasii.* By the beginning and concluding words (a transcript of which has been sent me by a worthy member of

[o] Wanley, *Catalog. MSS. Septentr.*, p. 168.
[p] No. 96 in Mr. Coxe's Catalogue, and referred by him to the end of the eleventh century. It formerly belonged to the Church of St. Kykian, in Wurtzburgh.
[q] No. 17 in Mr. Coxe's Catalogue, and referred by him to the twelfth century.
[r] No. 208 in Mr. Coxe's Catalogue, and referred by him to the thirteenth century.
[s] No. 31 in Mr. Coxe's Catalogue, and referred by him to the thirteenth century.

that society) I am well assured that it is Bruno's comment.

7. There is another in Balliol College (Catal. No. 210. marked B. 9ᵗ.) *Athanasii Symbolum cum Commentario.*

8. Another I have seen in the Cathedral library at York, which may be 500 years old. No title.

9. There is another in the library of St. German de Prez, about 500 years old. Montfaucon, having met with it, published it[u] as an Anecdoton; not knowing that it was Bruno's comment. It is not indeed quite so full, nor anything near so correct as the printed copy: but still it is plainly Bruno's comment, the title, *Tractatus de Fide Catholica.*

10. There is also in my Lord Oxford's library[v], a modern manuscript of this comment, written at Augsburg, in the year 1547: copied from Bruno's original MS. (by order of Charles Peutenger, son to the famous Conrad), where the title is, *Fides Catholica Sancti Anastasii Episcopi.* The mistake of *Anastasii* for *Athanasii,* we find, had crept into the German copies some centuries before: wherefore this is not to be wondered at. All the older copies, as well as the original manuscript, have *Athanasii* in the title, where there is a title, and *Athanasius* in the beginning of the comment.

The manuscripts which I have here recited, all but the first, seem now to be of no great use; if it be true, as I suppose, that the first prints were taken from the

---

[t] No. 32 in Mr. Coxe's Catalogue, and referred by him to the end of the twelfth century. He describes it as *Symbolum Athanasianum cum commento Brunonis Herbipolensis.*

[u] Montfaucon, *Athanas. Oper.*, vol. ii. p. 735.

[v] Now the Harleian Collection in the British Museum.

very original at Wurtzburgh. It is certain that they
are very imperfect, and uncorrect (I have collated
three of them) in comparison of the printed copies:
I could not observe above two or three places, and
those not very material, where the printed copies seem
to have followed a false reading, or may be corrected
by those manuscripts. One thing I a little wondered
at, that the three manuscripts of St. Germans, Trinity
College, and York, should all leave out some paragraphs which appear in the printed copies, and the
same paragraphs: but I have since found that those
very paragraphs were taken out of Fortunatus's comment, and belong not properly to Bruno's. This, I
presume, the first copiers understood, and therefore
omitted them. Probably Bruno's own copy might at
first want them, (though they must have been added
soon after,) or, if Bruno himself inserted them, yet he
had left some mark of distinction which was understood
at that time, though not by the editors of this comment
so many years after. But to proceed.

1120. In the next age, the famous Peter Abelard
wrote comments upon this Creed, which are printed
amongst his other works. The title in the prints is,
Petri Abaëlardi Expositio Fidei, in Symbolum Athanasii.
I suspect that the editor has added the latter part, *in
Symbolum Athanasii*, as a hint to the reader. The
comment is a very short one, scarce three pages in
quarto, and, for the age it was wrote in, a pretty
good one; though, as I conceive from some flaws in it,
printed from a copy not very correct.

1170. Of the same century is Hildegarde, the celebrated Abbess of St. Rupert's Mount, near Binghen on

the Rhine. She wrote "Explications of St. Benedict's Rule, and of the Athanasian Creed," which may be seen, Bibl. Max. PP., vol. xxiii. p. 596.

1210. Simon Tornacensis, priest of Tournay, in the beginning of the thirteenth century taught divinity at Paris with great reputation. His manuscript works are in many libraries, and among his other writings there is "An Exposition of the Athanasian Creed[x]." Oudin reckons up four manuscript copies of it, in as many distinct libraries, and acquaints us where they are to be found, and of what age they probably are.

1215. Contemporary with the former is Alexander Neckham, an Englishman, Abbot of Cirencester, or Circeter, in Gloucestershire. He wrote a comment on the Athanasian Creed, which is extant in manuscript, in the Bodleian, at Oxford, (marked E. 7, 8. Catal. No. 2339.) co-eval, probably, with the author[y].

There is another copy of the same comment in the Bodleian also, E. 6. 11. No. 2330. The title, *Expositio Fidei Catholicæ a Magistro Alexandro Edicta*. This copy is about fifty years later than the former. It may be of use to note down the first words of the comment[z]. It is drawn up in the scholastic way, and is pretty large, making ten folio leaves with double columns, in E. 7, 8. and four folio leaves with three columns, and a very small hand in E. 6. 11.

---

[x] " Expositio Symboli, per Simonem Tornacensis Ecclesiæ Canonicum, et Parisiensem Doctorem, quæ incipit ; Apud Aristotelem argumentum est ratio faciens fidem, sed apud Christum argumentum est fides faciens ra ionem."—Oudin, *De Scriptor. Eccles.*, vol. iii. p. 5.

[y] The title of this copy is, *Expositio super Symbolum Athanasii*.

[z] " Hæc est enim victoria quæ vincit mundum, fides nostra. Signanter dicit ' vult,' et non dicit, ' Quicunque Salvus erit.'"

1230. Not long after, Alexander Hales, before mentioned, wrote comments upon the same Creed, which are published in his *Summa*, part the third, under Quæst. 82. His method of commenting is, to raise doubts and scruples all the way he goes, and to answer them in the scholastic form; referring sometimes to the Fathers of the Church, and particularly to St. Austin, to whom he ascribes Gennadius's treatise *de Ecclesiasticis Dogmatibus*, according to the common error of that time. But I proceed.

1340. There is another commentary upon this Creed, written, as is said, by Richardus Hampolus, Richard Rolle, of Hampole, a native of Yorkshire, and a monk of the order of St. Austin. It contains, in a manner, Bruno's comment entire, with several additions and insertions, either of the author's own, or such as he had borrowed elsewhere. It has been twice printed, first at Cologne, in the year 1536, and afterwards in the Bibl. Max. PP., vol. xxvi. p. 624.

I am in doubt concerning the author of that comment, having reason to believe that the three copies mentioned by Tentzelius[a], preserved in the Gotha, Basil, and Leipsic libraries, are so many copies of this very comment which passes under the name of Hampole, and yet one of them is judged to be above 500 years older[b] than 1686, which is 150 years before

---

[a] Tentzel., *Jud. Erud.*, Præfat. et p. 224.
[b] Tentzelius writes thus:—" Opportune ad manus meas pervenit responsio Ampl. Felleri, qua rationem Codicis Latini Lipsiensis in præfatione a me citati prolixius exposuit. Ait enim, membranaceum istum codicem ante CCCCC. annos et ultra, eleganter scriptum videri; additas etiam esse non interlineares tantum notas, sed et marginales utrinque; in dextro videlicet et sinistro paginarum latere: rubricam autem Symboli nostri ita se habere; Fides Anas-

Hampole's days. It is possible that Joachim Fellerus, the compiler of the catalogue of the Leipsic library, might mistake in judging of the age of the manuscript, but it appears much more probable that the editors of that comment were mistaken in ascribing it to Hampole. However that be, I would here observe, that there is in Magdalen College, in Oxford, a comment intituled *Expositio in Symbolum Athanasianum per Januensem* (Catal. No. 2256, 115 [e]) which is no other than this very comment that passes in the prints under the name of Rich. Hampole. The catalogue's ascribing it to Januensis, was owing, I suppose, to an occasional passage in that manuscript relating to the Athanasian Creed, cited from Johannes Januensis's *Catholicon*, or dictionary, under the word *Symbolum*. The comment, however, I say, is the same with that which passes for Hampole's, as may plainly appear from the beginning of it, which I have transcribed into the margin [d]; only filling up an omission in it, occasioned, as is very common, by the repetition of the same word. There may be a good use made of that manuscript in Magdalen

---

tasii Papæ. In dextro primæ paginæ hæc legi verba: Hæc ratio Fidei Catholicæ traditur in veteribus Codicibus, et reliqua, quæ antea ex MS. Bibliothecæ Ducalis attuli. Unde patet, easdem plane Glossas in utroque Codice reperiri; præsertim quum in sinistro alterius margine, hæc etiam verba legi referat Fellerus: Hic beatus Anastasius liberum arbitrium posuit," &c.—*Ib.*, p. 225.

[e] No. 115 in Mr. Coxe's Catalogue, and referred by him to the beginning of the fifteenth century.

[d] "Hæc ratio Fidei Catholicæ traditur etiam in veteribus Codicibus a beato Athanasio Alexandrino conscripta. Et puto, quod idcirco tam plano et brevi sermone tradita sit, ut omnibus Catholicis, et minus eruditis, tutamen defensionis præstaret adversus illam tempestatem [quam contrarius ventus, hoc est, diabolus, excitavit per Arrium; quam tempestatem] qui fugere desiderat, hanc Fidei unitatem (al. veritatem) integram et inviolabilem teneat. Ita enim incipit ipsum opusculum, dicens, 'Quicunque vult Salvus,' &c. Hic beatus Athanasius liberum arbitrium posuit," &c.

College, for correcting the printed copy, which is very faulty both in words and order. The comment ought to begin as it begins in that manuscript, and not with the words, *Hic beatus Athanasius*, as in the prints. The editors did not understand, or did not consider, the nature and composition of that comment. The author, whoever he was, had made two columns, one on each hand, with the Athanasian Creed in the middle. On the left-hand, which is the first place, he set Bruno's comment, and on the right-hand, in the other column, he carried down another comment either of his own or borrowed. The first note on the right-hand was plainly designed for an introduction to the rest, and therefore ought to be set first, though the editors, considering only the position of the notes, began from the left-hand, with the first words of Bruno's comment. The Oxford copy observes the true natural order, and may very probably be of good use all the way through for the better digesting and methodizing that comment or comments, being in reality two comments mixed and blended together.

I should observe of the Oxford copy, that after the comment there is in the same hand this note, *Hæc conscripta sunt a quodam antiquo libro*. Possibly this may be of some use for the determining whether that comment be really Hampole's or no. For if the manuscript be not much later than 1415 (it must be so late, since it fixes that very date to Dr. Ullerston's Exposition of the Six Psalms) it may be probably argued that anything of Hampole's, who flourished but about eighty years before, would not have been called *antiquus liber*, an 'ancient book.' But this I leave to farther enquiries, not insisting upon it, since the argument is but probable at the best; and I do not know but the manuscript may be several years later than 1415, though hardly later than the middle of that century. Ullerston is undoubtedly the latest author in that collection. Petrus Florissiensis, or Floreffiensis (otherwise called Petrus de Harentals), wrote in 1374[e]: Januensis, Gorrham, Lyra, and Hampole are all older than he: the last, therefore, is Ullerston, who was probably still living when that manuscript was written. But enough of this.

1380. To the Latin comments here mentioned I may add an English one, which I may suppose to be Wickliff's. If it be not his, yet certainly it is of his time, and not far from the middle of the fourteenth century. I will first give some account of this English comment, and then shew both why I ascribe it to Wickliff, and why I do it not with full assurance, but with some degree of diffidence. I first met with it in a manuscript volume (in 12mo.) belonging to the library of St. John's College in Cambridge. The volume contains an English version of the Psalms and Hymns of the Church, with the Athanasian Creed, produced paragraph by paragraph in Latin, interspersed with an English version of each paragraph, and commented upon quite through, part by part. After the comment follow Proverbs, Ecclesiastes, Song of Songs, Wisdom, and Ecclesiasticus, all in old English, without gloss or comment. Now the reasons why I incline to ascribe the comment to Wickliff are these:—

   1. Dr. Langbaine, of Queen's College in Oxford, in

[e] See Oudin, *de Scriptor. Eccles.*, vol. iii. p. 1218.

a letter to Bishop Usher bearing date A.D. 1647, testifies that he had seen such a comment, and that he found it to be Wickliff's by comparing the beginning of it with Bale [f]. This, very probably, is the same comment, though there is no such manuscript now in Magdalen College, Oxon., as was in Dr. Langbaine's time.

2. All those parts of Scripture which go before and after this comment in the same volume, are of the same version with that of Wickliff's Bible in the library of Emmanuel College, without any difference (except that St. John's copy, being older, retains the more ancient spelling,) as I am well assured by comparing them together, so that if those parts be Wickliff's, it may appear very probable that the comment is his too. Indeed, our very learned Wharton was of opinion that the version commonly ascribed to Wickliff [g] was really John Trevisa's, who flourished in the time of Richard the Second, was a Cornish man by birth, and Vicar of Berkely in Gloucestershire about the year 1387 [h]; in which year he finished his translation of the *Polychronicon*. But Mr. Wharton's reasonings in this matter have appeared to others not satisfactory [i], and have in

---

[f] "While I was there (in Magdalen College Library), tumbling amongst their books, I light upon an old English comment upon the Psalms, the Hymns of the Church, and Athanasius's Creed; which I presently conjectured (though there be no name to it) to be Wickliff's. And comparing the beginning with Bale, found that I had not erred in the conjecture."—Langbaine, among Usher's Letters, p. 513.

[g] Wharton, *Auctar. Histor. Dogmat.*, p. 425—427.

[h] In that year he finished his version of Higden's *Polychronicon*, as the MSS. testify; and as is plain from its being finished in the thirty-fifth year of Thomas Lord Berkely, the fourth of that name, which agrees exactly with that year, and with no other.

[i] Oudin, *de Scriptor. Eccles.*, vol. iii. p. 1044.

part been confuted[k]. I shall not enter far into that dispute, being almost foreign to my purpose, and it is not very material whether Wickliff or Trevisa (if either) be judged the author of the comment. This only I may observe by the way, that Mr. Wharton's argument, drawn from the Norfolk manuscript of the Gospels (Cod. 254), which he is positive belongs to Wickliff, appears to be of some weight, so far as concerns the New Testament, and the inference may reach to several parts of the Old Testament also. Either Mr. Wharton must have been mistaken in ascribing the Norfolk copy to Wickliff, or else, for anything I see, his argument will stand good. The characteristic which he lays down whereby to distinguish Wickliff's version (namely, the frequent insertion of synonymous words) will by no means agree with the common version: and then the specimen he gives of the two different renderings of Luke ii. 7, is directly contrary[l]. But a fuller discussion of that point may be left with those who have more leisure, and have more particularly studied it. I am content to suppose that the common version ascribed to Wickliff is really his: perhaps he might give two editions of it[m]; or

[k] Le Long, *Bibl. Sacr.*, vol. i. p. 426.
[l] Wiclefus sic reddit: "And puttide Him in a Cratche; for place was not to Him in the comyn Stable."
Alter interpres sic: "And leide Him in a Cratche; for there was no place to Him in no Chaumbre."—Wharton, p. 426.
I have a manuscript of the New Testament, belonging to our College library, which reads Luke ii. 7 according to the first reading, and which has many instances of synonymous insertions everywhere: it is a different version from that which is commonly ascribed to Wickliff.
[m] "Patet, aut antiquiorem fuisse quandam S. Scripturæ translationem Anglicam, aut duplicem fuisse translationis Wicleviana Editionem."—Wharton, p. 436.

else Trevisa's may be little more than Wickliff's version, corrected and polished with great liberty, both as to sense and expression, where it appeared needful. That Trevisa really did translate the whole Bible into English, is positively asserted by Caxton, in his preface to Trevisa's translation of Higden's *Polychronicon* [n], and by Bale [o], who gives us the first words of the preface to it. To proceed.

3. A third reason I have for the ascribing the comment to Wickliff is, that some parts of it seem to suit exactly with his humour, and manner, and way of thinking, particularly the gird upon Popes and Cardinals in the close [p].

Nevertheless, I am far from being positive in this

---

[n] "Ranulph Monke of Chestre first Auctour of this Book, and afterward Englisbed by one Trevisa Vicarye of Barkley; which atte request of one Sr. Thomas Lord Barkley translated this sayd Book, the Byble, and Bartylmew de proprietatibus rerum out of Latyn into Englysh."—Caxton, Prohemye to his Edit. 1482.

[o] "In Anglicum idioma, ad petitionem prædicti sui domini de Barkeley, transtulit totum Bibliorum opus: Utrumque Dei Testamentum lib. ii. (His preface beginning) Ego Johannes Trevisa Sacerdos."—Bal., *Cent.* vii. c. 18, p. 518.

N.B. Bale seems to be mistaken in saying that Trevisa continued the *Polychr.* to 1397. For Trevisa ended with 1357. And Caxton declares that himself continued the history for 103 years farther, to 1460. (In this Dr. Waterland appears to have been misled by a mistake of Caxton's, since the true date of the end of John Trevisa's translation is 1387. as Dr. Waterland himself states above. The last date mentioned in Trevisa's text is 1357; which is perhaps the cause of Caxton's mistake. See Pabington's Preface to Higden, vol. i. p. lxii. n.)

[p] "And algif this Crede accorde unto Prestis, netheles the higher Prelatis, as Popis and Cardynals, and Bisshops shulden more specially Kunne this Crede, and teche it to Men undir hem."—Comm. on the Athan. Creed.

Compare some words of Wicklif's Bileve.

"I suppose, over this, that the Pope be most oblishid to the keping of the Gospel among all Men that liven here; for the Pope is highest Vicar that Christ has here in Erth."—Collier, *Eccl. Hist.*, vol. i. p. 728.

matter: much may be offered to take off the force of these reasons, or to counterbalance them. 1. This very comment is annexed to a manuscript commentary upon the Psalms and Hymns of the Church, now in Trinity College Library in Cambridge; which commentary appears not to be Wickliff's, though supposed to be his by Mr. Wharton ^q. The English version of the Psalms, going along with that commentary, is not the same with that of Wickliff's Bible: I have compared them. The commentary and version, too, are reasonably judged to be Hampole's. I find by a note left in a blank page at the beginning (signed J. Russel) that there is a copy of this commentary in the Royal Library (E. 15, 12), but imperfect; the prologue the very same, and expressly ascribed to Richard of Hampole, from whence it may be justly suspected that the comment upon the Athanasian Creed at the end, appearing in part (for two leaves are cut out), is Hampole's as well as the rest. There is in Bennet Library, in Cambridge, another manuscript copy of the same commentary (marked 1—1. Catal., p. 69) with the comment upon the Creed entire. The prologue I found to be the same as in the other, as also the comment on the first Psalm; by which I judge of the rest [r]. The comment on the Canticles at the end is likewise the same, only the Canticles are not all placed in the same order. At the

---

[q] "Commentarius in Psalmos, aliosque Sacræ Scripturæ ac Liturgiæ Ecclesiasticæ Hymnos, MS. in Collegio S. Trinitatis Cantab. F. Commentarius in priores 89 Psalmos habetur MS. in Bibliotheca Lambethana."—Wharton, see. Wicklef., *Append. ad Cav. II. L.*, p. 54.

[r] Qy. whether there be not one or two more copies of the same in the Bodleian. See the Bodleian Manuscripts in the General Catalogue, No. 2438, 3085.

bottom of the second leaf of the commentary there is left this note by an unknown hand, *Author hujus Libri, Richardus, Heremita de Hampole.* Now if this commentary really be Hampole's, of which I can scarce make any question, it will appear highly probable that the comment on the Creed is his too. 2. What favours the suspicion is, that here the comment is annexed to other comments in like form with itself, and not to mere versions, as in the manuscript of St. John's library. Nay, further, this comment on the Creed, as it appears in St. John's copy, has the several parts of the Creed in Latin, and in red letter, prefixed to the respective version and comment; just as we find in Hampole the several parts of each Psalm exhibited first in Latin and in red letter, which circumstance is of some weight. 3. Add to this, that there are some expressions in the comment on the Creed very like to those which are familiar with the author of that commentary on the Psalms, such as these, "it is seid comunly, that ther ben, &c. Clerkis sein," thus and thus: so that from similitude of style an argument may be drawn in favour of Hampole as well as for Wickliff. These considerations suffer me not to be positive on the other side. The comment may be Hampole's, or it may be Wickliff's; which latter opinion I the rather incline to for the reasons before given, appearing to me something more forcible than the other. And I may farther observe that there is in Sidney College, in Cambridge, a very old copy of Hampole's commentary, which runs through the Psalms, and all the ordinary Hymns and Canticles, but has no comment upon the Athanasian Creed annexed, though the MS. appears very whole and entire. This makes me less inclinable to suspect the comment upon the Creed being Hampole's; it is more probably Wickliff's, as I before said. However it be, the comment may be useful, and if it should prove Hampole's, it must be set forty years higher than I have here placed it. The distance of thirty or forty years makes no great alteration in any language, so that merely from the language, especially in so small a tract, we can draw no consequence to the author, excepting such peculiarities as may have been rather proper to this or that man, than to this or that time.

1478. To the comments before mentioned I may add one more, a Latin one, printed as I suppose, about the year 1478, though it carries not its date with it. The author is Peter d'Osma, called in Latin, Petrus de Osoma[s], or Petrus Oxomensis, or Uxomensis. The comment makes about seventy pages in quarto, and is drawn up in the scholastic way, with good judgment and accuracy, considering the age it was written in. The book was lent me by Mr. Pownall of Lincoln, a gentleman of known abilities, and particularly curious in searching out and preserving any rare and uncommon pieces, printed or manuscript. I do not find that this comment has been at all taken notice of in any of our *Bibliothèques*, or in any of the catalogues of the books printed before 1500. Even those that give account of the author, yet seem to have known nothing of the printing of this piece: probably there were but very few copies, and most of them soon de-

---

[s] "Commentaria magistri Petri de Osoma in Symbolum 'Quicunque vult,' &c., finiunt feliciter. Impressaque Parisiis per magistrum Uuulricum, cognomento Gering."

stroyed upon the author's falling under censure in the
year 1479. The author, if I judge right, was the same
Peter Osma who was Professor of Divinity in Salamanca, and adorned the chair with great reputation
for many years. He began to be famous about the
year 1444, and at length fell under the censure of
a provincial synod, held under Alphonsus Carrillus,
Archbishop of Toledo, in the year 1479 [t]. He was
condemned for some positions advanced in a book which
he had written upon the subject of Confession. The
positions, nine in number, are such as every Protestant
professes at this day [u]; being levelled only at the corruptions of popery in doctrine and discipline; but the
good man was forced to submit and abjure, and to
profess an implicit belief in whatsoever was held for
faith by the then Pope Sixtus IV. Such, in short, is
the account of our author, one of the most learned and
valuable men of his time, by confession even of his
enemies. At what particular time he composed his
comment on the Athanasian Creed, I cannot say; only
that it was between 1444 and 1479. I have placed
it according to the time it was printed as nearly as
I am able to judge of it.

These are all the ancient comments upon the Athanasian Creed that I have hitherto met with, or heard
of, excepting only such as have no certain author, or
none mentioned.

Muratorius informs us of two comments without
names, which are in manuscript, in the Ambrosian

---

[t] Nicol. Antonius, *Bibliotheca Hispana vetus*, lib. x. c. 16, § 900,
&c., (vol. ii. p. 203.)
[u] See the Positions and Censure in Carranza.—*Summ. Concil.*,
p. 463, &c., (880, &c.)

Library, near 600 years old. One of them bears for its title, *Expositio Fidei Catholicæ;* the other has no title. By the age of the manuscripts, (if Muratorius judges rightly thereof,) one may be assured that they are distinct and different from any of the comments below Abelard: and that they are neither of them the same with Bruno's or Fortunatus's, may reasonably be concluded, because Muratorius was well acquainted with both, and would easily have discovered it. Whether either of them may prove to be Abelard's, which has for its title, *Expositio Fidei,* and may suit well with the age of the manuscripts, I know not. Muratorius, while he makes mention of Bruno and Hildegardis, whose comments he had seen, says nothing of Abelard's; so that possibly one of his manuscript comments may prove the same with that. But if neither of them be the same with Abelard's, nor with each other, they must be allowed to pass for two distinct comments, whose authors are not yet known.

Nothing now remains but to close this chapter with a Table, as I have the former, representing in one view a summary of what is contained in it.

A TABLE OF THE ANCIENT COMMENTS.

A.D.	Commentators.	Country.	Title of the Creed.
570	Venant. Fortunatus.	Poictiers.	*Fides Catholica.*
852	Hincmar.	Rheims.	*Symbolum Athanasii.*
1033	Bruno.	Wurtzburgh.	*Fides Catholica Sancti Athanasii*
1110	MS. Ambrosian.	Italy.	*Fides Catholica.* [*Episcopi.*]
1110	MS. alter Ambros.	Italy.	
1120	Pet. Abaelardus.	France.	*Symbolum Athanasii.*
1170	S. Hildegardis.	France.	
1210	Simon Tornacensis.	France.	*Symbolum Athanasii.*
1215	Alex. Neckham.	England.	*Fides Catholica.*
1230	Alexander Hales.	England.	*Athanasii Symbolum.*
1340	Rich. Hampolus.	England.	*Athanasii Symbolum.*
1380	John Wickliff.	England.	Crede, or Salm, of Attanasie.
1478	Petr. de Osoma.	Spain.	*Athanasii Symbolum.*

F

CHAPTER IV.

LATIN MANUSCRIPTS OF THE ATHANASIAN CREED.

I CONFINE myself in this chapter to the Latin manuscripts, since the Creed was undoubtedly written originally in Latin, and therefore the manuscripts in any other languages will be more properly treated of in another chapter among the versions. None of the learned at this day make any question but that the Creed was originally a Latin composure. This they pretend to be certain of, and unanimously agree in, however doubtfully they may speak of other things, or however they may differ in their opinions about the age or author. Even those, many of them, who have ascribed the Creed to Athanasius, have yet been obliged by plain and irresistible evidence to acknowledge, with the legates of Pope Gregory IX., that it was originally Latin. The style and phraseology of the Creed; its early reception among the Latins, while unknown to the Greeks; the antiquity and number of the Latin manuscripts, and their agreement (for the most part) with each other, compared with the lateness, scarceness, and disagreement of the Greek copies, all concur to demonstrate that this Creed was originally a Latin composure rather than a Greek one: and as to any other language besides these two, none is pretended.

I proceed, then, to recount the Latin manuscripts as high as we can find any extant, or as have been known to have been extant; and as low as may be necessary, or useful to our main design.

A.D. 600. The oldest we have heard of is one mentioned by Bishop Usher, which he had seen in the Cotton Library, and which he judged to come up to the age of Gregory the Great [a]. This manuscript has often been appealed to since Usher's time, and upon the credit of Usher, by the learned on this subject: as particularly by Comber, L'Estrange, Tentzelius, Tillemont, Le Quien, Muratorius, Natalis Alexander, and perhaps several more. Montfaucon takes notice of Usher's manuscript; but observes that Usher himself allowed the character to be much later than the time of Gregory [b]: which would have been a strange inconsistency in Usher, who forms his argument for the antiquity of the manuscript from the character itself, and from the ancient kind of picture. But Montfaucon is plainly mistaken, confounding what Usher had said of another manuscript, in Bennet Library at Cambridge [c], with

---

[a] "Latino-gallicum illud Psalterium in Bibliotheca Cottoniana vidimus: sicut et alia Latina duo, longe majoris antiquitatis; in quibus, præter Hymnum hunc (sc. Te Deum) sine ullo authoris nomine, Hymni ad Matutinas, titulo inscriptum, et Athanasianum habebatur Symbolum, et Apostolicum totidem omnino quot hodiernum nostrum continens capitula. In priore, quod Gregorii I. tempore non fuisse recentius, tum ex antiquo picturæ genere colligitur, tum ex literarum forma grandiuscula, Athanasianum quidem, Fidei Catholicæ, ... alterum vero Symboli Apostolorum præfert titulum. In posteriore, quod Regis Æthelstani aliquando fuit, Apostolicum, vice versa, Symbolum simpliciter, alterum autem Fides Sancti Athanasii Alexandrini nuncupatur."—Usher, *de Symb. Præf.*, p. 4 (2, 3).

[b] "Codicum omnium qui hactenus visi memoratique sunt, antiquissimus ille est qui ab Usserio laudatur, ævo Gregorii Magni conscriptus; si tamen ea vero sit ejus MS. ætas: nam addit Usserius, scripturam ævo Gregorii longe esse posteriorem."— Montf., *Diatr.*, p. 721.

[c] "In Psalterio Græco Papæ Gregorii, ut præfert titulus (scriptura enim ævo Gregorii longe est posterior) Psalterio videlicet

what he had said of the Cotton manuscript at Westminster. The two manuscripts are very distinct, and different as possible; nor has the Bennet manuscript any Athanasian Creed in it: only its being called Gregory's Psalter occasioned, I suppose, the mistake of making it the same with the other. Tentzelius[d] seems first to have confounded them together; and probably Montfaucon followed him implicitly, not having Usher at hand to consult, which would immediately have discovered the fallacy. Were there no other objection against Usher's manuscript beside what hath been mentioned, all would be well; but it is of greater weight to observe, that there is not at this day in the Cotton Library any such manuscript copy of the Athanasian Creed, nor indeed any Latin Psalter that can come up to the age of Gregory, or near it. There is an ancient Psalter (marked Vespasian A.) written in capitals and illuminated, and which might perhaps, by the character, be as old as the time of Gregory the Great, were it not reasonable to think, from a charter of King Ethelbald, written in the same hand and at the same time, and formerly belonging to it[e], that it

Græco et Romano, Latinis utroque literis descripto, quod iu Benedictini, apud Cantabrigienses, Collegii Bibliotheca est reconditum."
—Usher, *de Symb.*, p. 9. This MS. is marked N. 15 in the Catalogue of MSS. of C. C. C., Cambridge, p. 44.

[d] Tentzel., *Judic. Erudit.*, p. 49; *Exercit. Select.*, vol. i. p. 29.

[e] "Constat vero ex Historia et Synopsi Bibl. Cottonianæ, quam in ingens Reip. literariæ beneficium edidit amplificandis bonis literis Latus doctissimus Thomas Smithus noster, et indiculo Psalterii Latini in majusculis scripti cum versione Saxonica interlineari, quod notatur Vespasian. A. 1. Chartam hanc (Æthelbaldi R. Australium Saxonum) ex isto MS. exscissam esse. Quod etiam illius quum mensura quæ cum foliis illius MS. quadrat, tum etiam manus in utroque prorsus eadem, tum denique Locus MSS., unde scissa est, inter folia x. et xi., codicem vertentibus ostendit."— Hickes, *Dissert. Epist.*, p. 67, (at the end of vol. ii. of his *Thesaurus*.)

cannot be set higher than the date of that charter, A.D. 736. But I should here observe, that that charter is not in the larger capitals, as the Psalter itself is, but in the smaller capitals, the same hand that the several pieces in that manuscript, previous to the Psalter, are written in; and how far this may affect our present argument I cannot say. Possibly the Psalter itself, being in a different hand, may be older than those previous pieces, as it is certainly much older than the additional pieces at the end, which are not in capitals, great or small.

This Psalter has the *Te Deum* annexed to it, with the title of *Hymnus ad Matutinum*, as Usher's had; and also the Athanasian Creed, with the title of *Fides Catholica;* but both in a very different and much later hand than that of the Psalter itself, later by several centuries, as the very learned Mr. Wanley[f] judges, who sets the age of the Psalter about 1000 years, but of the Athanasian Creed, &c., at the time of the Norman Conquest. A suspicion, however, may from hence arise, that this very Psalter, with what belongs to it, might be the Psalter, &c., which Usher spake of, especially since there is none other in the Cotton Library at all like it. But, on the contrary, it is to be considered, that this manuscript has no Apostolical Creed at all in it, which Usher affirms his to have had; nor has it the *Hymnus Matutinus*, beginning with *Gloria in excelsis Deo*, which Usher's also had[g]; nor is the Creed

[f] Wanley, *Catal. MSS. Septentr.*, p. 222.
[g] "Ad finem veterum Psalteriorum Latinorum, cum Apostolico et Athanasiano Symbolo, etiam Hymnus iste (sc. Gloria, &c.) habetur adjectus. In antiquissimo Cottoniano ἀνεπίγραφος est: in

in capitals, as one would imagine Usher's to have been by what he says of it; neither is it at all probable, that if Usher had intended the Psalter now extant in the Cotton, he should give no hint of the Saxon version going along with it, especially considering that it might be made an objection to its antiquity; nor do I think that so inquisitive a man as Usher could either have been ignorant of the age of Ethelbald, or of his charter having been once a part of that manuscript. In his *Historia Dogmatica*[h], he takes notice of this very Psalter (now marked Vespasian A.), and of the Saxon version in it, and likewise of its being in the same hand with Ethelbald's charter; and there he sets the age of it no higher than the year 736 (that is, above 130 years later than Gregory I.), without the least hint that he had ever mistaken the age of it before, or had thought otherwise of it than he did at the time of his writing this later treatise. These considerations persuade me that Bishop Usher had seen some other manuscript, which has since that time, like many more[i], been lost or stolen from the Cotton Library. He that was so accurate in every tittle of what he says of King Athelstan's Psalter (mentioned at the same time), could never have been so negligent, or rather plainly careless, in respect of the other. I conclude, therefore, that there really was such a Psalter as Usher describes, with the Athanasian Creed in it, such as he judged to

Æthelstaniano proximo, Hymnus in die Dominico ad Matutinas, inscribitur."—Usher, *de Symbol.*, p. 42 (33).

[h] "In Bibliotheca D. Roberti Cotton extat Psalterium Romanum vetustissimum, cum versione interlineari Saxonica: character i tem cum charta Æthilbaldi Anglorum Regis, anno 736 data."—Usher, *Hist. Dogmat.*, p. 104.

[i] T. Smith, *Præf. ad Catalog. MSS. Bibl. Cotton.*

be of the age of Gregory I., from more marks than one; and how good a judge he was in those matters is well known to as many as know anything of that great man. But how far his judgment ought to sway, now the manuscript itself is lost, I must leave with the reader.

660. Next to this of Bishop Usher we may place the famous manuscript of Treves, from which the Colbert manuscript (to be mentioned hereafter in its place) was copied. Mr. Antelmi [k] sets it as high as the year 450, upon a presumption that the Colbert manuscript is as old as the year 600, and that 150 years may reasonably be allowed between the Colbertine copy and that from which it was copied. Tillemont, supposing or admitting the Colbertine to be near the age that Antelmi mentions, yet thinks fifty years difference might be sufficient, and that therefore the age of the Treves manuscript might be fixed at 550, or thereabout [l]. But, since the Colbert manuscript cannot reasonably be set much higher than 760, as we shall see in its proper place, I shall not pretend to set the Treves manuscript above 660, and that only under the favourable allowance of a probable conjecture. The authority of this manuscript of Treves stands upon the credit of a passage prefixed to the Colbertine copy [m], which declares that the latter was copied from a manuscript found at Treves. It was not a copy of the entire Creed, but began at the Second Part, which relates to the Incarnation; for, after the words "believe rightly the In-

[k] Antelm., *de Symb. Athan.*, p. 26.
[l] Tillemont, *Mémoires*, vol. viii. p. 283 (670).
[m] "Hæc inveni Treviris in uno libro scriptum, sic incipiente, Domini nostri Jesu Christi et reliqua. Domini nostri Jesu Christi fideliter credat."—Apud Montf., *Diatrib.*, p. 728.

carnation of our Lord Jesus Christ" (being only part of the foregoing sentence) follows; "for the right faith is, that we believe," and so on to the end of the Creed. This remaining part of the Creed is very different from the common copies, and seems to have been so contrived with design, as I shall have occasion to observe more at large in the sequel. And it is to me an argument that the manuscript was written while the Eutychian controversy was at the height, about the end of the fifth century, or beginning of the sixth, though I here set it a great deal lower, because this is not the place to explain that matter fully, nor would I too far indulge a bare conjecture. It is sufficient to suppose it written in the seventh century, as it was undoubtedly copied from as early if not earlier than the eighth.

700. After the manuscript of Treves may justly follow the Ambrosian manuscript, which is in the Ambrosian Library at Milan, a copy of which has been published by Muratorius, in his second tome of *Anecdota*. It was brought thither from the famous monastery of Bobbio, (of High-Lombardy, in the Milanese,) founded by Columbanus, A.D. 613. The character of the manuscript is Langobardick, and it is judged by Muratorius (who has more particularly examined it) to be above 1000 years old[n]. By his account then, who

---

[n] "In alio etiam Vetustissimo Ambrosianæ Bibliothecæ Codice ante mille et plures annos scripto, Symbolum idem sum nactus."— Murator., vol. i. p. 16.

" Cæterum opusculum Hoc (Bachiarii Fides) mihi depromptum est ex antiquissimo Ambrosianæ Bibliothecæ Codice, quem ante annos minimum mille conscriptum, characterum forma non dubitanter testatur. Fuit autem olim celebris Monasterii Bobiensis, et ex illo in Ambrosianam translatus a magno Card. Federico Borromæo," &c.—Murator., vol. ii. pp. 8, 224.

wrote in the year 1698, we ought to set the age of this manuscript higher than 698. Yet, because Montfaucon, who in his travels through Italy had also seen it, puts it no higher than the eighth century [o], we shall be content to place it between the seventh and eighth, or in the year 700, to make it a round number. There are in this manuscript some readings different from the common copies, which shall be carefully noted hereafter. It is without any title.

703. We may next set down King Athelstan's Psalter, of which Bishop Usher had taken notice, making it next in age to the other most ancient one of the age of Gregory I. He and Dr. Grabe both fix the date of it to the year 703, from the Rule of the Calendar found in it [p]. Dr. Smith, in his Catalogue of the Cotton Manuscripts, inclines to think that the manuscript is later than that time, but taken from one that was really as early as the year 703, the later copyist transcribing (as sometimes has been) the book and the Rule word for word, as he found them [q]. Allowing

---

[o] "Codex VIII. Sæculi, charactere Langobardico, in quo Gennadii de Ecclesiasticis Dogmatibus, Bachiarii Fides, Symbolum Athanasii, omnia eadem manu."—Montfauc., *Diar. Ital.*, p. 18.

[p] "Psalterium illud anno æræ nostræ Christianæ 703, longe ante Æthelstani regnantis tempora, ex regulis Kalendario in libri initio subjunctis scriptum fuisse deprehendi."—Usher, *de Symb.*, p. 8 (6).

"Quod Regis Æthelstani fuisse dicitur, atque anno 703 scriptum est."—Grabe, *Prolegom. in Vetus Test.*, vol. iv. c. 3, § 7.

[q] "Hic vero venerandæ antiquitatis liber fere ante mille annos descriptus; ut quibusdam ex Calendario, quod annum Christi 703, certo designat, illic præfixo videtur. Sed cum librarios eandem temporis adnotationem, quæ ad vetustissimos codices proprie et peculiariter spectat, suis exemplaribus apposuisse sæpissime observaverim.... an sit ille ipse codex autographus qui tantam præ se ferat ætatem, vel annon potius sæculo, aut circiter, ante tempora Æthelstani descriptus, vix pro certo præstarem; ad posteriorem sententiam faventiori animo inclinaturus."—Smith, *Bibl.*

this to have been the case here (though it be only conjecture), it may still be true that there was a manuscript of the age of 703 with this Creed in it, from whence the later one, now extant, was copied, which serves our purpose as well, and the rest is not material. But it should not be concealed that the Psalter (in this manuscript) is in small Italian, and the above-mentioned Rule in a small Saxon hand, which may, in some measure, weaken the argument drawn from the age of one to the age of the other; so that at length our evidence from this manuscript will be short of certainty, and will rise no higher than a fair probable presumption. I have nothing farther to observe, but that the Psalter wherein this Creed is, is the Gallican Psalter, not the Roman, and the title is, *Fides Sancti Athanasii Alexandrini,* "The Faith of St. Athanasius of Alexandria."

760. We may now take in the Colbertine copy, of which I have before spoken, referring the date of it to the year 760, or thereabout. Montfaucon sets it above the age of Charles the Great [r], allowing it to have been written about the time of Pepin, who began to reign in the year 752; so that I cannot be much out of time in placing it as I have done. It is written in Saxon

---

Cotton. Histor., p. 44. (This passage could not be found in Dr. Smith's Preface.)

[r] "Nongentos superat annos Colbertinus codex 784. Saxonicis descriptus literis, et mea quidem sententia, ante ætatem Caroli Magni exitus . . . . Sunt qui codicem illum 1100 annorum esse adfirmarunt: verum periti quique ævo circiter Pipini exaratum arbitrantur."—Montf., *Diatr.,* p. 721.

"Nec tamen Codicis Colbertini auctoritate nititur hæc opinio, quem arbitratur Anthelmius 1100 annorum. Etenim (quod pace viri eruditissimi, et amicissimi dicatur) multo minoris ætatis eo tex esse comprobatur; nemo enim peritus cui librum exhibuerim, octavo cum sæculo antiquiorem æstimavit."—Ib., p. 724.

character, and is imperfect, wanting the first part, above one-half of the Creed, just as the manuscript of Treves, from which it was copied.

760. The manuscript of St. Germans at Paris is entire, and of the same age with the former[s]. It is marked No. 257, and written in a Saxon letter as well as the other. A specimen of the hand, with the three first paragraphs of the Creed, may be seen in Mabillon[t]. The title, *Fides Sancti Athanasii Episcopi Alexandriæ*. It differs in some places from the common copies (as shall be noted hereafter), though not near so much as the Colbert manuscript before mentioned.

772. Next to these is the famous manuscript of Charles the Great, at the end of a Gallican Psalter, written in letters of gold, and presented by Charlemagne, while only king of France, to Pope Adrian 1., at his first entrance upon the Pontificate, in the year 772. Lambecius, in his catalogue of the Emperor's Library at Vienna, where this manuscript is, gives a large account of it[u]. The title is, *Fides Sancti Athanasii Episcopi Alexandrini*.

800. There is another manuscript in the Royal Library at Paris, marked 4908, which Montfaucon judges to be near 900 years old[v]. He wrote in the

---

[s] "Paris saltem antiquitatis est Sangermanensis noster, num. 257. Saxonicis pariter literis exaratus, qui titulum habet, ' Fides Sancti Athanasii Episcopi Alexandriæ.' "—Ib., p. 721.

[t] Mabill., *de re Diplom.*, lib. v. p. 351.

[u] Lambecius, *Catal. Biblioth. Vindobonens.*, lib. ii. c. 5, pp. 261, 296, &c. "Carolus Magnus proprio carmine suo testatur se illum codicem summo Pontifici Hadriano I. dono misisse; et quidem, ut ego arbitror, illo ipso anno 772, cujus die decimo Februarii jam memoratus Hadrianus in summum Pontificem electus est."

[v] "Regius Codex, num. 4908, annorum pene nongentorum, nul-

year 1698. So if we place it in the year 800, we shall want a little of 900 years from that time. He supposes it of very near the same age with the Vienna manuscript. It bears no title, nor any name or note of the author. It contains no more than the first part of the Creed, as far as the words *et tamen non tres æterni, sed unus* ——; the rest is torn off and lost.

850. I may here place a manuscript of Bennet College Library in Cambridge, whose age I cannot certainly fix to a year, but by all circumstances it cannot well be supposed later than this time. It is at the end of a Psalter, which, by comparing, I find to be a Gallican Psalter. Bishop Parker left a remark in it about its being in the possession first of one of the Archbishops of Canterbury, and at length conveyed down to the hands of Becket[x], who was Archbishop of Canterbury in the year 1162. The great antiquity of the manuscript appears from the martyrs, confessors, and virgins addressed to in it, all of the early times[y]. There are some few variations in this copy, such as are also found in the most ancient manuscripts of this Creed, particularly the word *et*, frequently inserted before *Spiritus Sanctus*, which has been since erased

lum habet titulum, nullumque auctoris nomen. Æqualis ipsi est, qui memoratur a Lambecio," &c.—Montf., *Diatr.*, p. 721.

[x] " Hoc Psalterium [N. X.] laminis argenteis deauratum, et gemmis ornatum, quondam fuit N. Cantuar. Archiep. tandem venit in manus Thomæ Becket quondam Cant. Archiep. Quod testatum est in veteri scripto."—Matth. Cant., Catal. MSS. C.C.C., C. p. 43.

[y] " In Litaniis, Orate pro nobis, Sancte Contestor, Sancte Horasme, Sancte Oswolde, &c. Martyres. Sancte Cuthberte, Sancte Germane, Sancte Placide, Sancte Columbane, Sancte Caurentine, &c. Confessores. Sancta Brigida, Sancta Eugenia, Sancta Eulalia, Sancta Petronella, &c., Virgines. Et non sunt hisce recentiores."—Catal. MSS. C. C. C., C., p. 43.

by some officious hand. The title is observable, *Fides Sancti Anasthasii Episcopi; Anasthasii* for *Athanasii*, by a transposition of syllables.

860. Montfaucon informs us of a manuscript in the Colbert Library, No. 1339, which once belonged to Charles the Bald[z], who died in the year 877; began to reign 840. It cannot therefore be much amiss to fix upon 860 for the date of it. The title it bears is, *Fides Athanasii*.

883. There is a second manuscript copy of the Athanasian Creed in the library of Bennet (or Corpus Christi) College, marked N. O. V. It is at the end of a Gallican Psalter, in the same hand, and carrying its certain date with it. It was written in France, by order of Count Amadeus, or Achadeus[a], and in the year 883, as appears from the Litany[b]. The title is, *Fides Catholica*.

930. Mr. Wanley gives us an account of a Roman Psalter in the Royal Library (formerly of St. James's), with an interlinear Saxon version to it, written about the time of King Athelstan[c]. Among the Canticles at the end there is also this Creed, under the title of *Hymnus Athanasii de Fide Trinitatis, quem tu concelebrans discutienter intellige*. This is in red ink. The

---

[z] "Colbertinus No. 1339, qui fuit Karoli Calvi imperatoris, inscribitur; Fides Athanasii."—Montfauc., *Diatrib.*, p. 721.

[a] "Ad finem Psalterii, Achadeus, misericordia Dei comes hunc Psalterium scribere jussit."—Catal. MSS., C. C. C., C., p. 46.

[b] "Oratur, ut Marinum Apostolicum in Sancta religione conservare digneris, ut Karlomannum Regem perpetua prosperitate conservare digneris: ut Leginam conservare digneris: ut Fulconem Episcopum cum omni grege sibi commisso in tuo apto servitio conservare digneris."—Catal. MSS. C. C. C., C., p. 47.

[c] Wanley, *Catal. MSS. Septentr.*, p. 182. Wanley, however, only gives the title *Hymnus Athanasii*.

title seems to have been then customary in England, as may be probably argued from a Saxon version (to be hereafter mentioned) of the same age, or very near, and bearing the same title [d].

957. In the Archbishop's Library at Lambeth there is a Gallican Psalter, written, according to Mr. Wanley [e], in the time of King Edgar, or a little before. At the end there is the Athanasian Creed in the same ancient hand, with an interlinear Saxon version. The title, *Fides Catholica Sancti Athanasii Episcopi*.

970. There is another manuscript copy of this Creed, much of the same age with the former, in my Lord Oxford's elegant library, richly furnished with all kinds of curious and valuable manuscripts. This Creed is at the end of a Gallican Psalter, and has an interlinear Saxon version to it. Mr. Wanley, who was so kind as to acquaint me with it, and to favour me with a sight of it, refers it to the time of King Edgar, who began his reign in 959, and died in 975. The title is, *Fides Catholica Athanasii Alexandrini Episcopi*.

1031. In the Cotton Library there is a Gallican Psalter, with Saxon interlined (marked Vitellius, E. 18), which Mr. Wanley refers to the year 1031 [f]. The Athanasian Creed, at the end as usual among the other Canticles, bears the title of *Fides Catholica Athanasii Episcopi Alexandrini*.

[d] *Hymnus Athanasii de Fide Trinitatis.* Wotton, *Conspectus Brevis operis Hickesiani*, p. 77.
[e] Wanley, *Catal.*, p. 269. "Eadgari Regis Anglosaxonum temporibus, aut paulo ante, ut videtur, exaratus."
Wharton, *Auctar. Hist. Dogm.*, p. 374, "Alfredo parum recentior videtur."
[f] Wanley, *Catal.*, p. 222, 224. Smith, *Catal. Cotton.*, p. 101.

1050. In the Norfolk Library, now belonging to the Royal Society at London, there is also a Gallican Psalter, whose age is fixed by Mr. Wanley[g] to the time of Edward the Confessor. The Creed is in it, and has an interlinear Saxon version running along with it. The title, *Fides Catholica Athanasii Alex.*

1064. In Bennet College Library is a manuscript copy of this Creed without any title. The Psalter, wherein it is, is called *Portiforium Oswaldi*, and is marked K. 10. An account of the book may be seen in Mr. Wanley[h], and in the Catalogue, p. 30.

1066. I may here place the Cotton Manuscript before mentioned, bound up with the ancient Roman Psalter, marked Vespasian A., though of a very different and much later hand. The Creed has an interlinear Saxon version, as usual, and its title is *Fides Catholica.* Mr. Wanley judges it to be as old as the coming in of the Normans[i].

1066. Of the same age[k] is the Roman Psalter in our Public Library at Cambridge, with the Latin text in black letter, a Saxon version in red, and the titles in green. The Creed is interlined with Saxon, as well as the Psalter, but has no title; for from this time, I conceive, the title began to be left out in some copies for brevity sake, or because it was thought superfluous.

It will be needless to take notice of any manuscripts below this time, excepting only such as contain something particular.

[g] Wanley, *Catal.*, p. 291.   [h] Ibid., p. 110.
[i] Ibid., p. 222. Smith, *Bibl. Cotton. Histor.*, p. 35.
[k] Wanley, *Catal.*, p. 152.

1087. Quesnel[1], and after him Pagi[m], speaks of a manuscript copy of this Creed in a Breviary and Psalter for the use of the monks of Mount Cassin, judged to be about 600 years old. This is the same Breviary that Quesnel has made observations upon in another work[n]; and there he fixes the age a little below 1086—*paulo post annum* 1086. The title of the Creed is, *Fides Catholica edita ab Athanasio Alexandrinæ sedis Episcopo*. There is the like title to the Creed in the triple Psalter of St. John's College, Cambridge, about the same age, or older, (marked B. 18,) *Incipit Fides Catholica edita ab Athanasio Archiepiscopo Alexandrinæ civitatis*. And there is such another title in a Psalter of the Norfolk Library, (No. 155,) *Fides Catholica edita a Sancto Athanasio Epo.;* but the hand is modern.

1120. In my Lord Oxford's Library I had a sight of a manuscript written in Germany about 600 years ago, for the use of the Church of Augsburg, which bears for its title, *Fides Anastasii Episcopi*.

1150. In the Norfolk Library is a Psalter (marked No. 230) with an interlinear version Normanno-Gallican; the Psalter is Gallican, and the title of the Creed at the end, *Fides Catholica*.

1240. Usher takes notice of a copy of this Creed then in the Royal Library at St. James's, (formerly belonging to Louis IX.); the title, *Fides Catholica*.

1300. Montfaucon informs us of a Latin and a French copy of this Creed found in a manuscript about 400

---

[1] Quesnel, Dissert. xiv. *ad Leon. Oper.*, p. 732.
[m] Pagi, *Critic. in Baron. Ann.* 340, § 8. p. 121, (vol. i. p. 441.)
[n] Quesnel, *Observat. ad Breviarium*, p. 327.

years old, placed in opposite columns. What is remarkable is, that the Latin has for its title *Canticum Bonifacii,* and the French over against the other, *Ce chant fust St. Anaistaise qui Apostoilles de Rome*[o].

1400. In the Bodleian at Oxford there is a manuscript copy of this Creed (No. 1205), which has for its title, *Anastasii Expositio Symboli Apostolorum.* It is about 300 years old, and belonged once to the Carthusian monks at Mentz. The Carthusians are particularly noted for their more than common veneration for this Creed, reciting it every day at the Prime, as Cardinal Bona testifies both of them and the Ambrosians[p], which I remark by the way. I observe that the German copies of this Creed, for five or six hundred years upwards, have most commonly Anastasius instead of Athanasius. I make no question but that this first arose from a mistake of the copyists, and not out of any design. One may perceive that Anastasius is sometimes written where Athanasius of Alexandria must have been intended. I suppose, at first, some copies had accidentally Anasthasius for Athanasius (as one in Bennet College Library mentioned above), by a transposition of letters or syllables, as easily happens in writing or speaking: thus Phrnnutus for Phurnutus, Marivadus for Varimadus, and the like. Now when the copyists had thus introduced Anasthasius (Anas-tha for Atha-nas), those that came after left out the *h* to make it Anastasius, that being a common name, which the other was not. This I thought proper to hint, that it may appear how little reason there is for ascrib-

[o] Montfaucon, *Diatrib.*, pp. 722, 727
[p] Bona, *de Divin. Psalmod.*, c. 18, §§ 5, 10, pp. 897, 900.

G

ing this Creed to Anastasius, whether of Rome, or of Antioch, or any other.

I have now run through the manuscripts of greatest note or use, either for antiquity or for anything particular, to give light to our further enquiries. Two only I have omitted, which have been thought considerable; not so much in themselves, as upon account of the other tracts they were found to be joined with. The one is the manuscript found in the library of Thuanus (*Codex Thuaneus*), annexed to some tracts which were once supposed to belong to Vigilius Tapsensis, though now certainly known to be none of his. Quesnel was much pleased with the discovery of this manuscript, as favouring his hypothesis about Vigilius Tapsensis[q]. And Antelmius has taken some pains in confuting him, shewing that the supposed works of Vigilius are none of his[r], and that if they were, yet no certain argument could be drawn from thence to make Vigilius author of the Creed, since it is a common thing for tracts of several authors, especially if they relate to the same subject, to be tacked to each other.

The second manuscript is one that was found annexed to the "Fragments of Hilary of Poictiers[s];"

[q] "Absoluta Dissertationum nostrarum editione, inveni Codicem Tuuaneum, in quo Dialogus Vigilii Tapsensis adversus Arianos, Sabellianos, et Photinianos legitur, sub hoc titulo: 'Incipit Altercatio Athanasii cum Haeresibus.' Post hunc Tractatum habetur Symbolum Nicaenum, et Formula Fidei Ariminensis Concilii, quam proxime sequitur Symbolum Athanasianum cum hac Epigraphe: 'Fides dicta a Sancto Athanasio Episcopo.' Porro, conjecturae nostrae de autore hujus Symboli, Vigilio, non parum suffragatur, quod in antiquissimo codice illigatum reperiatur Opusculo cui nomen Athanasii pariter praefixum legitur, sed quod Vigilii Tapsensis esse indubitatum habetur," &c.—Quesnel, in *Addend.*, p. 913.

[r] Montfauc., Athan. Op., vol. ii. pp. 603, 724.

[s] "Invenitur id similiter in Fragmentis Hilarii historicis in Cod.

which circumstance was thought a reason for ascribing this Creed to Hilary. Vossius first, and after him many others, throw it off as a very slight argument, since the manuscript pretended is very modern; nor is the Creed ascribed to Hilary in that manuscript, but only bound up with his " Fragments," as any other work might be, however little akin to them. Montfaucon takes notice of this matter in few words[t]; Tentzelius more at large[u]. It is sufficient for me just to have hinted it.

Having now given as particular account as was needful of the more ancient Latin manuscripts of this Creed, I may just observe, that as to modern ones they are innumerable, there being scarce any manuscript Latin Psalter of modern date but what has the Creed in it, and generally without a title. I may next subjoin a table of the manuscripts here recited, representing in one view the age, the title, the country where written, and the kind of Psalter wherein found: all which circumstances will be of use to us in our following enquiries. Particularly, as to the Psalters, it will be of moment to observe whether they be Roman or Gallican, because from thence we may be able to discover in what places or countries this Creed was first re-

---

vetori Part. 2, sub finem."—Felckman, *Var. Lect. Oper. Athan.*, p. 83.

[t] "Hilario nonnulli adscriptum voluerunt, quia nimirum in codice quodam exstat post Hilarii Fragmenta. Quasi vero id non vulgo et in plerisque codicibus observetur, ut multa diversorum opera consequenter in manuscriptis describentur. Cum autem in ejusmodi codice post Hilariana opera, nullo præmisso auctoris nomine compareat; hinc, uti jam supra diximus, inferendum, tum exaratum fuisse cum pro Athanasiano nondum vulgo haberetur."—Montfauc., *Diatrib.*, p. 723.

[u] Tentzel., *Judic. Erud.*, pp. 2, 3, &c.

ceived, according to their use of this or that Psalter. But because, perhaps, some readers may be at a loss to know what we mean by those different names of Roman and Gallican Psalters, it may not be improper here to throw in a few previous instructions relating to the different kinds of Latin Psalters, and the names they have gone under.

There are four kinds or sorts of Latin Psalters, which have passed under the names of Italic, Roman, Gallican, and Hebraic. One of them was before Jerome's time; the three last are all Jerome's, as he had a hand, more or less, in every one of them. I shall treat of them distinctly in their order as follows :—

I. The Italic Latin Psalter is of the old translation, or version, such as it was before Jerome's time. I shall not enter into the dispute whether it were one version, or many. The common opinion is, that there were several Latin versions before Jerome[v], but one more eminent than the rest, called Italic[x], as being received into common use in Italy[y]. However that be, it is become customary with such as treat of this subject to speak of all that was extant before Jerome as of one version, under the name of *Vetus Vulgata*, or *Versio*

---

[v] "Qui enim Scripturas ex Hebræa Lingua in Linguam Græcam verterunt numerari possunt, Latini autem interpretes nullo modo: ut enim cuique primis Fidei temporibus in manus venit Codex Græcus et aliquantulum facultatis sibi utriusque linguæ habere videbatur, ausus est interpretari."—August., *de Doctr. Christian.*, lib. ii. c. 11, vol. iii. p. 25.

[x] "In ipsis autem interpretationibus Itala cæteris præferatur: nam est verborum tenacior cum perspicuitate sententiæ."—August., ib., c. 15, p. 27.

[y] "Ecclesia Latina a principio, vel ferme a principio, usa est versione Latina Testamenti Vet. ex Græca τῶν ό translatione facta, quæ Itala vulgo dicebatur, quoniam in Italia prius usitata in alias inde Latinorum Ecclesias recipiebatur."—Hodius, *de Biblior. Text. Origin.*, lib. iii. pars 2, c. 1, p. 342.

Italica. There are entire Psalters of this old version, printed and manuscript [1], though now nowhere in use in Divine offices, except such parcels of it as, having been anciently taken into the Roman missals, or other old Liturgies, remain there still, the people being accustomed to them, and there being no great necessity for changing them; but all the entire Psalters in use are of another kind. Martianay, in his edition of Jerome's works, once intended to give us an entire and correct Psalter (with some other of the sacred books) of the old Italic version; but the various lections were so many and so different, that the work appeared too laborious and difficult, for which reason he then laid it aside [a]. This version, or versions, is what all the Latins used before Jerome, and many also after him, the Africans especially, down to the sixth century at least, or beginning of the seventh.

2. The Roman Psalter is not very different from the old Italic. It is nothing else but that old version, cursorily and in part corrected by Jerome in the time of Pope Damasus, A.D. 383. It has had the name of Roman, because the use of it began the soonest and continued the longest in the Roman offices. It obtained in Gaul near as soon as at Rome, but was laid aside in the sixth century, when Gregory of

[1] Le Long, *Bibl. Sacr.*, vol. i. p. 243.
[a] "Appendicem Sacrorum aliquot voluminum, juxta Veterem Vulgatam usu receptam ante Hieronymum, hoc loco edendam statueramus: sed quum operi manus jamjam accederet, tantam inter MSS. Codices hujus versionis Latinæ deprehendimus dissonantiam, ut impossibile esset vel solas variantes horum codicum lectiones adnotasse nisi maximo temporis intervallo. Quare ne in sequentem annum differretur editio hujus Divinæ Bibliothecæ, Appendicem prædictam latiori operi, ac majori otio reservavimus."—Martian., *Not. ad Hieronym.*, vol. i. p. 1419.

Tours [b] introduced the other Psalter, since called Gallican. The Roman Psalter, however, still obtained at Rome till the time of Pope Pius V.[c], and it is still used in the Vatican church, and some few churches besides.

3. The Gallican Psalter is Jerome's more correct Latin translation made from Origen's *Hexaplar* [d], or most correct edition of the Greek Septuagint, filled up, where the Greek was supposed faulty, from the Hebrew, distinguished with obelisks and asterisks, denoting the common Greek version in those places to be either redundant or deficient. Many of the old manuscripts [e] still retain those marks; but more have left them out, I suppose, to save trouble. This more correct Psalter was drawn up by Jerome in the year 389, and obtained first in Gaul about the year 580, or, however, not later than 595; from which circumstance it came to have the name of Gallican, in contradistinction to the Roman. From Gaul, or France, it passed over into England before the year 597, and into Ger-

---

[b] " Psalmos autem cum secundum LXX. interpretes Romani adhuc habeant ; Galli et Germanorum aliqui secundum emendationem quam Hieronymus Pater de LXX. Editione composuit, Psalterium cantant: Quam Gregorius, Turonensis Episcopus, a patribus Romanis mutuatam, in Galliarum dicitur Ecclesias transtulisse."— Walafrid. Strab. *de Reb. Eccles.*, c. 25, p. 196 (p. 690).

[c] Bona, *de Rebus Liturg.*, lib. ii. c. 3, p. 506. Hodius, lib. iii. pars 2, c. 4, p. 383. Mabill., *de Curs. Gallic.*, p. 398.

[d] Hieron., *Epist. ad Sunn. et Fretet.*, in vol. ii. p. 627.

[e] The Cotton Manuscript of 703, and the Bennet of 883, Lambeth of 957, Lord Oxford's of 970, and Bruno's own manuscript of 1033, besides many more in France, England, and other countries. " Quanta porro fuerit diligentia nostratium in describendo hocce Psalterio, cum asteriscis et obelis, non aliunde testatum volumus quam ex infinita copia Codicum MSS. qui cum talibus distinctionibus supersunt usque hodie in Gallicanis Bibliothecis."— Martian., Hieronym. Op., vol. i. *Prolegom.* ii. c. 5.

many, and Spain, and other countries. The popes of Rome, though they themselves used the other Psalter, yet patiently connived at the use of this in the Western Churches and even in Italy, and sometimes privately authorized the use of it in churches and monasteries [f], till at length it was publicly authorized in the Council of Trent, and introduced a while after into Rome itself by Pius V. It was admitted in Britain and Ireland before the coming of Augustine the Monk, and prevailed after, except in the church of Canterbury [g], which was more immediately under the Archbishop's eye, and more conformable to the Roman offices than other parts of the kingdom. It has been said [h] that this very Gallican Psalter is what we still retain in our liturgy, called the reading Psalms, in contradistinction to the other Psalms in our Bibles of the new translation. But this is not strictly true: for the old translation, though it be taken in a great measure from the Gallican, has yet many corrections from the Hebrew, (where they were thought wanting,) first by Coverdale in 1535, and by Coverdale again, 1539, and, last of all, by Tonstall and Heath in 1541; according to which

[f] "Anno 1369, Urbani V. autoritate Sancitum, ut Cassinenses Psalterio Gallicano uterentur."—Montfauc., *Diar. Ital.*, p. 331. P. Adrian, long before, had recommended the Gallican Psalter to the Church of Bremen. See below in c. vi., and Bona, *de Rebus Liturg.*, p. 506.

[g] "Ante adventum Augustini Monachi, primi Archiepiscopi Cantuariensis, in Angliam, i.e. ante annum 597, Ecclesiæ Britannicæ et Hibernicæ Psalterium Gallicanum receperant. Augustinus huc a Gregorio M. missus Romanum secum advexit, et Ecclesiæ suæ Cantuariensi tradidit. Sed loco illius invaluit tandem, per omnes Ecclesias Anglicas, usus Gallicani."—Hodius, lib. iii. pars 2, c. 4, p. 384.

[h] "Hodienum in Liturgia Ecclesiæ Anglicanæ retinetur editio Gallicana: at versio illa quæ habetur in Bibliorum voluminibus, quæque pro authentica agnoscitur, ex Hebræo est."—Ibid.

edition is the Psalter now used in our liturgy, as I have learned by comparing: and it had been before taken notice of by Durell [i]. But this in passing.

4. The Hebraic Latin Psalter means Jerome's own translation, immediately from the Hebrew, made in the year 391. This, though otherwise of great esteem, was never used in the public Church offices [k]. There are but few copies of it in comparison, because this Psalter, as before hinted, having never been in common use like the Roman and Gallican, has been confined to a few hands. We are not to expect an Athanasian Creed in this Psalter, as not being intended for the use of the choir, neither are we to expect to meet with it in the Italic Psalters, which are few, and which were grown, or growing out of use before the Athanasian Creed was brought into the public offices. But in the Roman and Gallican Psalters we may find it; and it will be of moment to observe in which of them it is found. Indeed, some manuscript Psalters there are which have the Roman and Gallican together in opposite columns, the Gallican always set first [l]. Others have the Hebraic and Gallican set column-wise, as the former, and some have all the three versions of Jerome placed in the like order. Dr. Hody informs us of two such manuscripts, to which may be added

---

[i] Durell, *Eccles. Anglican. Vindic.*, c. 27, p. 306.

[k] "Tertium est de Hebræo in Latinum quod Ieronymus transtulit de Hebræo in Latinum. Sed non est in usu Ecclesiæ, sed viri studii literati et sapientes eo utuntur."—Roger Bacon, apud Hodium, l. c.

"Hæc autem (versio ex Hebræo) ideo recepta non fuit, quia duæ priores, quotidiano usu in Ecclesiis frequentatæ, sine magna divini officii perturbatione non poterant abrogari."—Bona, *de Rebus Liturg.*, lib. ii. c. 3, p. 506; cf. Hodium, p. 385.

[l] Hodius, l. c.

a third, now in Trinity College in Cambridge, which has the Athanasian Creed with Bruno's comment in it, as intimated above. Another such triple Psalter there is in St. John's College of the same University, as before hinted; and in my Lord Oxford's library is a fine old Latin Bible, where the Psalms appear under all the three versions. Nay, some manuscripts have the Greek also with the other, making a fourth column: an account of this last sort may be seen both in Dr. Hody and Le Long [m]. These double, triple, or quadruple Psalters came not in, I presume, before the end of the tenth century or beginning of the eleventh; for Berno Augiensis of that time acquaints us with the occasion and use of them, and how they came to be so contrived [n]. When the Roman way of singing, first adapted to the Roman Psalter, had been introduced into France and Germany (which was first done in the eighth century), in process of time it bred some confusion in the two Psalters, mixing and blending them one with the other, that it was difficult to distinguish which words belonged to this, and which to that. To remedy this

[m] Le Long, *Bibl. Sacr.*, vol. i. p. 244.
[n] "Inter cætera, ex emendata LXX. interpretum translatione Psalterium ex Græco in Latinum vertit (Hieronymus) illudque cantandum omnibus Galliæ, ac quibusdam Germaniæ Ecclesiis tradidit. Et ob hoc Gallicanum Psalterium appellavit, Romanis adhuc ex corrupta vulgata editione Psalterium canentibus: ex qua Romani cantum composuerunt, nobisque usum cantandi contradiderunt. Unde accidit quod verba, quæ in diurnis vel nocturnis officiis canendi more modulantur, intermisceantur, et confuse nostris Psalmis inserantur; ut a minus peritis haud facile possit discerni quid nostræ, vel Romanæ conveniat editioni. Quod pius pater ac peritus magister intuens, tres editiones in uno volumine composuit: et Gallicanum Psalterium, quod nos canimus, ordinavit in una columna; in altera Romanum, in tertia Hebræum."—Berno Augiens. Epist. inedit., apud Mabill., *de Cvrs. Gallic.*, § 21, p. 396. Hodius, *de Biblior. Text. Origin.*, p. 382.

inconvenience, a way was found out to have both the Psalters distinctly represented to the eye together, in two several columns, and thus came in the kind of Psalters before mentioned. We easily see why the Gallican used to be set in the first column, namely, because those Psalters were contrived by the French and Germans, who made use of the Gallican, and so gave the preference to their own. If I have detained my reader a little too long in this digression about the Psalters I hope the usefulness of the subject may make him some amends and be a just apology for it. I now return to our Creed, and what more immediately belongs to it; closing this chapter, as I promised, with a table, representing a summary or short sketch of what hath been done in it.

A TABLE OF MANUSCRIPTS.

A.D.	Manuscripts.	Psalters.	Titles of the Creed.
600	Bp. Usher's.		Fides Catholica.
660	Treves.		
700	Ambrosian.		
703	Cotton 1.	Gallican.	Fides Sancti Athanasii Alexandrini.
760	Colbert 1.		
760	St. Germans.		Fides Sancti Athanasii Episcopi.
772	Vienna.	Gallican.	Fides Sancti Athanasii Episcopi Alexandrini.
800	Regius, Paris.		
850	Benet Coll. Cant. I.	Gallican.	Fides Sancti Anasthasii Episcopi.
860	Colbert 2.		Fides Athanasii.
883	Benet C. 2.	Gallican.	Fides Catholica.
930	St. James's 1.	Roman.	Hymnus Athanasii.
957	Lambeth.	Gallican.	Fides Catholica S. Athanasii Episcopi.
970	Harleian 1.	Gallican.	Fides Catholica Athanasii Alexandrini Episcopi.
1031	Cotton 2.	Gallican.	Fides Catholica Athanasii Episcopi Alexandrini.
1050	Norfolk 1.	Gallican.	Fides Catholica Athanasii Alexandrini.
1064	Benet C. 3.		
1066	Cotton 3.		Fides Catholica.
1066	Cambridge.	Roman.	
1087	Cassinensis.		Fides Catholica edita ab Athanasio, &c.
1120	Harleian 2.		Fides Anastasii Episcopi.
1150	Norfolk 2.	Gallican.	Fides Catholica.
1240	St. James's 2.		Fides Catholica.
1300	Friars Minors.	Gallican.	Canticum Bonefacii. [Rome.
			Ce Chant fust St. Anaistaise qui Apostoilles de
1400	Bodleian.		Anastasii Expositio Symboli Apostolorum.

CHAPTER V.

ANCIENT VERSIONS, PRINTED OR MANUSCRIPT.

SOME account of the ancient versions of the Athanasian Creed may be of use to shew when and where it has been received, and what value hath been set upon it, at several times and in several countries. I shall note the time in the margin when the first version into any language appears to have been made; and I shall rank the versions of the several countries according to the chronological order of those first versions respectively.

FRENCH VERSIONS.

A.D. 850. Under the name of French versions I comprehend all versions made at any time into the vulgar language then current in France, whatever other name some may please to give them. I beg leave also to comprehend under the same name all oral versions delivered by word of mouth, as well as written ones; otherwise I am sensible that I ought not to have begun with French versions. I do not know that the Gauls, or French, had any written standing version of this Creed so early as 850, or for several centuries after. Their oldest versions of the Psalter are scarce earlier than the eleventh century[a], and of the entire Scripture

[a] See Le Long, *Bibl. Sacr.*, vol. i. p. 313, &c.

scarce so early as the twelfth; and we are not to expect a written version of the Athanasian Creed more ancient than of their Psalter. But what I mean by setting the French versions so high as I here do, is, that the Athanasian Creed was, as early as is here said, interpreted out of Latin into the vulgar tongue for the use of the people by the clergy of France in their verbal instructions. This is the same thing, in effect, with a written standing version, as supplying the place of it, and is as full a proof of the general reception of the Creed at that time as the other would be. Now that the Athanasian Creed was thus interpreted into the vulgar tongue in France as early as the year 850, or earlier, I prove from the words of Hincmar, above cited [b], giving orders to the clergy of his province to be able to express this Creed *communibus verbis*, that is, in their vulgar or mother tongue. What that mixed kind of language which they then used should be called is of no great moment to our present purpose to enquire. Some perhaps, with Vitus Amerbachius and Bishop Usher [c], will call it Teutonic, or German, because Franks and Germans, being originally the same, spake the same language. But I see no consequence that because Franks and Germans used the same language, therefore Franks and Gauls, mixed together, must still keep the same, any more than that a mixed nation of Normans and Saxons must all agree either in Norman or Saxon. One would rather expect in such a mixed people a mixed language too, as usually happens in such cases. As to France in particular at that time, Mr. Wharton has plainly shewn that the language there

[b] See above, p. 28.   [c] Usher, *Histor. Dogmat.*, p. 111.

spoken was very widely different from the Teutonic or German.

The *Concordate* between the two brothers, Lewis and Charles, at Strasburgh, puts the matter out of dispute, where one expressed himself in the Teutonic, the other in the language then current in France, called Romanensis, or Rustica Romana, corrupt Roman, or Latin [d], nearer to the Latin than to the German, but a confused mixture of both. Such was the language then vulgarly spoken in France, as appears from the specimen of it given by Wharton from Nithardus. And this, I presume, is the language into which our Creed was interpreted in Hincmar's time; for which reason I have set the French versions first. If any one shall contend that the Teutonic prevailed then in the diocese of Rheims, though not in the other parts of Gaul more remote from Germany, I shall not think it of moment to dispute the point, since it is not material to our present purpose.

As to the French versions, properly so called, written standing versions, I have said that none of them reach higher than the eleventh century. Montfaucon gives us one, though imperfect, 600 years old [e]; that is, of the eleventh century, and very near the end of it, about 1098, 600 years before the time of his writing; and this is the oldest that I have anywhere found mentioned. Next to which, perhaps, we may reckon that in Trinity College, in Cambridge; I mean the interlinear version, which Mr. Wanley [f] calls Normanno-Gallican,

[d] Wharton, *Auctar. Histor. Dogmat.*, p. 344.
[e] Montfaucon, *Diatrib.*, pp. 721, 727, and 733, where it is quoted at length.
[f] Wanley, *Catal. MSS. Septentr.*, p. 168.

about 580 years old. And next to that the Norfolk manuscript (No. 230), before mentioned, about the same age with the other; and Mr. Wanley informed me of two more in my Lord Oxford's library. There is one in the Cotton Library (Nero, C. 4) above 500 years old, according to Mr. Wharton [g]. Montfaucon gives us another above 400 years old [h]. But it is needless, and foreign to my purpose, to number up all the versions: the first in its kind is what will be chiefly serviceable to our following enquiries.

GERMAN VERSIONS.

870. As to written and standing versions, the German, so far as we find any records, ought to have the first place. There is in the Emperor's library at Vienna [i] a German, or Teutonic, version of this Creed, made by Otfridus, monk of Weissenberg, in the ninth century: the manuscript, as Lambecius assures us, is coeval with the author. There have been several later German versions, a brief account of which may be seen in Lambecius [k], Tentzelius [l], and Le Long [m], but more particularly in Tentzelius. It is sufficient to my purpose to have taken notice of the first and most considerable in its kind.

ANGLO-SAXON VERSIONS.

930. There have been Anglo-Saxon versions of this Creed as early as the time of King Athelstan, as appears from the manuscript of the Royal Library, with

[g] Wharton, *Auctar. Histor. Dogmat.*, p. 390.
[h] Montfaucon, *Diatrib.*, p. 722.
[i] Lambec., *Catal. Biblioth. Vindobon.*, lib. ii. c. 5, pp. 460, 768.
[k] Ibid., c. 8, p. 763.
[l] Tentzel., *Judic. Erud.*, Præf. and p. 226.
[m] Le Long, *Bibl. Sacr.*, vol. i. p. 376.

an interlinear version, noted above, and which I place in 930. The Lambeth manuscript of 957 has also an interlinear Saxon version, both which manuscripts confirm the account given of an Anglo-Saxon copy of this Creed, printed from a Latin manuscript, interlined with Saxon, out of the church of Salisbury. The version itself seems to have been made about the middle of the tenth century, or about 950, which suits very well with the age of the manuscripts before mentioned. Only this we may expect, that the Saxon copies of those manuscripts will be found much more correct than the Sarum copy (and so I find that of Lambeth is, having a copy of it by me, which I owe to the civility of the very learned Dr. Wilkins), being written at a time when the Saxon language was less corrupted, and retained more of its primitive purity; whereas the Sarum copy was written ⁿ, as is conjectured, after both Danes and Normans had much altered the language. I before observed that the title in Dr. Wotton's copy is *Hymnus Athanasii*, as in St. James's copy; and there is something farther worth the noting, which is the Rubric following the title, directing the Creed to be sung alternately º, which confirms the account given by

---

ⁿ "Versionem istam circiter medium decimi sæculi esse factam ipsius sermonis cum puritate (ubi non hallucinatur interpres) conjuncta proprietas ostendit. Recentius vero descriptam fuisse, sub Nortmannorum in Angliam Adventum, non tautum librarii linguæ Saxonicæ haud gnari recentior manus in qua exaratur, sed pravum illud Anglo-Danicum, vel forsan Anglo-Nortmannicum, scribendi genus demonstrat."—Wotton, *Not. ad Brevem Conspect. Operis Hickesiani*, p. 75.

º *Hymnus Athanasii, de Fide Trinitatis.*

* "Quem tu concelebrans, discutienter intellege. Incipit de fide." On which Dr. Wotton makes this note:—

* "Ita MS. Hoc est, Quem tu antiphonatim, vel alternatim psallens, animo percipe."—p. 77.

Abbo Floriacensis [p] of the custom of the Gallican and English Churches in that age. But to proceed. From the time we have had any version of this Creed into our country language, we may reasonably conclude that such versions have varied by little and little in every age, in proportion to the gradual alteration in our language, till at length the version became such as it stands at this day. Such as are desirous of having a specimen of the Creed in very old English verse may find one in Dr. Hickes's *Thesaurus* [q]; and they may see a good part of a prose version in old English (though considerably later than the other) in Wickliff's Comment, before mentioned; or an entire version into the English of that time in a manuscript of Pepys's Library, now belonging to our college, No. 2498, p. 368. I may here note, that all our Saxon and English versions down to the time of the Reformation, or to the year 1548, were from the Latin only, and not from any Greek copy; and after that time, upon the return of Popery, the old version from the Latin came again into use for a while, as appears by the Primer set forth by Cardinal Pole in Queen Mary's days, A.D. 1555. But these and the like observations are out of the compass of my design, and so I pass on.

GREEK VERSIONS.

I have before intimated that this Creed was originally Latin, and therefore the Greek copies can be no more than versions; and they appear to be very late also, in comparison to the former. However, since the

[p] See above, p. 31.
[q] Hickes, *Thesaur. Linguar. Septentr.*, vol. i. p. 223.

Greek is one of the learned languages, since the Creed has been ascribed to a Greek author, and has been also supposed by many to have been written in Greek, it will therefore be proper to give as particular and as distinct account as is possible of the Greek version or versions. Our enquiries here will lie within a little compass, for the Greek copies are neither many nor ancient. Montfaucon, a very diligent searcher into these matters, frankly professes that he had never seen any Greek copy of this Creed so old as 300 years, nor ever heard of any that was ancient[r]. He scruples not to say farther, that there had not been yet seen any Greek record, of certain and undoubted credit, whereby to prove that this Creed had been known to the Greek Church for more than 500 years upwards[s]. He speaks only of Greek records; as to Latin ones, they afford sufficient proof that this Creed was pleaded against the Greeks in the dispute about the Procession, in the eighth or ninth century at latest, and therefore must have been in some measure known to them. The Greeks and Latins had some dispute on that head in the Synod of Gentilly, not far from Paris, in the year 767, under King Pepin. But perhaps this Creed was not

[r] "Sane nullum vidimus Græcum hujus Symboli Codicem qui trecentorum sit annorum ; nec antiquum alium a quopiam visum fuisse novimus."—Montfaucon, *Diatrib.*, p. 727.
[s] "Adjicere non pigeat non visum hactenus fuisse Græcorum quodpiam monumentum (certum scilicet ac indubitatum) quo ab annis plus quingentis notum Ecclesiæ Græcæ fuisse Symbolum, Quicunque, possit comprobari."—Ib., p. 721.
To the same purpose speaks Combefis of this Creed:—
"Vix enim extat præterquam in recentiorum collectaneis, librisque eorum polemicis, quibus ipsum vel impugnant, vel etiam defendunt ; idque volunt illi qui aiunt non haberi in Græcorum libris ; non enim sic stupidi videntur ut negent Græce haberi."—Combef., *Not. ad Man. Calec.*, p. 297.

pleaded at that time; at least it does not appear that it was.

It cannot be doubted but that the Greeks had heard something of this Creed from the Latins as early as the days of Ratram and Æneas Parisiensis, that is, above 850 years ago, when the dispute about the procession between the Greeks and Latins was on foot; this the testimonies above cited plainly shew. But this is not enough to prove that the Greek Church had yet any value for this Creed, or that there was then extant any Greek copy of it.

1200. Nicolaus Hydruntinus, cited above, who flourished under Alexius IV., Emperor of the East, and Pope Innocent III., that is, in round numbers about 1200, gives us the first notice of this Creed being extant in Greek in his time. He observes, that the Article of the Procession from the Son was not in the Greek copy of this Creed, as neither in the Nicene, blaming the Latins, as I apprehend, for interpolating both. The censure was just with respect to the Nicene Creed, but not with respect to the Athanasian, which certainly never wanted that Article, as is plain from the agreement of the Latin copies, and the earliest of them, those of a thousand years date, which I remark by the way. As to our present purpose, this is certain, that some time before Nicolaus of Otranto wrote, the Creed had been translated into Greek by a Greek, or at least by one that took part with the Greeks in the question about the Procession. It can hardly be imagined that Nicolaus had translated it himself, and that he appealed to his own version. There must have been a version before, undoubtedly; and one can scarce suppose less than fifty or one hundred years before, since both the time and author of it were forgotten, and this Greek version passed with Nicolaus for Athanasius's original. Manuel Calcca [t], who wrote about the year 1360, intimates that there had been Greek copies long before his time, and that the most ancient of all had the Article of the Procession from the Son, and that the older Greeks who wrote against the Latins did not pretend to strike out that Article, as those did that came after. Could we depend upon this report we might then be certain that the Greek copies of the time of Nicolaus Hydruntinus, were late in comparison, and that there had been other Greek copies much more ancient. But this I leave to the consideration of the learned. However this fact be, one thing is certain, that the oldest Greek copy could be only a version, whether sooner or later.

As to Greek copies now extant in manuscript, they are but few and modern. I may here give a short account of them, of as many as I have hitherto found mentioned in books or catalogues of manuscripts.

1. There is one in the Emperor's Library at Vienna, said to be in paper, ancient, and of good value [u]. These

---

[t] "Testantur autem hanc ipsam fidei confessionem sancti viri (Athanasii) esse, atque id dictum ita se habere, qui contra Latinos multo ante scripserunt; quam sibi ut adversum frustra labefactare nituntur. Atque, ut intelligi datur, tunc quidem adhuc servabatur; postmodum vero pertinaciores ad contradicendum facti, omnino illam auferre voluerunt: etsi modo nihilominus curiose inquirentibus raro, licet in vetustissimis codicibus, ita habere invenitur." —Man. Calec., contr. Græc., lib. ii.; in Bibl. Max. PP., vol. xxvi. p. 414.

[u] "CCXLV. Codex MS. Theologicus Græcus est Chartaceus, antiquus, et b·næ notæ in 4to., constatque foliis 341.

"Continentur eo Hæc.

"Primo, &c.

words are too general to fix any certain date upon. One may guess from the paper, that the manuscript is not very ancient, since paper came not into frequent or common use before the thirteenth century. But not to insist upon a disputable argument (since cotton paper, though not common, was however sometimes used as early as the tenth century), one may judge more certainly from what is written in the same volume, and, I suppose, in the same hand (for Nesselius makes no distinction), that the copy of the Creed is not earlier than the middle of the fourteenth century. Maximus Planudes makes a part of the manuscript: he flourished about the year 1340.

2. There is another Greek manuscript of this Creed in the same library, a paper one too, and said to be pretty ancient, by Nesselius, who gives account of it [v]. From the mention therein made of the Creed's being presented to Pope Julius, I should be apt to conclude that the manuscript is not earlier, nor copied from any earlier, than Manuel Caleca's time, or the fourteenth century; but there are other marks, particularly some pieces of Julianus Cardinalis, which demonstrate that

---

"IIdo et quidem a fol. 77, ad fol. 79: S. Athanasii Archiepiscopi Alexandrini Symbolum Fidei, cujus titulus et principium, Τοῦ ἁγίου 'Αθανασίου τοῦ μεγάλου. Ὅστις δ' ἂν βούληται σωθῆναι, πρὸ πάντων χρὴ κρατεῖν πίστιν," &c.—Nessel., *Catal.*, vol. i. p. 344.

[v] "CXCmus Codex MS. .... est Chartaceus, mediocriter antiquus, et bonæ notæ, in 4to. Constatque nunc foliis 332, et ad Johannem Sambucum—olim pertinuit. Continentur eo Hæc. I. primo," &c.

"XVIII. Et quidem a fol. 303, ad fol. 304. S. Athanasii magni, Archiepiscopi Alexandrini, Confessio Catholica Fidei, ad S. Julium Pontificem Romanum; cujus et titulus et principium Τοῦ ἐν ἁγίοις πατρὸς ἡμῶν 'Αθανασίου τοῦ μεγάλου Ὁμολογία τῆς καθολικῆς πίστεως ἣν ἔδωκε πρὸς Ἰούλιον Πάπαν 'Ρώμης. Τῷ θέλοντι σωθῆναι," &c.—Nessel., *Catal.*, vol. i. p. 281.

the manuscript cannot be much older than the middle of the fifteenth century.

3. Felckman had a manuscript copy of this Creed in Greek, without any title to it, or any author named [x]. I can say nothing to the age of it, for want of further particulars.

4. Felckman had another manuscript out of the Palatine Library (which library is since transferred partly to the Vatican, the rest to Munich, &c.), with a title to it, σύμβολον τοῦ ἁγίου 'Αθανασίου, St. Athanasius's Creed [y]. The title alone is a sufficient argument of its being modern to any that consider what were the more usual and ancient titles represented above. It is to be noted, that those two manuscript copies are so nearly the same, that they make but one copy in print, which has been inserted in all the editions of Athanasius's works after Felckman's, as well as in his, and makes the fifth in Gundlingius [z], who gives us six Greek copies of this Creed. It is observable that this copy owns not the Procession from the Son; from whence we may infer that it was not made by the Latins, or, however, not by any who were not friends to the Greeks.

[x] "Extat hoc Symbolum in nostro Codice II. anonymo, sed absque titulo et nomine authoris ; unde et sic editum."—Felckman, *Var. Lect. in Athan.*, p. 83.

"Incipit ; εἴ τις θέλει σωθῆναι, πρὸ πάντων χρὴ αὐτῷ τὴν καθολικὴν κρατῆσαι πίστιν," &c.

[y] "Invenimus id ipsum etiam post in codice quodam Palatinæ Bibliothecæ, expresse Athanasio inscriptum (licet id recentiores Græci nolint, ut videre est ex epistola Meletii Constantinopolitani Patriarchæ ad Douzam) ex quo etiam discrepantias quasdam notabimus.

"Incipit ; εἴ τις θέλει σωθῆναι, πρὸ πάντων χρεία ἐστὶν ἵνα τὴν καθολικὴν κρατήσῃ πίστιν," &c.—Felckman, *ib.*

[z] Gundling., *not. ad Zialowsk.*, p. 76.

5. Lazarus Baifius's copy [a], which he had from Venice in the time of Francis I., in the year 1533, was published by Genebrard, in the year 1569. This copy probably was contrived by a Latin (having the Procession from the Son in it), or, at least, by some honest Greek who would not vary from the original. I conclude this Greek copy to be modern, from the title, for a reason before hinted.

6. There was another manuscript copy [b] of this Creed, which Nicolaus Bryling first printed at Basil, and afterwards H. Stevens in France, in the year 1565. This also must, in all probability, be very modern, because of σύμβολον in the title. It acknowledges the Procession from the Son, conformable to the original.

7. In the Royal Library at Paris (No. 2502) there is another manuscript Greek copy of this Creed [c], written in the year 1562, published by Genebrard, 1569, and said by him to belong to the Church of Constantinople. This was taken from an older manuscript,

[a] "Titulus: Ἔκθεσις ὁμολογίας τῆς καθολικῆς πίστεως τοῦ μεγάλου Ἀθανασίου πατριάρχου Ἀλεξανδρείας πρὸς Ἰούλιον Πάπαν.
"Incipit. Ὅστις ἂν βούληται σωθῆναι, πρὸ πάντων χρὴ κρατεῖν τὴν καθολικὴν πίστιν."—Genebrard, p. 3.

[b] "Titulus: Σύμβολον τοῦ ἁγίου Ἀθανασίου.
"Incipit: Ὅστις βούλεται σωθῆναι," &c.—Genebrard, l. c.

[c] "De Græcis autem codicibus pauca suppetunt dicenda, cum unum tantum nobis inspicere licuerit, scil. Reg. 2502. In quo extat Symbolum superiore sæculo exaratum."—Montf., *Diatrib.*, p. 722.
"Secunda, quam elimus formula, jam olim publici juris facta per Genebrardum anno 1569, quam ait ille esse Ecclesiæ Constantinopolitanæ, extat in Regio Codice Num. 2502, olim ex Bibliotheca Johannis Huralti Boistallerii a Carolo IX. Venetiis legati: in quo Codice hæc leguntur, ante Dialogum S. Athanasii cum Ario.
.... Transcriptus et recognitus liber hic est, ex vetustissimo exemplari Cretico ; Venetiis an. 1562, impensa facta aureorum X. Zacharias Sacerdos transcripsit et habuit."—Montf., *Diatrib.*, p. 727.

but how much older cannot certainly be known [d]. One may imagine from the title [e], and beginning of it, that the form is the same with one of those in the Emperor's Library, and that they were copied one from the other, or both from a third copy. This manuscript acknowledges the Procession from the Son. I had understood, from Mountfaucon's general way of expression, that Genebrard had published his copy from this very manuscript of the Royal Library (No. 2502). But observing that Genebrard's wants some words (ἀίδιος ὁ πατήρ, ἀίδιος ὁ υἱός, ἀίδιον τὸ πνεῦμα τὸ ἅγιον) which Mountfaucon's copy has, I conclude that he meant only the same form, as to matter and words, for the most part, not the same manuscript.

8. There is another manuscript Greek version, or rather paraphrase of this Creed, having several interpolations, published by Bishop Usher, in 1647, from a copy sent him by Patrick Young. It has been often since printed: in the Councils, in Gundling, and in Montfaucon.

It leaves out the Article of Procession from the Son; from whence we may judge that it was composed by a Greek, or Grecizing Latin. The title insinuates that the Creed was drawn up in the Nicene Council [f], an

[d] "Incertum autem utrum ex illo quod memorat vetustissimo exemplari, Symbolum etiam sit mutuatus; Codex quippe amplæ molis multa et varia complectitur, quæ dubitare licet ex uuone Codice exscripta fuerint, an ex compluribus."—Montf., *ib.*

[e] "Titulus: Τοῦ ἐν ἁγίοις Πατρὸς ἡμῶν 'Αθανασίου τοῦ μεγάλου Ὁμολογία τῆς καθολικῆς πίστεως ἣν ἔδωκε πρὸς Ἰούλιον Πάπαν Ῥώμης.

"Incipit: Τῷ θέλοντι σωθῆναι," &c.—Montf., p. 729.

[f] Ἐκ τῆς ἁγίας καὶ οἰκουμενικῆς τῆς ἐν Νικαίᾳ, περὶ πίστεως κατὰ συντομίαν, καὶ πῶς δεῖ πιστεύειν τὸν ἀληθῆ χριστιανόν.— Usher, *de Symb.*, p. 33 (26).

opinion entertained by Johan. Cyparissiota, about the year 1360, as observed above. When this story or fiction first came in I cannot pretend to determine. Bishop Usher speaks of a very ancient manuscript, partly in Irish and partly in Latin, which hints at the same thing: but he fixes no date to the manuscript; the words, "very ancient," are too general to give satisfaction in it. The Creed is there said to have been composed in the Nicene Council by Eusebius and Dionysius, and a third left nameless [g], as not being known. The author of that book of hymns must have been very ignorant not to know Athanasius, who was undoubtedly the third man, and for whose sake (to account for the Creed's being written in Latin) the whole story seems to have been contrived. By Eusebius must have been intended Eusebius of Vercell, in Piedmont, a Latin, and a great friend and intimate of Athanasius: by Dionysius undoubtedly is meant Dionysius, Bishop of Milan, of the same time and of the same principles, and well acquainted with Eusebius [h]. Had the contrivers of the fable laid their scene at Alexandria, where Athanasius and this Eusebius, with several other Latins, met together in the year 362, they had made

---

[g] "In Hymnorum, partim Latino partim Hibernico Sermone scriptorum, Codice vetustissimo . . . notatum reperi, trium Episcoporum opera in eadem Nicæna Synodo illud fuisse compositum, Eusebii, et Dionysii, et nomen tertii (sic enim ibi legitur) nescimus."—Usher, de *Symb.*, præf. p. 2.

[h] It seems highly probable, that the whole fable about Eusebius and Dionysius was first raised out of a passage of St. Ambrose, which might be thought to hint some such thing. The words are:—

"Itaque ut Eusebius Sanctus prior levavit vexillum confessionis, ita Beatus Dionysius in exilii locis, priori martyribus titulo vitam exhalavit."—Ambros., ad *Vercellens.*, Ep. 63, vol. ii. p. 1039.

it the more plausible. But let us return to our Greek copies, from which we have a little digressed.

This is observable of the Greek copies in general, that they differ very widely from each other, and therefore cannot be copies of one and the same version. Possibly three or four of them may be thrown into one, admitting, however, many various lections; but still there will be as many remaining which cannot be so dealt with, but must be looked upon as distinct and different versions. Such as desire to see all the copies together may find them in Gundling and Montfaucon; four at large, the rest exhibited only by various lections. I do not know whether the manuscripts of the Vienna Library have been collated for any of the printed editions: perhaps not; I do not remember that I have met with any mention of them in any of the editors of the printed copies.

It may be of use to set the printed editions, after our account of the manuscripts, in chronological order, as distinctly as may be, since we cannot fix the dates of the manuscript copies.

1540. 1. The first printed edition was by Nicolaus Bryling[i], a printer of Basil. My authors have been deficient in not setting down the date of it. I have endeavoured to fix the year, but have not yet been so happy as to come to a certainty in it. Wherefore, I hope, my reader will excuse it, if, rather than set no

---

[i] "Quod olim evulgavit Basileæ Nicolaus Bryling; deinde in Gallia an. 1565, Henricus Stephanus."—Genebrard, *in Symb. Athanas.*, p. 8.

"Quam post Nic. Brylingium et Mich. Neandrum, H. Stephanus in lucem edidit anno 1565."—Fabric., *Bibl. Græc.*, lib. v. c. 2, § 88, in vol. v. p. 315.

year at all, I choose one which I know cannot be very much over or under, because of other pieces printed by the same Bryling about that time. Fabricius mentions Michael Neander as editor of the same copy after Bryling, and before Stephens, but what year is not said. Sebastian Lepusculus's[k] edition of the same was in 1559[l], and Stephens's in 1565.

1569. 2. The second printed copy was taken from the manuscript of Lazarus Baiffius, which he received from Dionysius[m], a Greek, in the year 1533, as before hinted. This was first printed by Genebrard in the year 1569, again in 1585, and oftentimes since. This copy is sometimes called the Dionysian copy; and it is observed by Gundling to differ from the first copy but in seven places, and therefore these two have been commonly thrown into one by the editors of both.

1569. 3. The third copy was also first printed by Genebrard, at the same time with the other. It has gone under the name of the Constantinopolitan copy, because Genebrard supposed it to have been in use at Constantinople[n]. It differs considerably from both the

[k] Lepusculus, *Compend. Josephi Gorionidis*, p. 49.
[l] Nic. Serarius, who wrote in the year 1590, speaking of that first copy printed by Bryling and Stephens, says as follows:—
"Quarum prima vulgata dici potest, eo quod hactenus ea sola hic apud nos, Germania et Gallia, typis evulgata fuerit."—Nicol. Serar., *de Symbol. Athanas.*: in *Opusc. Theolog.*, vol. ii. p. 9.
[m] "Hoc Symbolum reperi in libro Græco MS. de Processione Spiritus Sancti, quem Lazaro Baiffio Oratori Regis Francisci I. apud Venetos, obtulit Dionysius Græcus, Episcopus Ziencnsis et Firmionsis an. 1533."—Genebrard, p. 8.
"In manus meas pervenit liber quidam Græcus, de Processione Spiritus Sancti, oblatus Lazaro Bayffio claro Regis nostri Francisci I. apud Venetos Oratori, anno Christi 1533. Quem manu sua elegantissime pinxerat Nicolaus Sophianus patrum nostrorum ævo vir valde doctus."—Genebrard, p. 2; cf. Gundling, p. 69.
[n] "Superius Symbolum Athanasii verbis aliquantulum immu-

other, and is never thrown into one with them, but kept distinct by itself.

1600. 4. The fourth is the Commeline, or Felckman's copy, from the Palatine manuscripts, often reprinted with Athanasius's works. This also stands by itself, as a distinct version.

1647. 5. The fifth was first published by Usher, in the year 1647. This differs extremely from all the rest, having, besides many variations, and slight insertions, one very large interpolation. It hath been often reprinted since Usher's time [o].

1671. 6. The sixth and last was first published by Labbe and Cossart n the second tome of Councils. This copy comes the nearest to the two first, and therefore is sometimes thrown into one with them; but it differs from both in about forty places, according to Gundling's computation.

These are all the printed copies, which are sometimes called four and sometimes six: four, because the first, second, and sixth may be tolerably thrown into one; six, because they may also be kept distinct, and may be reckoned as so many copies at least, if not so many several versions. So much for the Greek versions of our Creed.

To the versions already mentioned may be added the Sclavonian, of several dialects, and, as I conceive, pretty ancient. But we have little or no account of them, only, as I shall shew in the sequel, we may be certain that there have been such. There are Italian, Spanish,

---

tatis Constantinopolitani sic Græce legunt, et recitant."—Genebrard, p. 14.

[o] Usher, de Symbolis, p. 33.

Irish, and Welsh versions; but whether any that can justly be called ancient I know not. Future searches into libraries may perhaps produce farther discoveries. Fabricius makes mention of an Hebrew version of late date, and of an Arabic one still later[p]: but these, or the like modern versions, will be of no use to us in our present enquiries.

[p] " Hebraice versum a Julio Marcello Romano MS. in Bibliotheca Vaticana memorat Imbonatus in Bibl. Latino-Hebraica, p. 149. Sed omitto recentiores versiones, ut Arabicam a Nisselio editam Lugd. Bat. 1656, 4to., una cum Cantico Canticorum."—Fabric., *Bibl. Græc.*, lib. v. c. 2, § 88, in vol. v. p. 315.

" Georgius Nisselius Symbolum Athanasii Arabico idiomate cum Cantico Canticorum Æthiopice et Arabice edito Ludg. Bat. an. 1656, conjunxit . . . id tamen non hausit ex Codice MS. sed ipse in Arabicum Sermonem transtulit."—Teutzel., p. 125.

CHAPTER VI.

OF THE RECEPTION OF THE ATHANASIAN CREED IN THE CHRISTIAN CHURCHES.

FROM the materials here laid down we may now be able to determine something about the reception of the Creed, especially in the Western Churches; among which the Churches of France, or Gaul, ought undoubtedly to be named first.

FRANCE, OR GAUL.

A.D. 550. This Creed obtained in France in the time of Hincmar, or about 850, without all dispute. We may advance higher up to 772; for it was then in Charles the Great's Psalter, among the Hymns of the Church. The Cotton manuscript Psalter, with this Creed in it, will carry us up to 703; and the Canon of the Council of Autun to 670; at which time the Gallican clergy, at least of the Diocese of Autun, in the Province of Lyons, were obliged to recite this Creed, together with the Apostles', under pain of episcopal censure, which shews of how great value and esteem the Creed was at that time, and affords a strong presumption (as Quesnel and Pagi[a] well argue in the case) that it had

---

[a] "Dubium non est quin multis ante synodum illam Augustodunensem annis compositum esset, et jam olim per totam Ecclesiam celebre evasisset: nunquam enim sapientissimi antistites id commisissent, ut istam fidei formulam omnium ordinum clericis amplectendam, et *irreprehensibiliter*, ut aiunt, *recensendam*, synodali edicto sub condemnationis pœna præciperent; imo et illam e re-

been in use there long before. There will be some doubt, as I intimated above, about the supposed Canon of the Council of Autun, which will in some measure abate the force of our evidence, and of the argument built upon it. But as it is certain, from other evidence, that this Creed was received in the Gallican Churches as high as 772 or 703, so it must be owned that this very much confirms the supposition of the Council of Autun; and the concurring circumstances give very great light and strength to each other. But what most of all confirms the foregoing evidence, and the reasoning upon it, is, that Venantius Fortunatus, a full hundred years before the Council of Autun, had met with this Creed in the Gallican parts, and found it then to be in such esteem as to deserve to be commented upon, like the Lord's Prayer and Apostles' Creed: accordingly he wrote comments upon it, as well as upon the other. This wonderfully confirms the reasoning of Quesnel and Pagi, that this Creed must have been in use there near a hundred years before the Council of Autun, that is, as high as 570, about which time Fortunatus flourished and wrote. And considering that this Creed must have been for sometime growing into repute before it could be thought worthy to have such honour paid it along with the Lord's Prayer and Apostles' Creed, I may perhaps be allowed to set the time of its reception in the Gallican Churches some

gione cum Symbolo Apostolico ponerent, nisi jam longo usu recepta, approbata, et inter Germanas Magni Athanasii lucubrationes numerata fuisset; quod nisi post plurium annorum seriem fieri vix potuit."—Quesnel, Dissert. xiv. p. 731.

" Quare jam ante centum fere annis opus illud Athanasio attributum fuerat."—Pagi, *Critic. in Baron.*, Ann. 340, § 6, p. 120. (vol. i. p. 441).

years higher: reception of it, I mean, as an excellent formulary, or an acknowledged rule of faith, though not perhaps admitted into their sacred offices. Upon the whole, and upon the strength of the foregoing evidences, we may reasonably conclude that the reception of this Creed in the Gallican Churches was at least as early as 670, understanding it of its reception into the public offices: but understanding it of its reception as a rule of faith, or an orthodox and excellent formulary and system of belief, it may be justly set as high as 550, which is but twenty years, or thereabout, before Fortunatus commented upon it. Le Quien scruples not to set it as high as 500 [b].

Spain.

630. Next to France we may mention her near neighbour Spain, which seems to have received this Creed very early, and within less than a hundred years after the time before fixed for its reception in France. As to the truth of the fact, it may be argued two several ways. 1. From the near affinity and relation between the Spanish and Gallican offices before either France or Spain had received the Roman. 2. From the fourth Council of Toledo, their quoting passages from this very Creed.

1. As to the first argument, though a general one, it must appear of great weight. If the sacred offices in France and Spain were in those times the same, or very nearly so, then the reception of this Creed in France

---

[b] "Non nisi ex eodem Symbolo, quod jam ante receptum esset, Avitus Viennensis ... alicubi scribebat," &c.—Le Quien, *Dissert. Damascen.*, p. 98.

will afford a very considerable argument of its reception in Spain also.

Cardinal Bona is very large and diffuse in setting forth the agreement and harmony of the old Gallican offices with the Spanish in sundry particulars[c]; and he supposes this uniformity of the two Churches to have been as early, at least, as the days of Gregory, Bishop of Tours, who died in the year 595. Mabillon, after him, frequently asserts the same thing[d], and with greater assurance than Bona had done, having met with new and fuller evidences to prove it, only he dates the agreement of the Spanish Mosarabick offices with the Gallican from the third and fourth Councils of Toledo[e], the latter of which was in the year 633. Mr. Dodwell, speaking of the same matter, says, "Nor does Mabillon himself judge it probable that the innovations attempted by Pope Vigilius in Spain held long, of what kind soever they were. All Spain was soon after united in one form, and that different from the Romans, and agreeing with the Gallican[f]." It is, therefore, a plain case that the Gallican and Spanish offices were very much the same in the beginning of the seventh century, and so continued for some time. If, therefore, the Gallican Churches received the Athanasian Creed into their public offices before the year 670, it will appear extremely probable that the Spanish received it also, and about the same time. I here make a distinction, as I did before, between receiving the Creed as

[c] Bona, *de Rebus Liturg.*, lib. i. c. 12, p. 372.
[d] Mabillon, *de Liturg. Gallican.*, Præf., §§ 2, 3; lib. i. c. 3, §§ 9, 14, pp. 20, 23.
[e] Ibid., lib. i. c. 4, §§ 8, 9, p. 30.
[f] Dodwell, of Incense, p. 190.

a rule of faith, and receiving it into the solemn offices, to be recited or sung in churches. The reception of it, in the first sense, I conceive to have been somewhat earlier, in Spain as well as in France, than its reception in the latter sense. But as different Churches in France had anciently different customs, so also was it in Spain; and therefore it is probable that the reception of this Creed into the public offices was in some Churches sooner, and in others later, according to the various rites, customs, and circumstances of the several Churches.

But I proceed to the Second Article, whereby we are to prove the reception of this Creed in Spain.

2. The fourth Council of Toledo cites a considerable part of this Creed, adopting it into their own Confession [g]. We may be confident that the Creed did not borrow the expressions from them, but they from the Creed, since we are certain that this Creed was made long before the year 633. The reference to this very Creed appears so plain in the words of that Council, that most of the learned have concluded from thence that the Spanish fathers had both seen and approved this Creed. Baronius is positive that the Council took their expressions from it [h]. Calvisius dates the publi-

[g] "Nec personas confundimus, nec substantiam separamus. Patrem a nullo factum, vel genitum dicimus: Filium a Patre non factum, sed genitum, asserimus: Spiritum vero Sanctum nec creatum, nec genitum, sed procedentem a Patre et Filio profitemur; ipsum autem Dominum nostrum Jesum Christum . . . ex substantia Patris ante sæcula genitum . . . æqualis Patri secundum divinitatem, minor Patre secundum humanitatem. . . . Hæc est Catholicæ Ecclesiæ Fides: hanc Confessionem conservamus, atque tenemus. Quam quisquis firmissime custodierit, perpetuam salutem habebit."
—Concil. Tolet. IV. Capitul I., in Labbe, *Concil.*, vol. v. p. 1704.

[h] "Ex eodem Athanasii Symbolo ea verba primi capituli Toletani quarti Concilii deducta noscuntur, quibus dicitur, Patrem

I

cation of the Creed from that Council[i]; so also Alstedius[k]. Gavantus, in his Comments upon the Roman Breviary, concludes from thence that this Creed had been read in the Church as high as that time[l]. Helvicus[m] falls in with the opinion of Calvisius and Alstedius, grounded upon the expressions of this Council being parallel to those of the Creed. These authors have perhaps carried the point too far in supposing this a sufficient proof of any public reception of the Creed in Spain at that time, or of its being read in their churches; but it is clear enough that the Spanish fathers had both seen and approved it, otherwise they could not, or would not, have borrowed so plainly from it. Thus much is allowed by most of the learned moderns, as Quesnel[n], Natalis Alexander[o], Montfaucon[p], Tillemont[q],

---

[a] nullo factum," &c.—Baron., *Annal.*, ann. 340, § 12, vol. iii. p. 529 (p. 436).

[i] "Repositum fuit in archivis, nec publicatum, nisi, quantum ex historiis conjicere licet, post trecentos fere annos, ubi in Concilio Toletano quarto quaedam ex eo translata verba recensentur."— Seth Calvis., *Op. Chronolog.*, ann. 340, p. 544 (396).

[k] "Symbolum Athanasii ab illo scriptum est Romae itidem contra Arium. Publicatum est post 300 fere annos in Concilio Toletano, et inde usque ad nostra tempora in Ecclesia usurpatum."— Alsted., *Thesaur.*, p. 178.

[l] "Athanasius dum esset Romae, scripsit Latine Symbolum .... et recitavit coram Pontifice et ei assidentibus, ann. 340, ut scribit Baronius; et est illud idem, immutatum, logique solitum in Ecclesia, ante annos nongentos sexaginta. Vide Annales ad annum praedictum."—Gavant., *Comment. in Breviar. Rom.*, vol. ii. p. 69 (p. 106).

[m] "Athanasius Symbolum scribit Romae, et Concilio offert; non tamen publicatur, nisi post 300 ferme annos in Concilio Toletano." —Helvic., *Theatr. Histor.*, ad ann. 339.

[n] "Imo et jam ab anno 633 aliqua ex isto Symbolo descripta mihi videntur in ea confessione fidei, quae edita est a Concilio Toletano iv. habeturque capit. i. ejusdem."—Quesnel, Dissert. xiv. p. 731.

[o] Natal. Alexand., vol. iv. p. 109.

[p] Montfauc., *Diatrib.*, p. 720.

[q] Tillemont, *Mémoires*, vol. viii. p. 283 (p. 670).

Muratorius, Oudin[r], and others, that the expressions of that Council and this Creed are parallel, and one borrowed from the other, and the words of the Council from the words of the Creed, only Muratorius hints as if a doubt might be made whether the Council took from the Creed, or the Creed from the Council[s], which may seem strange in him, who supposes the Creed to have been made by Fortunatus many years before that Council was held. But, I suppose, he is there speaking of the argument drawn from the words of that Council alone, abstracting from the other circumstance, and previous to the consideration of Fortunatus's comment, otherwise he is guilty of a very great oversight. It appears, then, that this Creed was known and approved in Spain as early as 633; and it is observable how exactly this falls in with the time when the Spanish Churches are supposed to have received the Gallican offices, according to Mabillon's account. Wherefore it is extremely probable, that about this time they received this Creed from the Gallican Churches; received it as an orthodox formulary, and an approved rule of faith. As to their taking it into their public service and Psalmody, I pretend not to set it so high, having no proof that they did receive it in that sense so early; but as soon as the Gallican Churches made it a part of their Psalmody, we may

---

[r] Oudin, *Comment. de Scriptor. Eccl.*, vol. i. p. 348.
[s] "Verum ne majoris quidem momenti sunt verba illa, quæ in Concilii Toletani quarti professione Fidei leguntur: quamvis enim phrases nonnullæ ibidem inveniantur Symboli phrasibus oppido similes, attamen ejusmodi non sunt ut iis patribus Symbolum jam innotuisse demonstrent. Quin ex eodem Concilio has formulas quis delibasse videri potest, ut inde Symbolum istud conflaret."—Murator., *Anecdot.*, vol. ii. p. 223.

reasonably think that the Spanish did so too, or within a very short time after.

GERMANY.

787. Next to France and Spain we may mention Germany; not only because of their nearness of situation to France, but also because of their mutual intercourse and affinity with each other. This Creed, very probably, was received in some parts of Germany soon after it obtained in the Gallican Church. The mutual intercourse of the German and Gallican Churches makes it probable; and the ancient manuscript of the Creed found at Treves, or Triers, in Germany, may persuade the same thing. Our positive evidence is, however, clear and certain for the reception of the Creed as early as 870, being then translated by Otfridus into the German or Teutonic language. Anscharius's instructions to his clergy (above mentioned) will afford an argument for the reception of this Creed in Germany from the time of his holding the See of Hamburg, or from 830; and it was received at Basil, as we learn from Hatto, bishop of the place, before 820. Indeed, I have above referred Basil to France, considering how it stood in Hatto's time, and that it was part of ancient Gaul; but then it was upon the confines of Germany, and has in later times been reckoned to it, and we have good reason to think that the customs of the German Churches in the ninth century were nearly the same with those of the Church of Basil in 820. What passed in the Council of Frankfort (if I mistake not in my construction of it) may warrant the carrying it up as high as 794; and it was seven years before that,

namely, in the year 787 [t], that Pope Adrian sent to St. Willehad, Bishop of Breme, the famous Psalter of Charles the Great [u], with this Creed in it, the same that I have spoken of above. No wonder, therefore, that Anscharius and Rembertus, afterwards Archbishops of Hamburg and Breme, so very highly valued this Creed. The particular regard paid to this Creed by Charles the Great, in the year 772, may plead perhaps in favour of a more early date; at least, no doubt can be made but as soon as he came to be Emperor, if not a great deal sooner, the German Churches (as well as the Gallican before) admitted this Creed even into their public offices. It is of this time that an anonymous author, cited above, in a tract directed to Charlemagne, then Emperor, says that this Creed was professed by the Universal Church. We cannot, however, be mistaken in setting the reception of it in Germany as high as the year 787. So high may pass for certain fact; and there is great probability for the running it up many years higher.

England.

800. As to our own country, we have clear and positive proof of the Creed's being sung alternately in our churches in the tenth century, when Abbo of Fleury,

---

[t] Mabill., *Act. Sanct.*, sæc. 3, part 2, vol. iv. p. 409.
[u] "Codex iste .... in Bibliotheca cubiculari summi Pontificis Hadriani I. permansit usque ad annum DCCLXXXVIII. quo S. Willehadus ab eodem cum consensu Caroli M. primus Episcopus Bremensis declaratus est. Tunc videlicet P. P. Hadrianus eundem illum Codicem Psalterii, quem ipse in principio Pontificatus sui tanquam munus gratulatorium a Carolo Magno acceperat, eadem ratione donavit S. Willebado, ut et ille, in novo Episcopatu suo, frueretur usu sacri istius muneris."—Lambec. *Catal. Bibl. Vindob.*, lib. ii. c. 5, p. 297.

an ear-witness of it, was here, and when the Saxon versions, still extant, were of standing use for the instruction and benefit both of clergy and people. These evidences alone will prove the reception of this Creed in England to have been as early as 950 or 930, or the time of Athelstan, whose Latin Psalter, with the Creed in it, remains to this day. The age of the manuscript versions will warrant us thus far; but, possibly, if those versions were thoroughly examined by a critic in the Saxon, it might appear that the version, or versions, were some years older than the manuscripts. But it may be worth the observing farther, that among several other ancient Professions of Faith drawn up by our Bishops of the Saxon times, there is one of Denebert, Bishop of Worcester, presented to Archbishop Athelard in the year 799, which contains in it a considerable part of the Athanasian Creed [v]. From whence may be concluded that this formulary was well known here and well approved, among the learned at least, in those times. Wherefore, upon the whole, and all circumstances considered, I may presume to name the year 800, or thereabout, for the reception of this Creed in England. Further enquiries may perhaps carry it up higher; but it cannot reasonably be brought lower, and so there I leave it.

ITALY.

880. We learn from Ratherius, above cited, that this Creed was in common use in some parts of Italy, particularly in the diocese of Verona, in Low Lombardy,

[v] "Orthodoxam, Catholicam Apostolicam Fidem, sicut didici, paucis exponam verbis, quia scriptum est, 'Quicunque vult Salvus esse,'" &c.—Profess. Deneberti Episc. Wigorn., in *Text. Roff.*, p. 252.

in his time ; that is, about 960. He then speaks of it as a man would do of a formulary that had been customary amongst them, and of long standing. He exhorts his clergy to make themselves masters of the three Creeds, Apostles', Nicene, and Athanasian, without the least intimation of the last of them being newly introduced. I incline to think, that from the time that Lombardy became a province of the French under Charles the Great (about the year 774), this Creed obtained there, by means of that prince, who had so great a value for it, and whose custom it was to disperse it abroad wherever he had any power or influence. He presented it to the Pope himself in 772; he delivered it, about the same time, or before, to the monks of Mount Olivet, in Jerusalem, of his foundation; and it appears to have been with his consent, or perhaps at his request, that Pope Adrian conveyed it to Willehad, the first Bishop of Breme, in 787. These circumstances make it highly probable that the same Charles the Great introduced this Creed into Lombardy soon after his conquest of it; and, indeed, nothing could be more serviceable at that time in a country which had so long before been corrupted with Arianism. Add to this, that it appears highly probable that the Gallican Psalter was introduced into the Churches of Italy soon after Lombardy became a province under the kings of France; and if their Psalter came in, no doubt but their Creed, then a part of their Psalter, came in with it. Cardinal Bona observes, and seems to wonder at it, that the Gallican Psalter obtained in most parts of Italy in the eleventh century[x]. He might, very probably,

[x] Bona, *de Rebus Liturg.*, lib. ii. c. 3, p. 506.

have set the date higher, as high perhaps, or very near, as the conquest of Lombardy by Charlemagne. Thus far, at least, we may reasonably judge, that those parts which were more immediately subject to the kings of France, Verona especially, one of the first cities taken, received the Gallican Psalter sooner than the rest. However, since I here go only upon probabilities, and have no positive proof of the precise time when either the Creed or the Psalter came in, and it might take up some years to introduce them and settle them there (new customs generally meeting with difficulties and opposition at the first), these things considered, I am content to suppose the year 880 for the reception of this Creed in Italy, which is but eighty years higher than Ratherius, and is above one hundred years from the entire conquest of Lombardy by Charles the Great. There may be some reason to suspect that this Creed had been known in Italy, and received, at least in some of the monasteries there, near two hundred years before. The manuscript of Bobbio, in Langobardic character, and written about the year 700, or sooner, will afford a very strong presumption of it; and if we consider how from the year 637, in the time of Rotharis, one of the Lombard kings of Italy, there had been a constant struggle between the Catholics and Arians, and a succession of bishops on both sides kept up, in almost every city of his dominions, for many years together, I say, from these considerations, one might reasonably presume that the Catholics had about that time procured this Creed, together with Bachiarii Fides and Gennadius's Tract, out of the Gallican parts, to arm themselves the better against the spreading heresy.

But as this does not amount to a public reception of it, nor is the fact so clear as not to be liable to dispute, I pretend not to insist upon it.

Rome.

930. Rome is of distinct consideration from the other parts of Italy, and was always more desirous of imposing her own offices upon other Churches, than of receiving any from them. The *Filioque* in the Constantinopolitan Creed had been long admitted into all the other Western Churches before Rome would accept it, which was not (at least it does not appear that it was) till the middle of the eleventh century, or about 1050. The custom of reciting the Nicene or Constantinopolitan Creed in the Communion Service had prevailed in Spain, France, and Germany for several centuries, and was at length but hardly admitted at Rome in the year 1014. It was thought civil enough of the popes of Rome to allow the other Western Churches to vary from the Roman customs in any thing; and those other Churches could not enjoy that liberty and privilege in quiet, without complying with the Roman Offices in most things besides. The use of the Athanasian Creed was one of those things wherein they were beforehand with the Church of Rome, and in which they were indulged, as was also the use of the Gallican Psalter, which the Western Churches in general were allowed[y] to have, while the Romans were

---

[y] "Alexander IV. in sua Constitutione quæ est Sexta in Bullario Ordinis Eremitarum Sancti August ni, mandat Priori Generali et reliquis Fratribus in Tuscia, ut recitent officium juxta morem Romanæ Ecclesiæ, excepto Psalterio."—Bona, *de Rebus Liturg.*, lib. ii. c. 3, p. 506.

"Sic quoque S. Franciscus, ut testatur Frassenius (Disqu. Bib.,

tenacious of their own. But though the Romans retained their own Psalter all the way down to the middle of the sixteenth century, yet they had long before borrowed this Creed from the Gallican, and received it into their Offices. This is certain fact; but as to the precise time when it was first done it may not be easy to determine: it was, without all question, before Thomas Aquinas's days, who tells us (as above cited) that this Creed was received by the authority of the pope: I wish he had told us what pope. That it was not received into the Roman Offices so soon as the year 809 may be probably argued from a case that then happened, which has been hinted above. The Latin monks of Mount Olivet (founded by Charles the Great) in their Apologetical Letter to Pope Leo III. made the best defence they were able of their own practice in their public professing that the Holy Ghost proceeds from the Son. They pleaded the open acknowledgment of the same doctrine in Charles the Great's own chapel, and that the same doctrine had been taught them in St. Gregory's Homilies, and in the Rule of St. Benedict, and in the Athanasian Creed, and in a Dialogue given them by Pope Leo himself[z]. Now, had the Athanasian

---

c. 6, § 1) illius Ordinis Frater, in Regula suorum præcipit: Clerici faciant Divinum Officium secundum Ordinem sanctæ Romanæ Ecclesiæ, excepto Psalterio."—Hodius, *de Text. Bibl.*, lib. iii. c. 2, § 4, p. 383. See also above, p. 44.

[z] "Benignissime Pater, dum essem Ego Leo, servus vester, ad Sancta vestigia vestra, et ad pia vestigia Domni Karoli, piissimi Imperatoris, Filiique vestri, audivimus in Capella ejus dici in Symbolo Fidei, Qui ex Patre Filioque procedit. Et in Homilia S. Gregorii, quam nobis Filius vester Domnus Karolus Imperator dedit, in parabola Octavarum Paschæ, ubi dixit: Sed ejus missio ipsa processio est, qui de Patre proce it et Filio. Et in Regula S. Benedicti, quam nobis dedit Filius vester Domnus Karolus, . . . et in Dialogo quem nobis vestra Sanctitas dare dignata est, simi-

Creed been at that time recited in the public Offices at Rome, those monks who were so particular in every little circumstance pleadable in their favour, could not have failed (especially upon their mentioning the Athanasian Creed) to have pleaded a thing so notorious, and which would have given the greatest countenance and authority possible to them and their doctrine, and must have been of the greatest weight and force with Pope Leo, to whom they were writing, and whose protection they were then seeking and humbly imploring. From hence then one may reasonably infer that this Creed was not received into the Roman Offices so early as the year 809. Let us now enquire whether we can fix upon any later time for its coming in.

Genebrard testifies that in the oldest Roman Breviaries he could meet with, or hear of, this Creed always made a part of the service[a]. But this is too general, nor can we be certain how ancient those oldest Breviaries were, nor whether they belonged to the Roman Church strictly so called, or to other Western Churches; and, indeed, I know not how we can come to any certainty in this matter, unless it be by examining into the Roman Psalters which have this Creed in them. Whenever the Creed came into the Roman Psalters we may justly conclude that at the same time it came into the Roman Offices. We have in our public library at Cambridge a Roman Psalter, written for the use of the Church of Canterbury (as

liter dicit. Et in Fide S. Athanasii eodem modo dicit."—Epist. Monach. Montis Oliveti ; in Le Quien, *Damasc. Dissert.*, p. 7.

[a] " In vetustissimis Romanæ Ecclesiæ ὡρολογίοις (hæc nunc vocamus vulgo Breviaria) sub Athanasii nomine ejus ad Primam recitatio usu recepta est."—Genebrard, p. 3.

our judicious Mr. Wanley reasonably conjectures [b], and about the time of the Conquest, or a little before, suppose 1060. The Church of Canterbury more especially used the Roman Psalter, as hath been observed above, and was in all things conformable, of old time, to the Roman Offices. Now, if this Creed, which had long before been introduced into the Gallican Psalters, did at this time obtain in the Roman also, it is obvious to conclude, that it at the same time made a part of the Roman Offices, even at Rome itself, as well as Canterbury, since one was conformable to the other. This argument may carry us up some years higher; for there is another, an older Roman Psalter, taken notice of above, which has this Creed in it, written about the year 930, in the time of King Athelstan. It is said to have belonged formerly to Archbishop Cranmer. Perhaps this also might have been written for the use of the Church of Canterbury: I know of no Church amongst us which at that time used the Roman Psalter but the Church of Canterbury. However, it is highly improbable that any Church which complied so far with Rome as to use the Roman Psalter should take this Creed into that Psalter before such time as Rome itself had done the same thing. Upon the strength of this argument, though it be not demonstrative, but probable only (such as the case will admit of, and such as may very well pass till we can fix upon something more certain), I say, upon the strength of this, I in-

---

[b] "Notandum vero in Litania extare hæc verba : Ut Archiepiscopum nostrum, et omnem congregationem illi commissam, in sancta religione conservare digneris, te rogamus : quibus pene inducor ut credam hunc Cod. olim pertinuisse ad Ecclesiam Christi Salvatoris Cantuariæ."—Wanley, *Catal.*, p. 152.

cline to date the reception of this Creed at Rome from the tenth century, and the beginning of it, about the year 930. From this time forwards, I presume, the Athanasian Creed has been honoured with a public recital among the other sacred hymns and Church Offices all over the West. The way has been to recite it at the Prime, or first hour (one o'clock in the Latin account, with us seven in the morning), every Lord's day[c], and in some places every day[d]. But as the custom of making it only a part of the Sunday Service is the most ancient, so has it likewise been the most general and prevailing, and is at this day the common and constant usage of the Churches within the Roman Communion. And let this suffice so far as concerns the Western Churches.

Of the Greek and Oriental Churches.

As to the Greek, or Oriental Churches, I reserved this place for them, that I might not entirely omit them. It has been questioned whether any of them ever received this Creed at all. Vossius[e] seems to

[c] "Die Dominico ad Primam recitetur."—Hatt. Basil, A.D. 820. See above, p. 27.

"Per omnes Occidentis Ecclesias Dominicis semper diebus psallitur .... in cunctis Ecclesiis publice cani præcepta."—Manuel Calec. cont. Græc., lib. ii. c. 20; in Bibl. Max. PP. vol. xxvi. p. 414.

[d] "Fidem, 'Quicunque vult,' quotidie ad Primam iterat. Honor. August. Ad Primam dicunt quotidie Symbolum Athanasii."—Bona, de Carthusianis; Divin. Psalm., c. 18, § 5, p. 897.

"Ad Primam .... quotidie subditur Symbolum Athanasii."—Bona, de Ambrosianis, ib., § 10, p. 900.

[e] "Nec qui nostra ætate Patriarcha Alexandrinus, et Præses Constantinopoleos fuit, pro germano illud Symbolum habuit. Sic enim Meletius litteris suis Constantinopoli, anno 1597, ad Johannem Douzam Nordovicem datis, et a filio Georgio Douza editis: 'Athanasio falso adscriptum Symbolum, cum appendice illa Romanorum Pontificum adulteratum, luce lucidius contestamur.'"—Voss., de Trib. Symb., Dissert. ii. c. 20, p. 521.

have thought that they never have; and so also Combefisius[f]; and Dr. Smith, in his Account of the Greek Church, is positive, that, as to the Creed of Athanasius, the Greeks are wholly strangers to it [g].

Nevertheless, I find some very considerable men of a contrary persuasion, and not Romanists only, as Baronius, Spondanus[h], Muratorius[i], Renaudot[k], and others, but Protestants also, as particularly Gundling, whose words I have put into the margin[l]. We may observe, however, that thus far is agreed on all hands, that this Creed is not received in all the Greek Churches; and if it is in any, yet it is there differently read in the Article of Procession. It is not pretended that any of the African Churches, Alexandrian, Nubian, or Ethiopian (which are most of them of the Jacobite or Eutychian sect) have received it. So far from it, that they have not (at least the Ethiopian or Abassine Churches

[f] Combef., *not. ad Calec.*, p. 297, *et notatione* 48 *in vitam Basilii Pseudo-Amphiloch.* . . . "Symbolum Athanasii Græci ut ejus non recipiunt."

[g] Smith, Account of the Greek Church, p. 196.

[h] Spondanus epitomizing the words of Baronius, ann. 340, § 4 : "Cum autem e Romanæ Ecclesiæ antiquis monumentis, veluti eruderatum emersit in lucem, a Latinis omnibus, a Græcisque susceptum est: necnon ab Ecclesia Serviana, Bulgarica, Russica, Moscovitica, et aliis; quamvis ab eis dempta inde pars illa fuerit, qua Spiritum Sanctum a Patre Filioque procedere expressum habetur."

[i] "Re vera, non Ecclesia tantum Constantinopolitana, sed Serviana, Bulgarica, Russica, Moscovitica, aliæque Ritui Græco addictæ, etsi Athanasiano Symbolo in Sacris Liturgiis utantur, hanc tamen particulam, et Filio, inde exclusere."—Murator., vol. ii. p. 227.

[k] "Quod dicitur Dei Filius assumpsi-se Hominem, &c., rectum est, Symbolo quod Athanasii dicitur, et a Græcis Latinisque recipitur, conforme."—Renaud., *Orient. Liturg., ad Nestorii Liturgiam*, n. 2, in vol. ii. p. 643.

[l] "Mirari quis posset cur Græci Processionem Spiritus Sancti a Filio negent, additionem ad Symbolum Nicænum tam ægre ferant, cum tamen Symbolum Athanasii recipiant."—Gundling, p. 68.

have not) so much as the Apostles' Creed amongst them, if we may believe Ludolphus [m]; so little are they acquainted with the Latin forms or Confessions. Nor is it pretended that the more Eastern Christians, belonging to the Patriarchates of Antioch and Jerusalem, have any acquaintance with the Athanasian Creed; no, not the Maronites, though they formerly submitted to the see of Rome, and are still supposed to hold communion therewith, and to acknowledge the Pope for their head. All that is pretended with respect to this Creed is, that the Churches of Constantinople, Servia, Bulgaria, Russia, and Muscovy, acknowledge it as Athanasius's, or make use of it in their common and sacred Offices. And for proof of this it has been usual to appeal to a passage of Cazanovius, a Polish knight, in a letter of his to Calvin, which letter I have not seen, but find quoted both by Genebrard [n] and Vossius [o], men of opposite principles, and therefore the more safely to be relied on where they agree. But what does Cazanovius confess? That the Greek, Servian, Russian, and Muscovite Churches acknowledge the Athanasian Creed as Athanasius's, only curtailed (or, as they would say, corrected) as to the point of the

---

[m] Ludolph., *Histor. Æthiop.*, lib. iii. c. 5, § 19: "Symbolo Fidei Catholicæ Nicæno communiter utuntur. . . . Illo quo nos utimur, uti cæteri Orientales, carent: haud levi indicio Apostolos illius autores non esse."

[n] "Si Athanasii est, cujusnam illud erit quod nunc Græcorum, Serviorum, Russorum, et Moscorum Ecclesiæ sub ejusdem Athanasii titulo retinent, ac pro genuino agnoscunt?"—Cazanov. *ad Calvin. Epist.*; in Genebrard, p. 7.

[o] "Cazanovius Sarmata . . . . etsi multum ei hoc Symbolum displiceat, agnoscit tamen Athanasianum vocari, non in Latina solum Ecclesia, sed etiam in Constantinopolitana, Serviana, Bulgarica, Moscovitica."—Voss., *de Symb.*, Diss. ii. c. i. p. 516.

Procession. A confession from a Socinian adversary in this case is of some weight, and especially if it can be enforced by any corroborating evidence. Let us see, then, what may be further learned concerning the several Churches here named, and the reception of this Creed in them. I may take them one by one.

1. To begin with Muscovy, where the matter of fact seems to be most fully attested of any. In the account given of the Lord Carlisle's embassy from King Charles II. to the great Duke of Muscovy, in the year 1663 [p], I meet with this passage relating to the Muscovites and their divine service:—"The whole service is performed by reading of certain Psalms, or chapters in the Bible; sometimes the priest adds Athanasius's Creed, or sings certain hymns and St. Chrysostom's Homily." In another treatise, intituled, "Of the Ancient and Modern Religion of the Muscovites," written in French, and printed at Cologne, 1698, and since translated into English, there is this account of the Muscovites: that "they receive the Creed of the Apostles, and that of Nice and Athanasius [q]." These two testimonies are undoubtedly sufficient, so far as concerns Muscovy. Now, the Muscovites received their religion and their orders from the Patriarch of Constantinople about the tenth century, or beginning of the eleventh; and their receiving of this Creed will be a presumptive argument in favour of its reception at Constantinople also, if there be no evident reason against it. That the Muscovites did not receive the

[p] Harris's Collection of Travels, vol. ii. p. 181. See also the Duke of Holstein's Travels, ib., p. 36.
[q] Harris's Collection of Travels, vol. ii. p. 238. See also pp. 240, 241.

Creed from the Latins, but from the Greeks, is very plain, because their copies of the Creed are without the Article of the Procession from the Son [r]. For they pretend that the Latins have interpolated the Creed, appealing to their own uncorrupted copies; and they blame the Latins, farther, for inserting the *Filioque* into the Nicene [s]. From what hath been said, it appears to be certain fact, that the Muscovites receive the Athanasian Creed: how long they have had it, or how far short of 700 years (reckoning from the time that Christianity was received or restored amongst them), I cannot say. I should observe, that the Muscovites always perform their service in their own vulgar tongue, as is allowed on all hands [t]. Since, then, the Athanasian Creed is a part of their Service, they must have had a version of it in the Muscovite language, which is a dialect of the Sclavonian. Wherefore this also, after our proof of the thing, may now be added to the other versions above mentioned.

2. Russia, as distinguished from Muscovy, must mean Russia Minor, or the Black Russia, a province of Poland. As many as there follow the Greek rites are

[r] Tentzel., *Judic. Erudit.*, p. 151.
[s] See Harris, l. c. p. 240.
[t] "In cæteris autem regionibus, videlicet in Servia, Mysia, Bosnia, Bulgaria, Russia Minori Regi Poloniæ subdita, in Voihinia, Podolia, et parte quadam Lituaniæ, aliisque finitimis provinciis. ritu Græco divinum peragitur officium, translatis Græcorum typicis in Sclavonicam Linguam. Eosdem Græcos ritus, eadem lingua, servant Moscovitæ, quorum Regio Russia major, seu Roxolania nuncupatur," &c.—Bona, *de Divin. Psalmod.*, c. 18, § 17, p. 911; cf. Usher, *Histor. Dogmat.*, p. 246.
"Armeni suo quoque nativo sermone dudum sacra celebrant, tum qui Orthodoxam Fidem retinuerunt, tum Jacobitæ, ut Muscovitæ seu Rutheni, Constantinopolitanæ sedi subjecti, Russico; et alii quidam de quibus pauca scimus."—Renaudot., *Liturg. Orient.*, vol. i. Disserta. 6, p. xliii.

of the same account with the Muscovites before spoken of; and therefore what has been said of the former, with respect to the use of the Athanasian Creed, will be applicable to these also, and so I need not be more particular about them. The Patriarch of Muscovy ordains their Archbishop, who is therefore subject to him, and follows the same rites and customs; and their language is also a dialect of the Sclavonian, like the other.

3. Servia, now a large province of the Turkish empire, part of Northern Turkey in Europe, first received Christianity about the year 860, by the means of Cyril and Methodius, who are said to have invented the Sclavonian letters, and to have translated the Scriptures into the Sclavonian tongue. Cyril was a Greek, and came from Constantinople; and Methodius was a Greek too, both sent by the Greek Emperor to convert the country, which therefore became instructed in the Greek rites and religion. It is not improbable that they should have the Athanasian Creed, as well as the Muscovites and Russians, or perhaps before them, being converted sooner; and they also must have received it from the Greeks, and not from the Latins, because of their varying in the Article of the Procession from the Western Churches.

4. Bulgaria is likewise part of Turkey in Europe, and has been so from the year 1396. Christianity was planted there in the year 845. There were of old great disputes between the two Bishops of Rome and Constantinople upon the question to whose Patriarchate the Bulgarians did of right belong. In conclusion, about the year 870, the Greek Patriarch prevailed over

the Roman, by the interest of the then Emperor of Constantinople. The Bulgarians of consequence fell to the share of the Greek Church, and so have been educated in their rites and customs. Their language is a dialect of the Sclavonian, in which they perform their sacred offices; and, therefore, if they make use of the Athanasian Creed, they must be supposed to have it in their own vulgar tongue. I have no particular evidence of their using it beyond what has been mentioned from Cazanovius and the Romish writers, which yet seems to be sufficient, since it has been fully proved that it is used in Muscovy and in Russia, to whom the Bulgarians are neighbours, and with whom they conform in their other religious rites derived from the same fountain, namely, the Constantinopolitan Greeks.

5. It remains, then, that we consider the fact in respect of Constantinople itself, and the Greek Church there; for this also, as we have seen, has been named with others as receiving the Athanasian Creed. Genebrard is positive in it, and gives us the very Creed itself, which the Constantinopolitans, as he says, use and recite[u]. He wrote in the year 1569. The truth of his report is very much doubted, because the form which he exhibits acknowledges the Procession from the Son, which the Constantinopolitans admit not; and even those who, as before seen, assert or allow that they receive this Creed, yet, at the same time, intimate that it is not the entire Creed, but curtailed in that Article. However, Genebrard might be in the right

[u] "Superius Symbolum Athanasii verbis aliquantulum immutatis Constantinopolitani sic Græce legunt, et recitant."— Genebrard, p. 14.

as to the main thing, that the Constantinopolitans do receive the Creed, though mistaken in the particular form; or, possibly, some Latinizing Greeks at Constantinople might have one form, and the rest another, and thus all will be well. But let us enquire what further evidence there is of this Creed's having been ever received at Constantinople, and by the Greeks properly so called. An argument thereof may be drawn from the Greek copies that vary from the Latin in the Article of Procession. For who should draw up and curtail the Greek copies but the Greeks? and why should they be at the trouble of correcting (as they will call it) the Creed if they did not receive it? A second argument may be drawn from the Creed's being found in the Horologia belonging to the Greeks; that is, in their Breviaries (as we should call them), their Books of Service for the Canonical Hours. How should the Creed come in there, unless the Greeks received it into their sacred Offices? As to the fact, Bishop Usher's copy found in such a Breviary, is a sufficient evidence; and it is plain from the copy itself that it was no Latinizing Greek that made it or used it, since the Procession from the Son is struck out. Further, this Horologion belonged to a monk of Constantinople [v], which argues the reception of the Creed in that very city; and as a token of their esteem of it, and value for it, it is ascribed to the Nicene Council itself, which all the Greeks receive and respect with the greatest

---

[v] "In Thecaræ, Constantinopolitani Monachi, Græcorum Hymnorum Horologio (a Ravio nostro ex Oriente huc advecto) Symbolum hoc, eo quo post finem hujus Diatribæ cernitur interpolatum modo, Nicenæ Synodo adscriptum .... reperi," &c.—Usher, *de Symb.*, præf., p. 2 (p. 1).

veneration. From hence, then, it is plain that the Constantinopolitan Greeks (some of them at least) receive, or have received, this Creed, but with some alterations proper to their peculiar tenets, in opposition to the Latins. This fact, of the Constantinopolitans their receiving this Creed, might be farther proved from the Confession of Metrophanes Critopulus (in the year 1620, published in 1667 [x]), who admits the Creed, and looks upon it as owing to a very particular Providence, that the Greek copies (as he supposes) have been preserved pure and entire, while the Latin ones have been corrupted or interpolated. We find by Nicolaus Hydruntinus, above cited, that such had been the general persuasion of the Greeks, 500 years upwards, in relation to this Creed; not rejecting the Creed, but the Latin interpolation only, as they take it to be.

Which when I consider, reflecting withal how the Muscovites, Russians, &c. (who derived their religion from the Greeks since the ninth century), have all come into this Creed, and that no good account has been given of such agreement, except it be that they all received the same form when they first received their religion; I say, when I consider, and compare these things together, it cannot but give me a suspicion that this Creed had been received by the Greeks soon after their first disputes with the Latins about the Procession, only they took care to strike out a part of it, hoping to solve all by charging the Latins with interpolation; or, possibly, the Latin Patriarchs of Constan-

[x] "Metrophanis Critopuli, Protosyngeli Constantinopolitani Ὁμολογία τῆς ἀνατολικῆς ἐκκλησίας."—Edit. Helmstad., in 4to. a Joann. Horneio; vid. cap. 1, p. 18, in Tentzel., p. 150.

tinople, between the years 1205 and 1260, might first introduce the Creed there. They made use of it, as it seems, then and there, in their Offices for the instruction of the Catechumens, as I learn from a Pontifical of the Church of Constantinople about 500 years old, published in part by Martene, who gives an account of it [y], and also an extract of the office relating to Catechumens, which I have transcribed [z] into the bottom of the page. It is not improbable that the use of the Creed at Constantinople might first come in such a way; and when it had prevailed there for forty or fifty years, the returning Greeks might think it not improper to continue its use, only taking out the Article which concerns the Procession.

However this be, one thing is certain, and, I think, hath been proved abundantly, that the professed Greeks, even under the Patriarch of Constantinople, have in former times received, and still do receive, this Creed, with such alterations or corrections as are proper to their principles; and so I understand Dr. Covel [a],

[y] "Constantinopolitanæ Ecclesiæ Pontificale vetus, ad Latinos ritus accommodatum, cujus character ad annos 500 accedit; scriptum proinde eo tempore quo urbe a Gallis occupata, Latinis ritibus serviebat. Ex Bibliotheca R. R. P. P. Prædicatorum majoris Conventus Parisiensis."—Martene, *Syllab. Ritual.*, prefixed to vol. i.

[z] "Interrogatio. Fides quid tibi præstat? R. Vitam æternam. Ait ei Sacerdos.... Fides autem est, ut unum Deum in Trinitate, et Trinitatem in Unitate veneieris, neque confundendo Personas, neque Substantiam separando. Alia est enim Persona Patris, alia Filii, alia Spiritus Sancti: sed horum trium una est, et non nisi una Divinitas. Exeat ergo de te spiritus malignus," &c.—Martene, *de Antiq. Eccl. Ritibus*, c. 1, art. 7, vol. i. pp. 44, 45.

[a] Covel, Account of the Greek Church, pref., p. 9. To which I may add a remark of the learned Dr. Hickes, that "this Creed, though of an uncertain author, was, for its excellent composure, received into the Greek and Latin Churches."—Hickes, Serm., vol. ii. p. 235.

where he says, speaking of what is done amongst the Greeks, that Athanasius's Creed is owned as corrupted, that is, with such corruptions as the Greeks have made to it. Upon the whole, therefore, I cannot but close in with those many learned Romanists who have affirmed, and still do affirm, that this Creed is received both by Greeks and Latins. If the expression be thought too general, since it is certain that the Creed is rejected by innumerable Greeks, or, more properly, Orientalists, in Asia and Africa, as the Cophtes, and Nubians, and Abassines, and Maronites, Armenians, Nestorians, &c.; I say, if this be objected, it is to be considered that the Romanists, under the name of Greeks, mean generally the orthodox Greeks only, the Melchite Greeks, or as many as hold communion with the Patriarch of Constantinople, making no account of the rest, as being by their heresies cut off from the Church, and therefore of little or no consideration [b]. Now, in this sense, it is excusable enough to say, that the Creed is received both by Greeks and Latins.

To sum up what hath been said of the reception of this Creed. From the foregoing account it appears that its reception has been both general and ancient; it hath been received by Greeks and Latins all over Europe; and if it hath been little known among the

[b] "Attamen hoc ævi sub Orientalis Ecclesiæ nomine diversarum Nationum Orientalium Ecclesiæ veniunt; quæ licet a Græca suam cognoscant originem, propter tamen variarum hæresium colluviem et alia præter mores Christianos pessime introducta a Græca longissime absunt. Græci enim illius religionis homines, tanquam a se disjunctos, atque improbissimos, arcent, et detestantur."— Leo Allat., *de perpet. Consens. Eccl. Occid. et Orient.*, lib. i. c. 1, § 5, p. 7.

African and Asian Churches, the like may be said of the Apostles' Creed, which hath not been admitted, scarce known, in Africa, and but little in Asia[c], except among the Armenians, who are said to receive it[d]; so that, for generality of reception, the Athanasian Creed may vie with any, except the Nicene, or Constantinopolitan, the only general Creed common to all the Churches. As to the antiquity of its reception into the sacred Offices, this Creed has been received in several countries, France, Germany, England, Italy, and Rome itself, as soon, or sooner, than the Nicene, which is a high commendation of it, as gaining ground by its own intrinsic worth, and without the authority of any general Council to enforce it. And there is this thing further to be said for it, that while the Nicene and Apostles' Creeds have been growing up to their present perfection in a course of years, or centuries of years, and not completed till about the year 600, this Creed was made and perfected at once, and is more ancient, if considered as an entire form, than either of the others, having received its full perfection while the others wanted theirs. No considerable additions

[c] "Illo quo nos utimur, uti cæteri Orientales, carent (Habessini) haud levi indicio, Apostolos illius autores non esse, quamvis doctrinæ ratione Apostolicum recte vocetur."—Ludolph., *Hist. Æthiop.*, lib. iii. c. 5, n. 19. Ἡμεῖς οὔτε ἔχομεν οὔτε εἴδομεν σύμβολον τῶν Ἀποστόλων. Marc. Ephesius in Concil. Florent. ann. 1439, in Sylvest. Sgurop. Hist., sect. vi. c. 6, p. 150. Compare the statement of Marcus Ephesius in the discussions at the Council of Florence: "Non habemus (*Symbolum Apostolorum*);" in Harduin., vol. ix. p. 842.

"Symbolum nec ab Apostolis, nec a Synodo ulla generali factum est: Ad hæc, nec in Græc. nec in Orient. ullis Ecclesiis obtinuit, sed in Ecclesia Romana."—Suicer., *Thesaur.*, vol. ii. p. 1093; sub voce *Symbolum*.

[d] Ricaut, Present State of the Greek Church, p. 409.

or defalcations have been made to it (it has needed none) since its first compiling till of late years, and in the Greek Church only, which yet are so far from correcting or amending the form, that they have rendered it so much the less perfect, and the only way of restoring it to its perfection is to restore it to what it was at the first. But I pass on.

CHAPTER VII.

OF THE TIME WHEN, AND PLACE WHERE, THE CREED
WAS COMPOSED.

HAVING observed when and where this Creed hath been received, we may now ascend higher, and consider when and where it was made. Our enquiries here will be in some measure dark and conjectural; strong probabilities will perhaps be as much as we can reach to, which made it the more necessary for me to begin, as I have, at the lower end, where things are more plain and clear, in hopes to borrow some light to conduct our searches into what remains still dark and obscure. Whatever we have to advance in this chapter must rest upon two things:—1. Upon external testimony from ancient citations, manuscripts, comments, versions, and the like, such as have been previously laid down. 2. Upon the internal characters of the Creed.

1. To begin with the external evidence:—Our ancient testimonies, above recited, carry up the antiquity of the Creed as high as the year 670, if the first of them be admitted for genuine, as it reasonably may, notwithstanding some objections. Our manuscripts, now extant, will bring us no higher than 700; but such as have been known to be extant may reach up to 660, or even 600. This must be thought very considerable to as many as know how great a rarity a manuscript of eleven hundred or of a thousand years date

is, and how few books or tracts there are that can boast of manuscripts of such antiquity. The injuries of time, of dust, and of moths, and, above all, the ravages of war and destructions of fire, have robbed us of the ancient monuments, and left us but very thin remains; that a manuscript of the fourth century is a very great rarity, of the fifth there are very few, and even of the sixth not many. So that our want of manuscripts beyond the sixth or seventh century is no argument against the antiquity of the Creed, however certain an argument may be drawn from those we have, so far as they reach. But, beyond all this, we have a comment of the sixth century, of the year 570, or thereabout, and this certain and unquestionable, which may supersede all our disputes about the ancient testimonies or manuscripts of more doubtful authority. Here, then, we stand upon the foot of external evidence. The Creed was, about the year 570, considerable enough to be commented upon, like the Lord's Prayer and Apostles' Creed, and together with them. Here is certain evidence for the time specified, and presumptive for much greater antiquity; for who can imagine that this Creed, or indeed any Creed, should grow into such repute of a sudden, and not rather in a course of years, and a long tract of time? Should we allow 100 or 150 years for it, though it would be conjecture only, yet it would not be unreasonable or improbable conjecture. But we will let this matter rest here, and proceed to our other marks of direction.

2. The internal characters of the Creed. The Creed contains two principal doctrines; one of the Trinity, and the other of the Incarnation. Possibly, from the

manner wherein these doctrines are there laid down, or from the words whereby they are expressed, we may be able to fix the true date of the Creed, or very nearly at least; certain, however, thus far, that it must be somewhere above 570.

From the doctrine of the Incarnation, as expressed in this Creed, we may be confident that it is not earlier than the rise of the Apollinarian heresy, which appeared first about the year 360, and grew to a head about 370, or a little later. This Creed is so minute and particular against those heretics (without naming them, as it is not the way of the Creed to name any), obviating every cavil, and precluding every evasion or subterfuge, that one cannot suppose it to have been written before the depths of that heresy were perfectly seen into, and the whole secrets of the party disclosed, which we have no reason to think could be before the year 370, if so soon. This consideration alone is to me a sufficient confutation of those who pretend that Athanasius made this Creed either during his banishment at Treves, which ended in the year 338, or during his stay at Rome in the year 343, or that he presented it to Pope Julius or Pope Liberius, who were both dead before the year 367.

I must add, that Epiphanius[a] marks the very time when the Creeds first began to be enlarged in opposition to the Apollinarian heresy; namely, the tenth year of Valentinian and Valens, and the sixth of Gratian (it should be seventh), which falls in with A.D. 373, the very last year of Athanasius's life, according to those that place his death the latest; some say he died

[a] Epiphan., *Ancoratus*, c. 121, p. 123.

a year or two sooner. If, therefore, he made this Creed at all, it must be about that time; and, indeed, were there no stronger objections against the antiquity of the Creed, or against its being made by Athanasius, than the common objection about the supposed condemnation of the Nestorian and Eutychian heresies, I should scarce think it at all improbable that Athanasius should be the author, admitting that he lived to the year 373; for Epiphanius's larger Creed, made about that time, appears to me as full and express against both those heresies as the Athanasian can be supposed to be, and in some respects more so; and yet neither of those heresies were then in being, nor for many years after. But there are many other reasons which convince me that the Athanasian Creed must be placed lower than this time. I take Epiphanius's larger Creed to have been the first that enlarged the Article of the Incarnation, in opposition chiefly to the Apollinarians; and that Creed being drawn up, as Epiphanius expressly testifies, by the joint advice of all the orthodox Bishops and the whole Catholic Church, became a kind of rule or model for most of the Creeds that came after, among which I reckon the Athanasian.

For, from the doctrine of the Trinity, as particularly and minutely drawn out in that Creed, it is to me very plain, that it must be some years later than the Creed of Epiphanius, which will evidently appear to any man who will be at the pains to compare the two Creeds together.

One very observable particular is the manner of expressing the Unity by a singular adjective: *Unus æternus, Unus immensus, &c.:* " one eternal, one incompreher sible," &c., and the condemning the expression of *Tres æterni, Tres immensi*, &c. The Greeks never laid down any such rule of expression, never observed or followed it, but have sometimes run counter to it [b], meaning, indeed, the very same thing, but not so expressing it. As to the Latins, we shall find none of them (at least, I have not observed any) coming into that way of expression before Ambrose [c] and Faustinus [d] (in the years 381 and 384), who are the first that use it, and that but once, or very sparingly, not repeating and inculcating it, like the Athanasian Creed, nor leaving it destitute of explication. But St. Austin, afterwards, in his books of the Trinity, in the fifth especially, enlarges in justification of this rule of expression, and is full and copious upon it. His proofs, illustrations, example, and authority gave new strength and credit to this rule, which might then pass current, and become fit to appear, without farther explication, in a Creed. For this reason, principally, I incline to think that this Creed was not made before St. Austin's books of the Trinity were public (which was not till 416), or not before 420, or thereabout, to allow some time for

[b] Τριῶν ἀπείρων ἄπειρον συμφυΐαν.—Greg. Nazianz. *in Bapt.*, *Orat.* xl. c. 47, p. 668.

[c] "Ergo Sanctus Pater, Sanctus Filius, Sanctus et Spiritus: sed non tres Sancti, quia unus est Deus Sanctus, unus est Dominus. Una est etenim vera Sanctitas, sicut una est vera Divinitas, una illa vera Sanctitas naturalis."—Ambros., *de Sp. S.*, lib. iii. c. 16, vol. ii. p. 688.

[d] "Sed ne duos omnipotentes intelligas, præcavendum est: licet enim et Pater sit omnipotens, et Filius, tamen unus est omnipotens, sicut et unus est Deus: quia Patris et Filii eadem Omnipotentia est, sicut et eadem Deitas," &c. . . . . "Ostenditur Unitas Divinitatis in Patre et Filio, sicut et Omnipotentiæ, et quicquid omnino Divinæ Substantiæ est; hoc solo differens a Patre Filius, quod ille Pater est, et Hic Filius."— Faustin., *de Trinit.*, c. 3 (pp. 123, 124); in Bibl. Max. PP., vol. v. p. 646.

his works to be read, considered, approved, and to gain a general esteem. If it be said that St. Austin might as well copy from this Creed as the Creed from him, I say, No, for the reason is different. Creeds and other the like formularies which are to be put into every one's hands, and spread round about, ought not to contain anything till it has been maturely weighed, long considered, and fully explained, as well as proved, and generally acknowledged by the Churches of Christ. It is, therefore, much more reasonable to believe that St. Austin's writings should go first, and a general approbation of them in that particular; and then the Creed might conveniently follow, the way being now opened for it[e].

I may observe the like of another Article of the Athanasian Creed, namely, the Procession from the Son —a doctrine entertained, indeed, both by Greeks and Latins (as may appear by the testimonies commonly cited for that purpose), and expressed frequently in sense, though rarely in terms, but such as came not to be much inculcated or insisted upon till St. Austin undertook to assert and clear it, and to render it less liable to any dispute hereafter. For which reason the modern Greeks have looked upon him, in a manner, as the father of that doctrine, being at least the principal

---

[e] Combefis, speaking to this point, seemed inclinable to suppose that St. Austin had borrowed from the Creed; but correcting himself afterwards, he supposes rather that the Creed borrowed from him. His words are these:—

"Ejus Symboli, seu Formulæ Fidei, antiquitatem produnt illi ejus versiculi quos totidem verbis habet August. in Libris de Trinitate et alibi, quos non aliunde desumpsisse videatur quam ex eo Symbolo... Quanquam nihil vetat dicere ipsum potius Symboli Auctorem ex Augustino, aliisque P. P. sua consarcinasse."—Combefis, not. in Calec.; Auctar., vol. ii. p. 296.

man that brought it into vogue, however weakly they may pretend that he invented it. Thus far is certain, that his elaborate arguments and solid proofs from Scripture of the truth and of the importance of the doctrine made it pass the more readily, and gave it credit and authority enough to have a place in a standing Creed or Confession, which is to me another argument of the Creed's being made after St. Austin's writings were well known in the world, in that place, at least, where the Creed was made. From the premises, then, I presume to infer, that the Athanasian Creed is not earlier than the year 420.

I will next endeavour to shew, that it cannot reasonably be set lower than the Eutychian times, not later than the Council of Chalcedon, or than the year 451; and this also I shall attempt from the internal characters of the Creed in like manner as above.

1. There is not a word in the Creed directly and plainly expressing two natures in Christ, or excluding one nature, which critical terms against the error of Eutyches are very rarely or never omitted in the Creeds drawn up in the Eutychian times, or the times immediately following. 'Tis true, there is in the Athanasian Creed what may be sufficient to obviate or preclude the Eutychian heresy, as there is also in the larger Creed of Epiphanius, A.D. 373, and in the works of Nazianzen and Ambrose, about the year 380, and in Pelagius's Creed, A.D. 417, and in the writings of Austin and Vincentius of Lerins, both before the year 435, many years before Eutyches. The strongest expression of the Creed against the Eutychians, and which has been most frequently urged in this case, is, *Unus*

omnino, non confusione substantiæ, sed unitate personæ: "One altogether, not by confusion of substance, but by unity of person:" which yet is used by Vincentius[f], and by Austin[g], too, almost in terms. And if this be no reason for making either of those authors, or the Tracts ascribed to them, later than Eutyches, why shall the like expression be of any force in respect to the Athanasian Creed? There is nothing in the Creed but what was common and ordinary in Catholic writers before the Eutychian times; but there are wanting those critical, distinguishing terms of two natures, or one nature, necessary to be inserted in the Creeds after those times, and never, or very rarely, omitted; which is one reason, and a very considerable one, for setting the date of the Creed higher than 451.

2. Another argument of the same thing, near akin to the former, is, that this Creed makes no mention of Christ being consubstantial with us in one nature, as He is consubstantial with the Father in another: a tenet expressly held by some of the ecclesiastical writers before Eutyches' time, but seldom or never omitted in the Creeds or Confessions about that time, or after. To be convinced of the truth both of this and of the preceding Article, one need but look into the Creeds and Formularies of those times; namely, into that of Turribius of Spain in 447, of Flavian of Constantinople, as also of Pope Leo in 449, of the Chalcedon Council in 451, of Pope Felix III. in 485,

---

[f] "Unus autem, non . . . Divinitatis et Humanitatis confusione, sed . . . unitate personæ."—Vincent. Lerin., c. 19, p. 46 (p. 58).

[g] "Idem Deus qui Homo et qui Deus, idem Homo; non confusione naturæ, sed unitate personæ."—August., Serm. 186, Nat. Dom. iii., in vol. v. p. 885.

and Anastasius II. in 496, and of the Church of Alexandria in the same year; as also into those of Pope Hormisdas, and the Churches of Syria, and Fulgentius, and the Emperor Justinian, and Pope John II., and Pope Pelagius I., within the sixth century. In all which we shall find either express denial of one nature, or express affirming of two natures, or the doctrine of Christ's consubstantiality with us, or all three together, though they are all omitted in the Athanasian Creed. This is to me a second reason for setting our Creed higher than the Eutychian times.

3. I may argue this point farther from a passage of the Athanasian Creed, running thus: "One, not by conversion of the Godhead into flesh, but by taking of the manhood into God." This would not, I conceive, have run in these words, or in this manner, in the Eutychian times. For though the Eutychians were sometimes (as well as the Apollinarians often) charged with the doctrine of a "conversion of the Godhead into flesh," yet nothing is more certain than that the generality of them absolutely disowned and detested any such tenet, teaching rather "a conversion of the manhood into God," just the reverse. And, by the way, I would here offer it to the learned reader to consider, whether we may not from hence give a probable account of a very noted variation observable in many of the most ancient copies of this Creed, which run thus: *Unus autem, non conversione Divinitatis in carne, sed assumptione Humanitatis in Deo:* where there is *carne* for *carnem*, and *Deo* for *Deum*. A slight alteration in the words, but a very great one in the sense. A change of the Godhead in the flesh the Eutychians admitted, by making the two

natures become one, though they allowed not a change into flesh: so that by this little alteration of *carne* for *carnem*, the Creed would strike more directly at the Eutychian principles. Then, again, as to *Deum*, if that reading was to stand, the Creed, instead of confuting the Eutychians, would seem rather to favour them; for they taught that the manhood was assumed into God, and that in so literal and strict a sense as really to become God, or to be absorbed and lost in the Divine nature, both natures becoming one Divine nature. Such a construction might the words of the Creed be liable to. But put *Deo* for *Deum*, and it is entirely defeated; for then the sense is not that the manhood is assumed into God, but that God assumed the human nature; which is true, and not liable to any such misconstruction as the other. However this be, as to the variation of the copies, and the reason here assigned for it (which I offer only as a probable conjecture to be further enquired into), yet this is certain, that these words of the Creed, according to the common copies, are not so cautiously or accurately chosen as they might, or would have been, had the Creed been drawn up after the Eutychian times.

4. A fourth argument may be drawn from the similitude in the Creed, running thus: "As the reasonable soul and flesh is one man, so God and man is one Christ." This familiar and easy comparison was much made use of by the Catholics, down from the Apollinarian times to the time of Eutyches: by Nazianzen, Austin, Vincentius, Claudianus Mamertus, and others. But no sooner did the Eutychians wrest the comparison to their own sense, pleading for one nature in Christ,

like as soul and body make one nature in man, but the Catholics grew strangely averse to the similitude, and rarely made use of it; or when they did, it was either to dispute against it and condemn it, or else to guard and qualify it with proper cautions and restrictions. Wherefore it is by no means probable that this similitude would have been inserted at such a time in a Catholic Creed, and there left without guard or caution for the Eutychians to make an ill use of. This fourth argument I take from the learned and acute Le Quien, whose words may be seen in the margin [h]. And may we not from hence give a probable guess at the reason why the ancient manuscript of Treves, and the Colbertine copied from it, have entirely omitted this similitude, throwing in a few words, both before and after, to salve the breach, in some measure, and to preserve a connexion: which shews that it was no casual omission, but made with design. But I pass on.

These reasons convince me that the Creed was not made so late as the Council of Chalcedon, but before the year 451. It cannot therefore be ascribed to Vigilius Tapsensis in the year 484; not to mention that the phraseology of it agrees not with that writer's usual manner of expression, as Le Quien hath ob-

[h] "Quod quidem simile, quo Theologus etiam, aliique Patres Apollinaristas confutarant, tanti posthac non fecerunt insequentis seu quinti sæculi desinentis doctores, ut illud in Expositione Fidei insererent; cum Monophysitæ, Severo præsertim duce, eo vehementius contra Catholicos pugnarent, ut unam in Christo naturam esse ex Deitate et Humanitate compositam evincerent. Quinimo omnes ingenii vires explicare coacti sunt, ut varias discrepantias reperirent inter unionem Deitatis cum Humanitate in Christo, et unionem animæ cum corpore in homine." — Le Quien, *Dissert. Damasc.*, p. 10; compare Petav., *de Incarn.*, lib. iii. c. 9, &c., in Dogm. Theol., vol. v. p. 135, &c.

served[i]. Besides that the principal reasons on which Quesnel rested his opinion in regard to that author are now found to have been grounded on a false presumption of certain works being Vigilius's which are none of his[k]. And I may add, that to me there does not appear in Vigilius's pieces anything of that strength, closeness, and acuteness, which we find in the Athanasian Creed.

But I proceed to shew that this Creed is earlier than even the times of Nestorius, or the Ephesine Council of the year 431. It is certain that this Creed does not condemn the Nestorian heresy in such full, direct, critical terms as the Catholics found to be necessary against the wiles and subtleties of those men. There is not a word of the Mother of God, or of one Son only, in opposition to two sons, or of God's being born, suffering, dying: which kind of expressions the Creeds are full of after Nestorius's times, and after the Council of Ephesus, to guard the more certainly against equivocations, and to express the Catholic doctrine in strong terms, such as could not be eluded. As to what the Athanasian Creed really does express, and is conceived to strike directly at the Nestorian heresy, it is demonstration that the words are not more full or expressive

[i] "Sunt qui suspicentur expositionem istam Fidei fuisse concinnatam a Vigilio Tapsensi, qui scripsisse existimatur libros tres contra Varimadum Arianum: sed ab illorum opinione me deterruit versus iste, Unus omnino, non confusione substantiæ, sed unitate personæ. Nam Vigilius in libris quinque contra Eutychem nusquam unitatem personæ dicit, sed passim, et frequentissime unionem personæ ... Cumque variæ supersint hodie Vigilii Tapsensis Confessiones Fidei de Trinitate et Incarnatione, nulla earum similitudo et convenientia cum Symbolo Athanasiano, quoad stylum animadvertitur."—Le Quien, *Dissert. Damasc.*, p. 9.
[k] Vid Montf., *Diatrib.*, p. 724; Antelm., *Disquis.*, pp. 33, 34.

than may be found in elder Creeds, and in the Fathers that wrote against the Apollinarians and others, before ever Nestorius was heard of[1]. I know not how to give my reader a clear and just idea of this whole matter, but by setting down in chronological order the doctrine of the Incarnation, as expressed in Catholic writings from the Apollinarian times down to the Nestorian, from the year 373 to the year 431. One thing only I would remark beforehand, to make the following account the clearer, that the Apollinarians really held a doctrine very near akin to that which afterwards was called Eutychian, and they maliciously charged the Catholics with that very doctrine, which was afterwards called Nestorian; so that the Catholics, in their charge upon the Apollinarians, condemned the Eutychian doctrine long before Eutyches; and, in their defence of themselves, they also condemned the Nestorian tenets before Nestorius. I shall first justify the truth of this remark in both its parts, and then shall proceed farther to what I intend.

As to the first part, that the Apollinarians held a doctrine very near akin to that which was afterwards called Eutychian, it is a thing so well known, that I need not cite many testimonies for it. It was one of the commonest charges against the Eutychians, that they had revived the heresy of the Apollina-

---

[1] Le Quien is beforehand with me in the observation, whose words I may here cite:—

"Nec cuiquam negotium facessat, quod Nestorii et Eutychis hæreses ea (formula) prius possundatæ essent, quam ipsarum auctores emergerent. Alibi siquidem ostensum fuit SS. Patres, qui contra Apollinarium calamum strinxerant, disertissimis etiam verbis amborum impietates proscripsisse."—Le Quien, *Dissert. Damasc.*, p. 9.

rians [m] in some considerable branches of it: Petavius briefly shews what those branches were [n].

As to the other part of my remark, that the Apollinarians charged the Catholics with the opposite extreme, afterward called Nestorian, that has not been so much observed, but is no less true than the other; as may abundantly appear from the testimonies in the margin [o], besides others that will occur as we pass along. This also is observed by Le Quien in his Notes to Damascen [p]; whereupon he rightly infers, that it will be a false conclusion to argue that such or such writings must belong to the Nestorian times, only because of their treating of an unity of person in Christ.

[m] "Eutyches . . . per impios veterum hæreticorum volutatus errores, tertium Apollinaris dogma delegit; ut negata humanæ carnis atque animæ veritate, totum Dominum nostrum Jesum Christum unius asserat esse naturæ, tanquam verbi Deitas ipsa se in carnem animamque converterit."—Leon. Epist. 97, p. 633; cf. Ep. 134, p. 699.

[n] "Sane cum et multiplex, et ab autore suo interpolata sæpius Apollinaris hæresis fuerit, ut capite sexto docuimus; ea parte cum isto consensit Eutyches, qua carnem Christi non ex utero sumptam B. Virginis sed e Cælo delapsam Apollinaris credidit: tum quatenus uterque unicam naturam asseveravit, et utriusque permistam ac confusam substantiam."—Petav., de Incarn., lib. i. c. 15; in Dogmat. Theol., vol. v. p. 37.

[o] "Neque vero alium Jesum Christum, alium verbum dicimus, ut nova hæresis calumniatur, sed eundem, et ante sæcula, et post sæcula, et ante mundum et post Mariam; imo. ex Maria magnum Deum appellamus."—Hieronym., in Tit., c. 3, vol. iv. p. 431.

"Qui Apollinarii dogmata defendunt, per querimoniam quam adversus nos faciunt sua confirmare conantur, carnale verbum et dominum sæculorum, hominis Filium immortalem Filii Deitatem construentes. Proferunt enim quod aliqui quasi Ecclesiæ Catholicæ existentes, duos colunt Filios in dogmate; unum quidem secundum naturam, alterum autem secundum adoptionem postea acquisitam; nescio a quo talia audientes . . . nondum enim novi eum qui hæc subloquitur."—Gregor. Nyssen., quoted in Harduin, vol. iii. p. 106, Concil. v. Collat. 6. Cf. Ambros., de Incarn. Sacram., c. 7, p. 721; Athanas., Epist. ad Epictet., p. 454 (p. 497).

[p] "Ad Nestoriana tempora revocandi non sunt omnes libri quibus de una Christi persona disputandum est."—Le Quien, Not. in Damascen. de Hær., vol. i. p. 95.

These things premised, I now proceed to lay down the doctrine of the Incarnation as expressed in Catholic writers from the year 373, down to the year 431, inclusive.

I begin with the larger Creed of Epiphanius, which sets forth the Incarnation in the following terms:—

373. "The Word was made flesh, not by undergoing any change, nor by converting his Godhead into manhood, but by co-uniting it into his one holy perfection and Godhead. For there is one Lord Jesus Christ, and not two; the same He is God, the same He Lord, the same He King [q]."

Here we may observe that the Creed guards, just as the Athanasian does, against the two extremes: against the Apollinarian notion of the Godhead being converted into flesh, and against the Apollinarian calumny that the Catholics made two Christs instead of one.

380. Gregory Nazianzen, not long after, expresses himself in terms to the like effect:—"We divide not the man from the Godhead, but we make them one and the same (person) .... If any one imagines Mary not to be the mother of God, he has no part with God. ... If any man introduces two Sons, one of God and the Father, and a second of the Virgin Mother, and not one and the same Him, let him forfeit the adoption of sons promised to true believers: for God and man

---

[q] Ὁ γὰρ λόγος σὰρξ ἐγένετο, οὐ τροπὴν ὑποστὰς, οὐδὲ μεταβαλὼν τὴν ἑαυτοῦ θεότητα εἰς ἀνθρωπότητα· εἰς μίαν συνενώσαντα ἑαυτοῦ ἁγίαν τελειότητά τε καὶ θεότητα· εἷς γάρ ἐστιν Κύριος Ἰησοῦς Χριστὸς καὶ οὐ δύο, ὁ αὐτὸς Θεὸς, ὁ αὐτὸς Κύριος, ὁ αὐτὸς Βασιλεύς.—Epiph., *Ancoratus*, c. 21, p. 124. This Creed is given at length by Dr. Heurtley, in *De Fide et Symbolo*, pp. 13—15.

are indeed two natures, like as soul and body; but they are not two Sons, nor (two) Gods ʳ."

Here, again, we find the Nestorian tenets very fully obviated, while Nazianzen is answering the Apollinarian calumny against the Catholics: and at the same time, the Eutychian heresy (afterwards so called) is as plainly precluded, while Nazianzen is laying down the Church's faith in two natures against the Apollinarians who made but one.

382. Ambrose, in like manner, confutes the Apollinarians, without naming them:—"We ought also to condemn those, who, in another extreme, teach not one and the same Son of God, but that He who is begotten of God the Father, is one, and he that is generated of the Virgin, another: when the Evangelist saith that the Word was made flesh, to instruct us that there is but one Lord Jesus, not two.... There are others risen up who pretend that our Lord's flesh and Godhead are both of one nature.... And when they say that the Word was converted into flesh, hairs, blood, and bones, and changed from its own nature, after such a pretended change of the Divine nature, they may take the handle to wrest anything to the weakness of the Godhead which belongs to the infirmity of the flesh ˢ."

ʳ Οὐδὲ γὰρ τὸν ἄνθρωπον χωρίζομεν τῆς θεότητος, ἀλλ' ἕνα καὶ τὸν αὐτὸν δογματίζομεν. . . . εἴ τις οὐ θεοτόκον τὴν Μαρίαν ὑπολαμβάνει, χωρὶς ἐστὶ τῆς θεότητος. . . . εἴ τις εἰσάγει δύο υἱοὺς ἕνα μὲν τὸν ἐκ Θεοῦ καὶ Πατρὸς, δεύτερον δὲ τὸν ἐκ τῆς μητρὸς, ἀλλ' οὐχὶ ἕνα καὶ τὸν αὐτὸν, καὶ τῆς υἱοθεσίας ἐκπέσοι τῆς ἐπηγγελμένης τοῖς ὀρθῶς πιστεύουσι. Φύσεις μὲν γὰρ δ' ὁ Θεὸς καὶ ἄνθρωπος, ἐπεὶ καὶ ψυχὴ καὶ σῶμα, υἱοὶ δὲ οὐ δύο, οὐδὲ θεοί.—Gregor. Nazianz., Orat. 51, Ep. i. ad Cledon., p. 738.

ˢ " Et illos condemnare debemus qui adversa erroris linea, non unum eundemque Filium Dei dicunt, sed alium esse qui ex Deo

Ambrose seems here to intimate as if there were really some at that time who had run into that very error which the Apollinarians charged upon the Catholics, and which was afterwards called Nestorian. However that be, he condemns it in the name of the Catholics; as he condemns also the Apollinarian extreme, which afterwards became Eutychian. There is another passage of Ambrose cited by Theodoret, seemingly so full and express against the Nestorian and Eutychian heresies, that one can hardly be persuaded to think it really Ambrose's. But, on the other hand, it appears to be so well attested, that the late learned editor of Ambrose could not but yield to place it among his genuine Works, vol. ii. p. 729.

417. There is a Creed of Pelagius (as learned men now agree) inserted among the works both of Jerome[t] and Austin[u]. It was made several years before the Nestorian controversy. Our learned Dr. Wall has translated it into English[v], subjoining some excellent notes of his own to it. I shall transcribe as much as is to our purpose:—" We do in such a manner hold that there is in Christ one person of the Son, as that we say there are in Him two perfect and entire substances

Patre natus sit, alium qui sit generatus ex virgine; cum Evangelista dicat quia verbum caro factum est, ut unum Dominum Jesum non duos crederes . . . emergunt alii qui carnem Domini dicant et divinitatem unius esse naturæ . . . Deinde, cum isti dicant quia verbum in carnem, capillos, sanguinem, et ossa conversum est, et a natura propria mutatum est, datur illis locus ut infirmitatem carnis ad infirmitatem divinitatis, quadam facta divinæ naturæ mutatione, detorqueant."—Ambros., *de Incarn. Sacram.*, c. 6, vol. ii. pp. 714, 715.

[t] Hieronym., vol. v. p. 123: where it is called *Symbolum Damasi*.
[u] Augustin., Serm. 236, vol. v. App., p. 388.
[v] Wall's History of Inf. Bapt., part i. c. 19; vol. i. p. 406 (p. 200).

(or natures), viz., of the Godhead, and of the manhood which consists of soul and body.... We do abhor.... the blasphemy of those who go about by a new interpretation to maintain that since the time of His taking flesh, all things pertaining to the Divine nature did pass into the man [or manhood], and so also that all things belonging to the human nature were transferred into God [or the Divine nature]; from whence would follow (a thing no heresy ever offered to affirm) that both substances [or natures], viz., of the Divinity and humanity, would by this confusion seem to be extinguished, and to lose their proper state, and be changed into another thing. So that they who own in the Son an imperfect God and an imperfect man, are to be accounted not to hold truly either God or man."

Dr. Wall hereupon judiciously remarks, that there wanted only the accuracy of speaking, which Pelagius had here used, to clear and settle the dispute between the Nestorians and Eutychians. I would remark farther, that if Pelagius's Creed, in the year 417, had so plainly obviated both the Nestorian and Eutychian heresy before Nestorius or Eutyches was known, it may easily be conceived that the Athanasian Creed might do the same thing at or about the same time.

422. I might next shew how St. Austin likewise has expressed himself in as strong terms against both those heresies, as the Athanasian Creed has done; but, because I shall have another occasion to cite the passages, where I draw out a select number of expressions parallel to those of the Creed, I may spare myself the trouble of doing it here.

426. I might go on to observe what passed in the

case of Leporius, a man of the same principles, in the main, with Nestorius, but some years before him. His recantation treatise (*Libellus Satisfactionis*), supposed to be drawn up by St. Austin in the year 426, would furnish me with many full and strong expressions against the Nestorian principles beyond any to be met with in the Athanasian Creed; so that there is no just argument to be drawn from any expressions in that Creed for setting it so low as the Nestorian times.

431. I shall conclude this account with the recital of a Creed made about the same time, or in the same year, that the Council of Ephesus was held against Nestorius. It is the Creed of John, Patriarch of Antioch, approved by Cyril of Alexandria, and thought sufficient to wipe off all suspicion of Nestorianism from the author of it. It runs thus: " We confess, then, that Jesus Christ our Lord, the only-begotten Son of God, is perfect God and perfect man, of a reasonable soul and body; born of the Father before the worlds, as touching his Godhead; the same also in the end of days, for us and for our salvation, (born) of the Virgin Mary, as touching His manhood, consubstantial with us according to His manhood. But there was an union made of two natures, on which account we profess one Christ, one Lord, one Son. Conformable to this sense of an union without confusion, we acknowledge the Holy Virgin as Mother of God, because that God the Word was incarnate and made man, and from the very conception united to Himself a temple which He had taken of her [x]."

[x] Ὁμολογοῦμεν τοιγαροῦν τὸν Κύριον ἡμῶν Ἰησοῦν Χριστὸν τὸν υἱὸν τοῦ Θεοῦ τὸν μονογενῆ, Θεὸν τέλειον καὶ ἄνθρωπον τέλειον ἐκ

Here we may observe several expressions nearly resembling those of the Athanasian Creed; but withal several others more particular and explicit against the Nestorian principles than that Creed is: one Son, and Him consubstantial with us, in respect of his manhood; the Virgin, Mother of God, and the like. Such is the constant strain and tenor of the Creeds, and Confessions, and Catholic writings, treating of the Incarnation, at this time and after: as might be shewn at large from Cassian about 431, and Vincentius in the year 434, and from Flavian, and Pope Leo I., and others before the Council of Chalcedon. We have therefore very great reason to believe, that the Athanasian Creed was drawn up either before the Nestorian controversy had made much noise in the world, or, at least, before the compiler had notice of it. The sum, then, of my argument is this: there is nothing in the Athanasian Creed but what might have been said, and had been said, by Catholic writers before the time of Nestorius; but the Creed wants many of those particular and critical expressions which came into use after that time; therefore, since the internal characters of the Creed suit exactly with the Apollinarian times, and not with the Nestorian, it ought to be placed

ψυχῆς λογικῆς καὶ σώματος, πρὸ αἰώνων μὲν ἐκ τοῦ Πατρὸς γεννηθέντα κατὰ τὴν θεότητα, ἐπ' ἐσχάτων δὲ τῶν ἡμερῶν τὸν αὐτὸν δι' ἡμᾶς καὶ διὰ τὴν ἡμετέραν σωτηρίαν ἐκ Μαρίας τῆς παρθένου κατὰ τὴν ἀνθρωπότητα· ὁμοούσιον τῷ Πατρὶ τὸν αὐτὸν κατὰ τὴν θεότητα, καὶ ὁμοούσιον ἡμῖν κατὰ τὴν ἀνθρωπότητα, δύο γὰρ φύσεων ἕνωσις γέγονε· διὸ καὶ ἕνα Χριστὸν, ἕνα υἱὸν, ἕνα Κύριον ὁμολογοῦμεν. κατὰ ταύτην τῆς ἀσυγχύτου ἑνώσεως ἔννοιαν, ὁμολογοῦμεν τὴν ἁγίαν παρθένον θεοτόκον, διὰ τὸ τὸν Θεὸν λόγον σαρκωθῆναι, καὶ ἐνανθρωπῆσαι, καὶ ἐξ αὐτῆς τῆς συλλήψεως ἑνῶσαι ἑαυτῷ τὸν ἐξ αὐτῆς ληφθέντα ναόν.—Johan. Antioch., in Routh's Opusc., vol. ii. p. 206.

somewhere between Apollinarius and Nestorius, not lower than 430 or 431 at the utmost. And it is some confirmation of what hath been said, that Venantius Fortunatus, who lived in the Eutychian times, and commented upon this Creed about the year 570, as before observed, yet in his comment takes not the least notice of any part of this Creed being opposed to the errors of Nestorius or Eutyches, but only to those elder heresies of Sabellius, Arius, and Apollinarius, whom he specially makes mention of. I persuade myself, therefore, that this Creed ought not to be placed lower than 430, or thereabout; and I have before shewn why it should not be set higher than 420; so that now we have brought it within the compass of ten years, where we may let it rest awhile till we consider farther what place or country the Creed was most probably composed in, which may help us to settle the time of its date within somewhat stricter and narrower limits than before.

There is great reason to believe that this Creed was made in Gaul. The considerations which persuade us thereto are these following:—1. Its early reception in the Gallican Church, so far as appears, before all other Churches. 2. The great esteem and regard anciently paid to it by the Gallican Councils and Bishops [r]. 3. The Creed's being first admitted into the Gallican Psalter, and first received in those countries where that Psalter was received, as in Spain, Germany, and Eng-

---

[r] "Tanti namque apud Gallos Symbolum hoc fuit ut una cum Symbolo Apostolorum memoriæ commendari Presbyteris præcipiat Hincmarus idem in capitulis, Clericis omnibus Synodus Augustodunensis."—Sirmond., *in Theodulph. de Sp. S.*, vol. ii. p. 978; cf. Antelm., p. 30.

land. As the Gallican Churches delivered their Psalter to other Churches, so is it reasonable to believe that the Creed was received from them likewise. 4. The oldest version we hear of is Gallican, in the time of Hincmar. 5. The oldest authors that make mention of it are likewise Gallican; for proof of which I refer to the ancient testimonies above. 6. The first that cite the words of it (as it seems) are likewise Gallican. I will here mention two: Avitus of Vienne, in Gaul [z], and Cæsarius of Arles [a]. I have set their words in the margin. 7. The oldest commentator upon it, though an Italian by birth and education, had yet travelled into France, and was at length Bishop of Poictiers. 8. The number and antiquity of the manuscripts of this Creed found in France confirm the same thing; which has made several very learned men subscribe to

---

[z] The words of Avitus Viennensis, who was Bishop in 490, died in 523:—
"De Divinitate Spiritus Sancti, quem nec factum legimus, nec creatum, nec genitum."—In Sirmond., vol. ii. p. 159. "Nos vero Spiritum discimus ex Patre et Filio procedere... Sicut est proprium Spiritui Sancto a Patre Filioque procedere, istud Fides Catholica etiamsi renuentibus non persuaserit, in suæ tamen Disciplinæ Regula non excedit."—Le Quien, *Panopl. contr. Schism. Græc.*, cent. xi. c. 4, § 2, p. 241.
"Non nisi ex eodem Symbolo, quod jam ante receptum esset, Avitus Viennensis alicubi scribebat De Divinitate Sp. S.," &c.— Le Quien, *Dissert. Damascen.*, p. 98.

[a] The words of Cæsarius, who was Bishop in 503, died in 543:—
"Rogo et admoneo vos, Fratres carissimi, ut Quicunque vult Salvus esse, Fidem rectam et Catholicam discat, firmiter teneat, inviolatamque conservet.... Deus Pater, Deus Filius, Deus et Spiritus Sanctus: sed tamen non tres Dii, sed unus Deus. Qualis Pater, talis Filius, talis et Spiritus Sanctus. Attamen credat unusquisque Fidelis quod Filius æqualis est Patri secundum Divinitatem, et minor est Patre secundum humanitatem carnis, quam de nostro assumpsit."—Cæsar. Arelat.; in August., vol. v. App., p. 399.

N.B. The editors of St. Austin adjudge this to Cæsarius; as does also Oudinus, *Comment. de Scriptor. Eccl.*, vol. i. p. 1348.

this opinion [b], that the Athanasian Creed came first from Gaul. And it is certain that no other country or Church in the world has so fair, I may now say so clear, a pretence to it. Many circumstances concur to make good their title, as we have already seen; and more will appear in my next chapter, when I come to enquire who was the author.

Let it be allowed then, for the present, that our Creed was originally Gallican, and made between 420 and 430. We may next consider, whether we cannot come a little nearer towards fixing the time of its composition. We must point out some season when St. Austin's works were known, and studied, and well esteemed of in Gaul; and when the circumstances of the place might the most probably give occasion for the compiling such a Creed. Now it is observable that, about the year 426, St. Austin held a very close and intimate correspondence with the Gallican Churches. Leporius had for some time spread false doctrine in Gaul, chiefly relating to the Incarnation. His heresy was much the same with what Nestorius's was after-

[b] "Cæterum cum ex allatis supra testimoniis videatur in Galliis primum celebrari cœpisse hoc Symbolum, haud abs re conjectant eruditi viri, in Galliis illud fuisse elucubratum. Quod item forte suadeat antiquissimus ille in Galliis et in Anglia mos Symboli alternatim concinendi; itemque MSS. Gallicanorum copia et antiquitas."—Montfauc., *Diatrib.*, p. 726.

"E. Gallis primum prodiisse Symbolum Athanasianum animadvertimus, tum quod a Gallis scriptoribus ante omnes celebratum, a Synodis Episcopisque Galliarum receptum, et commendatum antiquitus fuerit, tum etiam quod Treviris in Galliarum Metropoli illud lucubratum fuisse opinio increbuerit. Quapropter Pithœus, ac Vossius, aliique eruditissimi viri Gallum hominem Symboli parentem opinati sunt; Antelmius vero, hac potissimum ratione ductus, non Vigilium in Africa Episcopum, sed Vincentium Lirinensem Opusculi hujus auctorem affirmavit."—Murator., *Anecd.*, vol. ii. p. 229.

wards. The Gallican bishops censured him; and he was forced to quit his country, having giving general offence to all there. He took his leave of Gaul, and passed over into Africa, with several others of the same party and principles; where lighting upon Aurelius, Bishop of Carthage, and St. Austin, he was by them brought to a sense of his error, and induced to sign a full recantation, called *Libellus Satisfactionis;* whereupon St. Austin, and Aurelius, and other African bishops, became intercessors with the bishops of Gaul in favour of Leporius, that he might be again received and restored by them. One can scarce imagine any more likely time, or more proper occasion, for the compiling such a Creed as the Athanasian is. All the lines and characters of it suit extremely well with the place, the time, the occasion, and other circumstances, which concur to persuade us that the Creed was, in all probability, composed in Gaul, sometime between the year 426 and the year 430: so that now we are confined to the narrow compass of four or five years, upon the most probable conjecture, and upon such evidences as a case of this nature can admit of, where more cannot be expected.

CHAPTER VIII.

OF THE AUTHOR OF THE CREED.

IF we have hitherto gone upon sure grounds about the time and place, we cannot long be at a loss for the author of this Creed. Who were the most considerable men, and best qualified for such a work, at that time in Gaul? Antelmius will point out Vincentius Lirinensis. But I have several reasons to persuade me that it was not, or could not be, Vincentius. No contemporary of his, nor any ancient writer, ever gives the least hint of his composing such a work. Antelmius supposes it to be after his Commonitory, that is, after 434; which if it had been, we should undoubtedly have found the Creed more particular and explicit against the Nestorian heresy: we should have read in it Mother of God, One Son only, and something of God's being born, suffering, dying, or the like; it cannot, therefore, be justly ascribed to Vincentius. Not to mention that such a work appears to have been much fitter for a bishop of a church, than for a private presbyter; inasmuch as bishops generally were obliged to give an account of their faith upon their first entrance upon the episcopate: and they had the privilege likewise of making Creeds and Forms of Prayer for their respective dioceses; for which reasons, *cæteris paribus*, this Creed ought rather to be ascribed to some bishop of that time than to an inferior presbyter. And who more likely to compose such a Creed than Hilary, Bishop of Arles, a celebrated man of that time, and of chief repute in the Gallican Church? His title to it will stand upon the following circumstances.

1. He was made bishop in Gaul within the time mentioned, about the year 429. 2. He is allowed to have been a man of great parts and capacity, of a neat wit and elegant style for the age he lived in; insomuch that Livius, a poet, and a celebrated writer of that time, did not scruple to say, that if Austin had come after Hilary, he would have been judged his inferior [a]. 3. Gennadius's character of Hilary's writings, that they were small Tracts [b], but extremely fine, suits well with our present supposition: but what most of all confirms and strengthens it, is what Honoratus of Marseilles, the writer of his life, tells us, that Hilary composed an admirable exposition [*Symboli Expositio ambienda*] of the Creed [c]. He calls it an Exposition of the Creed (not a Creed), which is the proper title for

[a] "Quid plura dicam? Nisi dicendi pausa desuper eidem advenisset, sermonem finire non potuerat, tanta gratia exundante, et miraculo et stupore crescente, ut peritissimis desperationem tunc autoribus sæculi ejus inferret oratio: in tantum ut Livius temporis illius poeta, et autor insignis, publice proclamaret; si Augustinus post te fuisset, judicaretur inferior."—Honoratus, *in Vita Sti. Hilarii*, c. 11, in Leo, vol. i. p. 740.

[b] "Ingenio vero immortali, aliqua et parva edidit, quæ eruditæ animæ, et fidelis linguæ indicia sunt; in quibus præcipua," &c.—Gennad., *Illustr. Vir. Catal.*, c. 71, p. 42.

[c] "Gratia ejus ex his operibus, quæ eodem dicendi impetu concepit, genuit, ornavit, protulit, possit absque hæsitatione dignosci: vita scilicet antistitis Honorati, homiliæ in totius anni festivitatibus expeditæ, Symboli Expositio ambienda, epistolarum vero tantus numerus," &c.—Honorat., *Vit. Hilar.*, c. 11, p. 740.

N. B. There is some doubt whether Ravennius of Arles, successor to Hilary, or Honoratus of Marseilles, be the author of this Life; but there is good reason to ascribe it to the latter. See Quesnel in Leo, vol. ii. p. 730; and Antelmius, *de veris operibus Leon. M.*, p. 367.

it, and more proper than that of *Symbolum*, or Creed, which it now bears. And so we find that it was but very rarely called *Symbolum* by the ancients; once, I think, by Hincmar, and never after for several centuries. And when it was, yet it was observed by Thomas Aquinas, that that was not so proper a name for it, not being composed *per modum Symboli*, in the way of a Creed; as indeed it is not. What the more ancient and usual titles were, may appear in one view in the tables above. Among others, we sometimes find the title of *Expositio Catholicæ Fidei*, or yet nearer, *Expositio Symboli Apostolorum*, An Exposition of the Apostles' Creed, which is as proper a title as any, and not unlike to this of Honoratus. 4. I may farther observe that this Hilary of Arles was a great admirer and follower of St. Austin[d], and had studied his writings; which may account for his often following St. Austin's thoughts in the compiling of the Creed, and sometimes his very expressions; and, indeed, forming the whole composition, in a manner, upon St. Austin's plan, both with respect to the Trinity and Incarnation. He did not indeed come heartily into St. Austin's doctrine about grace, predestination, free-will, &c., any more than the other Gallican bishops; but for other points, as Prosper observes, Hilary was entirely in Austin's sentiments. 5. Hence, likewise, we may account for the similitude of thoughts and expressions between Vin-

---

[d] "Unum eorum præcipuæ auctoritatis, et spiritualium studiorum virum, sanctum Hilarium, Arelatensem Episcopum, sciat Beatitudo tua admiratorem, sectatoremque in aliis omnibus tuæ esse doctrinæ: et de hoc quod in querelam trahit, jam pridem apud Sanctitatem tuam sensum suum per litteras velle conferre."
—Prosper, *ad Augustin.*, Ep. 225, vol. ii. p. 825.

centius Lirinensis and the author of the Creed, which Antelmius insists much upon to justify his ascribing it to Vincentius. Hilary and Vincentius were contemporaries and countrymen, both of the same monastery in the Isle of Lerin, much about the same time; so that it is natural to suppose that they should fall into the like expressions while treating on the same things; or that Vincentius might affect to copy from so great a man as Hilary (first, Abbot of Lerin, and then Archbishop of Arles) when writing on the same subject.

6. As to the style of Hilary, though we have but little of his left to compare the Creed with, yet what there is answers very well to the idea one should have of a man that might be able to draw up such a piece. His Life of the elder Honoratus, who was his predecessor in the see of Arles, is an excellent performance, and comes nothing short of the character he had raised for wit and eloquence. The style is clear and strong, short and sententious, abounding with antitheses, elegant turns, and manly strokes of wit. He does but touch a little in that piece upon the subject of the Trinity; so that one cannot from thence discover how he would have expressed himself upon that head. Only, that little there is there, is very like to a paragraph in the Athanasian Creed, both for turn and expression. Speaking of Honoratus, or rather to him, in the way of a rhetorical apostrophe, he observes [e] how clear and expressive he had been in his discourses con-

[e] "Quotidianus siquidem in sincerissimis tractatibus confessionis Patris ac Filii ac Spiritus Sancti testis fuisti : nec facile tam exerte, tam lucide quisquam de Divinitatis Trinitate disseruit, cum eam personis distingueres, et gloriae (gloriam,) aeternitate, ac majestate sociares."—Hilar., *Vit. Honorat.*, c. 38, p. 770.

cerning the Trinity in the Godhead; making the Persons distinct, but co-uniting them in glory, eternity, and majesty. Which may remind us of the words of the Athanasian Creed, "There is one Person of the Father, &c., but the Godhead of the Father, and of the Son, and of the Holy Ghost is all one, the glory equal, the majesty co-eternal." However that be, this we may learn from it, how great a commendation it was, in Hilary's account, to be able to speak clearly and accurately upon the subject of the Trinity, and how ambitious he might be of so doing himself: and we know, from his dying instructions[f] to his friends about him, how much he had the subject at heart. These, I confess, are but little circumstances; yet they are of some weight along with others more considerable, and therefore ought not to be entirely omitted. What weighs most with me is, that he was, in his time, a man of the greatest authority in the Gallican Church[g], without whose advice, or privity at least, such a Creed would hardly have passed; and that he actually was

[f] Among which this is one, and the first,—
"Fidem Trinitatis immobiliter retinete."—*Vit. Hilar.*, c. 20, p. 747.
[g] Quesnel quotes this eulogium of him, from Constantius Presbyter of the same time:—
"Illustrabatur haec civitas Hilario sacerdote, multimoda virtute pretioso: erat enim fidei igneus torrens, caelestis eloquii, et praeceptionis divinae operarius indefessus."—Quesnel, *Diss.*, vol. ii. p. 543.
To which may be added one line of his epitaph:—
"Gemma sacerdotum, plebisque, orbisque magister."—Honorat., *Vit. Hil.*, p. 751.
"Ubi instructos supervenisse vidisset, sermone ac vultu pariter in quadam gratia insolita excitabatur, seipso clarior apparebat ut Silvius Eusebius, Domnulus, auctores coaevi, admiratione succensi in haec verba proruperint: non doctrinam, non eloquentiam, sed nescio quid super homines consecutum."—Honorat., *Vit. Hilar.*, c. 11, p. 740.

the author of such a work as this is, and which must either be this, or else is lost. This Creed has been sometimes ascribed to the elder Hilary of Poictiers, though neither the diction, nor the matter, nor the manner of it, look anything like his: only it seems this Creed in one manuscript was found tacked to some pieces of that Hilary. I pretend not to draw any argument from hence in favour of our Hilary; though, had the manuscript been a very ancient one, or copied from one that was (neither of which appears), I should have thought it of some moment, since the similitude of names might possibly have occasioned it.

Having considered such reasons as seem to favour the conjecture about Hilary of Arles, it will next be proper to consider also what may be objected against it.

1. It may be objected, that this Hilary lived to the year 449; saw the rise, progress, and condemnation of the Nestorian heresy, and the beginning, at least, of the Eutychian. May it not therefore be reasonably presumed, that had he been to compile a Confession of Faith, he would have made it more full and particular against both those heresies than I have supposed the Creed to be? To this I answer, that the objection would be of weight if I supposed this Creed to have been made by him in the last years of his life: but as I take it to have been made a little after his entrance upon his episcopate, (to be a rule to his clergy all his time, as well as to satisfy his colleagues of his own orthodoxy,) the objection affects not me. Admit the Creed to have been drawn up by him about the year 429 or 430, and then it is just what it should be, exactly suited to the circumstances of time, and place:

and as to his enlarging or altering it afterwards, upon the rise of the two heresies, it might not be in his power when once gone out of his hands; nor would it be necessary, since both these heresies are sufficiently obviated in this Creed, though not so explicitly condemned as in many that came later.

2. It may be asked, how the author's name came to be so studiously concealed even by those that received and admired the Creed; and how it came to take at length the name of Athanasius, rather than of Hilary? I answer: This objection will equally lie against any other author assignable whatever, except Athanasius himself, whom we cannot with any colour of reason ascribe it to. It will be as easy to account for the studious concealment of the author's name, supposing it Hilary, as for any other, or perhaps easier. This Hilary had stoutly defended the rights of his see against Pope Leo's encroachments in the matter of appeals, and other branches of jurisdiction. This brought the good man under disfavour and disrepute; as must happen to the best of men when they have persons of greater figure and authority than themselves to contend with, however righteous and clear their cause may be. Besides this, Hilary had entertained a dislike to some of St. Austin's prevailing doctrines, about Grace, growing much in vogue; so that St. Austin's more zealous disciples had a pique against him on that account, and had the less value for his name. The way, then, to have this Creed pass current, and make it generally received, was to stifle as much as possible the name of the author, and to leave it to stand by its own intrinsic worth and weight. As to the name of

Athanasius, I take it to have come thus: upon the revival of the Arian controversy in Gaul, under the influence of the Burgundian kings, it was obvious to call one side Athanasians, and the other side Arians; and so also to name the Orthodox Faith the Athanasian Faith, as the other Arian. This Creed, therefore, being a summary of the Orthodox and Catholic faith, might, in process of time, acquire the name of the Athanasian Faith, or *Fides Athanasii*, in opposition to the contrary scheme, which might as justly be called *Fides Arii*, or the Arian Faith. The equivocalness of the title gave a handle to those that came after to understand it of a form of Faith composed by Athanasius; just as the equivocal title of Apostolical, given to the Roman Creed, occasioned the mistake about its being made by the Apostles. This appears to me the most probable account of the whole matter: and it is very much confirmed by what we see of several tracts wrote in the fifth and sixth centuries, dialogue-wise, where Athanasius is made the mouth of the Catholic side, and Arius of his party, and Photinus of his: not meaning that Athanasius, Arius, and Photinus were really the speakers in those conferences, but the readers were to understand the Athanasian, Arian, and Photinian principles, as being there fairly represented under those leading names.

3. If it be asked farther, why this Creed was not cited during the Nestorian and Eutychian controversy, when there was so frequent occasion for it; I answer, partly because the Creed was not particular and explicit enough to have done much service; but, chiefly, because the author had been eclipsed, and his repu-

tation obscured by greater names than his, so that his authority had weighed little; and to produce it without a name would have signified less. This objection, therefore, though it might be of great force in the question about Athanasius, is of no weight at all against our present supposition about Hilary of Arles.

These are all the objections which to me occur: and they seem to be so far from weakening the grounds upon which I proceed, that they rather tend to strengthen and confirm them. And though I do not pretend to strict certainty about the author of the Creed, yet I persuade myself that none that have been hitherto named have any fairer or so fair a claim to it as the man I have mentioned. Not Athanasius, not Hilary of Poictiers, not Eusebius of Verceil, not Pope Anastasius I., nor any of that name; not Vincentius Lirinensis, nor Vigilius Tapsensis, nor Athanasius of Spire, nor Fortunatus, nor Bonifacius, nor any other that has been thought on. From the many conjectures heretofore advanced by learned men, one may perceive that it has been judged to be a thing worth the enquiring after: and as others have taken the liberty of naming such author or authors as to them appeared most likely to have made the Creed, so have I, in my turn, not scrupling to add one more to the number.

The sum, then, of what I have presumed to advance upon probable conjecture, in a case which will not admit of full and perfect evidence, is this: That Hilary, once Abbot of Lerius, and next Bishop of Arles, about the year 430, composed the Exposition of Faith, which now bears the name of the Athanasian Creed. It was drawn up for the use of the Gallican clergy, and especially for the diocese or province of Arles. It was esteemed by as many as were acquainted with it, as a valuable summary of the Christian faith. It seems to have been in the hands of Vincentius, monk of Lerins, before 434, by what he has borrowed from it; and to have been cited in part by Avitus of Vienne, about the year 500, and by Cæsarius of Arles, before the year 543. About the year 570, it became famous enough to be commented upon like the Lord's Prayer and Apostles' Creed, and together with them. All this while, and perhaps for several years lower, it had not yet acquired the name of the Athanasian Faith, but was simply styled the Catholic Faith. But, before 670, Athanasius's admired name came in to recommend and adorn it; being in itself also an excellent system of the Athanasian principles of the Trinity [h] and Incarnation, in opposition chiefly to Arians, Macedonians, and Apollinarians. The name of the Faith of Athanasius, in a while, occasioned the mistake of ascribing it to him as his composition. This gave it authority enough to be cited and appealed to as standard in the disputes of the middle ages, between Greeks and Latins, about the Procession: and the same admired name, together with the intrinsic worth and value of the form itself, gave it credit enough to be received into the public service in the Western Churches: first in

[h] "Romanæ ego ecclesiæ quasi Symbolum, incerto Auctore, existimem, hinc Athanasii dictum et putatum quod dilucide Catholicam, ipsamque Athanasii Fidem (de Trinitate, maxime) complecteretur; cujus inter Catholicos sic spectata Fides, ut ejus Communio velut tessera Catholici esset; censereturque ejus condemnatio ipsa Nicænæ et Catholicæ Fidei ejuratio; uti se res habuit in Liberio Romano autistite," &c.—Combetis, *not. in Calec. in Auctar.*, vol. ii. p. 296.

France, next in Spain, soon after in Germany, England, Italy, and at length in Rome itself; while many other excellent Creeds, drawn up in councils, or recommended by emperors, yet never arrived to any such honour and esteem as this hath done. The truly good and great author (as I now suppose him) though ill-used by the then Pope of Rome, and not kindly treated with respect to his memory in after ages, has nevertheless been the mouth of all the Western Churches, and some Eastern too, for a long tract of centuries, in celebrating the glories of the co-eternal Trinity. And so may he ever continue, till the Christian Churches can find out (which they will not easily do) a juster, or sounder, or more accurate form of faith than this is.

CHAPTER IX.

The Creed itself in the Original Language, with Parallel Passages from the Fathers.

My design in this chapter is—

1. To exhibit the Creed in its native language, that is, in Latin, according to the most ancient and most correct copies. The Various Lections will be placed at the bottom, under the Creed. The manuscripts therein referred to, shall be denoted by such names or marks as appear above, in the Table of Manuscripts.

2. Opposite to the Creed, in another column, I place Parallel Passages, selected from authors that lived and wrote before 430, principally from St. Austin: and this with design to enforce and illustrate my main argument before insisted on, namely, that the Creed contains nothing but what had been asserted, in as full and express words as any words of the Creed are, by Church writers before the time specified.

3. I subjoin under these, at the bottom of the page, some farther select passages from Church writers before or after the time mentioned; partly to serve as comments upon some places of the Creed, and partly to shew how some writers of the fifth century, Vincentius especially, expressed themselves on the same heads, that the reader may from thence judge whether they appear prior to the Creed or the Creed prior to them.

I ought to ask my English reader's pardon for this part, which he may please to pass over, and to go on to the next chapter, intended chiefly for his satisfaction and to make him some amends for the present interruption: for my design in subjoining an English Commentary is to serve much the same purposes with what is here intended by the Latin; though not all of them, but as many as the nature of the thing will allow.

THE
ORIGINAL CREED,
WITH
PARALLEL PASSAGES.

Fides Catholica.

1. Quicumque vult salvus esse, ante omnia opus est ut teneat Catholicam Fidem.

2. Quam nisi quisque integram inviolatamque servaverit, absque dubio in aeternum peribit.

3. Fides autem Catholica haec est, ut unum Deum in Trinitate, et Trinitatem in Unitate veneremur:

4. Neque confundentes Personas, neque substantiam separantes.

5. Alia est enim Persona Patris, alia Filii, alia Spiritus Sancti.

Variantes Lectiones.

1. (*salvus esse*), esse salvus. Cod. Ambros. et Fortunat. in MS. Ambros.

2. (*quisque*), quis: Cod. Ambros. (*inviolatamque*), inviolabilemque: Cod. San-germ. (*absque dubio*), deest in Cod. Reg. Paris. (*in aeternum peribit*), peribit in aeternum. San-germ.

5. (*alia Filii*), alia Persona Filii. Cod. Ambros. item Fortun.[L.] (*alia Spiritus*), alia Persona Sp. Sanct. Cod. Ambros.

Loca parallela excerpta ex Variis; Ante An. 430.

1. "Catholicæ disciplinæ majestate institutum est, ut accedentibus ad religionem Fides persuadeatur ante omnia."—August., *de Utilit. Cred.*, c. 29, vol. viii. p. 64.
"Hæc est Fides nostra, quoniam hæc est Fides recta, quæ etiam Catholica nuncupatur."—August, *c. Maxim.*, lib. ii. c. 23, § 3, vol. viii. p. 729.

2. "Hæretici .... simplici Fide Catholica contenti esse nolunt; quæ una parvulis salus est."—August., *Enarr. in Psalm.* x., c. 3, vol. iv. p. 60.

3. Νῦν δὲ δίδασκε τοσοῦτον εἰδέναι μόνον· μονάδα ἐν τριάδι, καὶ τριάδα ἐν μονάδι προσκυνουμένην, παράδοξον ἔχουσαν καὶ τὴν διαίρεσιν καὶ τὴν ἕνωσιν.—Greg. Nazian., *Orat.* 23, *de Pace*, c. 33, vol. i. p. 422.

4. "Et hæc omnia nec confuse unum sunt, nec disjuncte tria sunt."—August., *Epist.* 170, § 5, vol. ii. p. 609.

5. "Impietatem Sabellii declinantes, tres personas expressas sub proprietate distinguimus—Aliam Patris,

Excerpta ex Patribus.

1. "Credamus ergo Deo, fratres: hoc est primum præceptum, hoc est initium religionis et vitæ nostræ, fixum habere cor in Fide."—August., *Serm.* 38, c. 3, vol. v. p. 195.

2. "Catholicorum hoc fere proprium, deposita Sanctorum Patrum et commissa servare, damnare profanas novitates: et sicut dixit, et iterum dixit Apostolus; Si quis annunciaverit, præterquam quod acceptum est, anathemare."—Vincent., c. 34.

3. "Catholica Ecclesia unum Deum in Trinitatis plenitudine, et item Trinitatis æqualitatem in una Divinitate veneratur."—Ibid., cc. 22, 18.

4. "Ut neque singularitas substantiæ personarum confundat proprietatem, neque item Trinitatis distinctio unitatem separet Deitatis."—Ibid., c. 22.

5. "Quia scilicet alia est persona Patris, alia Filii, alia Spiritus Sancti."—Ibid., c. 19.

6. Sed Patris, et Filii, et Spiritus Sancti, una est divinitas, æqualis gloria, coæterna majestas.

7. Qualis Pater, talis Filius, talis et Spiritus Sanctus.

8. Increatus Pater, increatus Filius, increatus et Spiritus Sanctus.

9. Immensus Pater, immensus Filius, immensus et Spiritus Sanctus.

10. Æternus Pater, æternus Filius, æternus et Spiritus Sanctus.

11. Et tamen non tres æterni, sed unus æternus.

---

6. (*coæterna*). Codd. nonnulli habent *et* coæterna. Deest *et* in Cod. Ambros. et in Fortunat. et Brunon., aliisque multis.

7. (*talis et Spiritus Sanctus*). Ita Codd. Ambros. Reg. Paris. C.C.C.C. 1, Cotton. 1. Jacob. 1. Fortunat. item Cæsarius Arelat. antiquissimus. MSS. recentiores, et editi omittunt *et*.

8. (*et Spiritus Sanctus*). Deest vocula *et* in recentioribus Codicibus: retinent plerique antiquiores hoc in loco, et similiter in subsequentibus, ante *Spiritus Sanctus*. Quæ lectio, opinor, vera est, ab autore Symboli profecta; scilicet, ad majorem emphasim, propter hæresim Macedonianam nondum penitus extinctam. Nostrum autem est Symbolum exhibere quale se primitus habuit.

aliam Filii, aliam Spiritus Sancti esse personam."— Pelag. *Symbol.*, in Lambec., vol. ii. p. 274.

6. "Confutantes Arium, unam eandemque dicimus Trinitatis esse substantiam."—Pelag. *Symb.*, *ib.*

"Patris et Filii et Spiritus Sancti unam virtutem, unam substantiam, unam Deitatem, unam majestatem, unam gloriam."—August. *c. Maxim.*, lib. ii. c. 26, § 14, vol. viii. p. 744.

7. "Qualis est Pater secundum substantiam, talem genuit Filium: et Spiritus Sanctus—est ejusdem et ipse substantiæ cum Patre et Filio ᵃ."—Faustin., *Fid.*

8. "Quicquid ad seipsum dicitur Deus, et de singulis personis singulariter dicitur, et simul de ipsa Trinitate."—August., *de Trin.*, lib. v. c. 8, § 9, vol. viii. p. 838.

9. "Magnus Pater, magnus Filius, magnus Spiritus Sanctus."—August., *ib.*, p. 837.

10. "Hoc et de bonitate, et de æternitate, et de Omnipotentia Dei dictum sit."—August., *ib.*, p. 839.

"Æternus Pater, coæternus Filius, coæternus Spiritus Sanctus."—August., *Serm.* 105, vol. v. p. 543.

---

6. "Sed tamen Patris et Filii, et Spiritus Sancti non alia et alia, sed una eademque natura."—Vincent., c. 19.

7. "Qualis immensa est Patris persona, talis est et Filii, talis est Sancti Spiritus."—Philastr., *Hær.*, 45, p. 112; (51, p. 106, cf. p. 178).

8. "Illud præcipue teneamus, quicquid ad se dicitur præstantissima illa et divina sublimitas, substantialiter dici; quod autem ad aliquid non substantialiter, sed relative: tantamque vim esse ejusdem substantiæ in Patre et Filio et Spiritu Sancto, ut quicquid de singulis ad seipsos dicitur, non pluraliter in summa, sed singulariter accipiatur."—August., *de Trin.*, lib. v. c. 8, § 9, p. 837.

ᵃ The exact words quoted are not to be found in the treatise of Faustinus *de Fide*; but in c. 4, p. 647, he says, "Qualis enim Pater Deus est, talis et Deus Filius est:" and in c. 7, p. 650, "Sic est Spiritus Dei ut sit ejusdem substantiæ cum Pater et Filio."

12. Sicut non tres increati, nec tres immensi, sed unus increatus, et unus immensus.

13. Similiter, omnipotens Pater, omnipotens Filius, omnipotens et Spiritus Sanctus.

14. Et tamen non tres omnipotentes, sed unus omnipotens.

15. Ita Deus Pater, Deus Filius, Deus et Spiritus Sanctus.

16. Et tamen non tres Dii, sed unus est Deus.

17. Ita Dominus Pater, Dominus Filius, Dominus et Spiritus Sanctus.

18. Et tamen non tres Domini, sed unus est Dominus.

---

12. (*unus increatus, et unus immensus*). Unus immensus et unus increatus. Cod. Ambros.

14. (*Et tamen*), deest *tamen* in Cod. Ambros.

16. (*est Deus*). Deest *est* in MS. Ambros.

18. (*est Dominus*). Deest *est* Cod. Ambros.

12. "Non tamen tres magni, sed unus magnus."— August., *de Trin.*, lib. v. c. 8, § 9, vol. viii. p. 837.

13. "Itaque omnipotens Pater, omnipotens Filius, omnipotens Spiritus Sanctus."—*Ib.*

14. "Nec tamen tres omnipotentes, sed unus omnipotens."—*Ib.*, p. 838.

15. "Deus Pater, Deus Filius, Deus Spiritus Sanctus."—August., *de Trin.*, lib. viii. c. 1, vol. viii. p. 865; et *Serm.* 105, c. 4, vol. v. p. 542.

16. "Nec tamen tres Dii . . . sed unus Deus."— August., *de Trin.*, l. c.

17. "Sic et Dominum si quæras, singulum quemque respondeo. . . . "—August., *c. Maxim.*, lib. ii. c. 23, § 3, vol. viii. p. 729.

18. "Sed simul omnes non tres Dominos Deos, sed unum Dominum Deum dico."—*Ib.*

12. "Nec magnos tres dicimus, sed magnum unum, quia non participatione magnitudinis Deus magnus est, sed scipso magno magnus est, quia ipse sua est magnitudo."—August., *de Trin.*, lib. v. c. 10, vol. viii. p. 838.

13. "Sed ne duos omnipotentes intelligas præcavendum est: licet enim et Pater sit omnipotens, et Filius, tamen unus est omnipotens, sicut et unus est Deus, quia Patris et Filii eadem omnipotentia est, sicut et eadem Deitas."—Faustin. (p. 123); *de Trinit.*, c. 3, p. 646.

14. "Sicut simul illi tres unus Deus, sic simul illi tres unus omnipotens est, et invisibilis unus, Deus Pater et Filius et Spiritus Sanctus est."—August., *Coll. cum Maxim.*, c. 12, vol. viii. p. 654. Cp. *de Trin.*, lib. viii. c. 1, vol. viii. p. 654.

16. "Unus Deus propter inseparabilem divinitatem; sicut unus Omnipotens propter inseparabilem Omnipotentiam."—August., *de Civit. Dei*, lib. xi. c. 24, vol. vii. p. 290.

"In illa summa Trinitate, quæ incomparabiliter rebus omnibus antecellit, tanta est inseparabilitas, ut cum Trinitas hominum non possit dici unus homo, illa unus Deus et dicatur et sit."—August., *de Trin.*, lib. xv. c. 23, § 43, vol. viii. p. 996.

18. "Non sunt enim duo Domini ubi Dominatus unus est; quia Pater in Filio, et Filius in Patre, et ideo Dominus unus."—Ambros., *de Sp. S.*, lib. iii. c. 15, vol. ii. p. 686.

19. Quia sicut singillatim unamquamque Personam et Deum et Dominum confiteri Christiana veritate compellimur; ita tres Deos, aut Dominos dicere Catholica religione prohibemur.

20. Pater a nullo est factus, nec creatus, nec genitus.

21. Filius a Patre solo est, non factus, nec creatus, sed genitus.

22. Spiritus Sanctus a Patre et Filio, non factus, nec creatus, nec genitus est, sed procedens.

23. Unus ergo Pater, non tres Patres; unus Filius, non tres Filii; unus Spiritus Sanctus, non tres Spiritus Sancti.

19. (*et Deum et Dominum*). Ita MS. Ambros. et MS. Oxon. Fortunat. rectissime. Cod. Fortunat. Ambros. aliique, tum MSS. tum impressi, habent Deum et Dominum. Brunonis Cod. et Coll. Joh. MS. Deum ac Dominum. Sau-germanensis, Dominum et Deum. Plerique editi, Deum aut Dominum. Quae lectio, me judice, omnium pessima est. [*aut Dominos*] Ita plerique MSS. et editi: sed nonnulli, ac Dominos.
(*prohibemur*). MS. Ambr. legit prohibemus: male.
22. (*sed procedens*). Cod. Ambros. adjecta habet ista; Patri et Filio coaeternus est. Glossa, uti videtur, ex margine in textum immissa: nisi forte librarius verba illa ex Bachiarii Fide, quam simul descripserat, huc transtulerit; sive oscitanter, sive majoris elucidationis gratia.—Vid. Bachiar. Fid., apud Murator., *Anecd.*, vol. ii. pp. 16, 18.

19. "Cum de singulis quæritur, unusquisque eorum et Deus, et omnipotens esse respondeatur; cum vero de omnibus simul, non tres Dii, vel tres omnipotentes, sed unus Deus omnipotens."—August., *de Civit. Dei*, lib. xi. c. 24, vol. vii. p. 290.

20. "Dicimus Patrem Deum de nullo."—August., *Serm.* 140, § 2, vol. v. p. 680.

"Non enim habet de quo sit, aut ex quo procedat." —August., *de Trin.*, lib. iv. c. 20, § 29, vol. viii. p. 829.

21. "Filius Patris solius—Hunc quippe de sua substantia genuit, non ex nihilo fecit."—August., *Ep.* 170 (*alias* 66), §§ 2, 3, vol. ii. p. 609.

22. "De Filio Spiritus Sanctus procedere reperitur."—August., *de Trin.*, lib. xv. c. 17, § 29, vol. viii. p. 988.

"Neque natus est sicut Unigenitus, neque factus," &c.—Id., lib. v. c. 14, § 15, p. 841.

23. "Unus est Pater, non duo vel tres; et unus Filius, non duo vel tres; et unus amborum Spiritus, non duo vel tres."—August., *c. Maxim.*, lib. ii. c. 23, § 3, vol. viii. p. 729.

---

22. "Spiritus quoque Sanctus non, sicut creatura, ex nihilo est factus; sed sic a Patre Filioque procedit, ut nec a Filio, nec a Patre sit factus."—August., *Ep.* 170, § 4, vol. ii. p. 609.

Τὸ ἅγιον πνεῦμα ... οὔτε γεννητὸν οὔτε κτιστὸν ... ἀλλ᾽ ἐκ πατρὸς ἐκπορευόμενον.—Epiphan. *adv. Hæres.*, lib. ii. c. 18, vol. i. p. 742.

23. Οὔτε οὖν τρεῖς πατέρες, τρεῖς υἱοὶ, οὔτε τρεῖς παράκλητοι· ἀλλ᾽ εἷς πατὴρ, καὶ εἷς υἱὸς, καὶ εἷς παράκλητος.—Pseud. Ignat., *ad Philipp.*, c. 2, p. 118; cf. Epiphan., l. c.

24. Et in hac Trinitate nihil prius aut posterius, nihil majus aut minus, sed totae tres personae coaeternae sibi sunt, et coaequales.

25. Ita ut per omnia, sicut jam supra dictum est, et unitas in Trinitate, et Trinitas in unitate veneranda sit.

26. Qui vult ergo salvus esse, ita de Trinitate sentiat.

27. Sed necessarium est ad aeternam salutem, ut Incarnationem quoque Domini nostri Jesu Christi fideliter credat.

28. Est ergo Fides recta, ut credamus et confiteamur, quia Dominus noster Jesus Christus, Dei Filius, Deus pariter, et homo est.

24. (*Et in hac*), deest *et* in Cod. San-germ.

28. (*confiteamur, quia*). Cod. Ambros atque editi nonnulli legunt *quod*. Plures habent *quia*.
(*Deus pariter, et homo est*). Ita Codd. Bened. 1, Colbertin. Jacob. 1, et Fortunat. Ambros. et San-germ. legunt, et Deus pariter et homo est. Editi, Deus et homo est.

24. " In hac Trinitate, non est aliud alio majus, aut minus."—August., *Serm.* 214, § 10, vol. v. p. 948.

" Nec enim prorsus aliquis in Trinitate gradus: nihil quod inferius, superiusve dici possit."—Pelag. *Symb.*, in Lambec., vol. ii. p. 274.

25. Vide supra, in Articulo 3.

26. Vide supra, Artic. 2.

27. " Dominus autem manens cum discipulis per quadraginta Dies, significare dignatus est quia per istud tempus necessaria est omnibus Fides Incarnationis Christi; quæ infirmis est necessaria."—August., *Serm.* 264, § 5, vol. v. p. 1077.

28. " Proinde, Christus Jesus, Dei Filius, est et Deus et homo."—August., *Enchir.*, c. 35, § 10, vol. vi. p. 210.

---

24. " Increata et inæstimabilis Trinitas, quæ unius est æternitatis et gloriæ, nec tempus nec gradum vel posterioris recipit vel prioris."—Ambros., *de Fid.*, lib. iv. c. 11, vol. ii. p. 547.

25. " Ita tota Deitas sui perfectione æqualis est, ut exceptis vocabulis quæ proprietatem indicant personarum, quicquid de una persona dicitur, de tribus dignissime possit intelligi."—Pelag., *Symb.*

26. "Si quis hanc Fidem non habet, Catholicus dici non potest, quia Catholicam non tenet Fidem; et ideo alienus est ac profanus, et adversus veritatem rebellis Fides."—Ambros., in Lambec., vol. ii. p. 268.

27. " Ideo conversatio ipsius in carne post resurrectionem per quadraginta dies erat necessaria, ut demonstraret tam diu esse necessariam Fidem Incarnationis Christi quamdiu in ista vita docetur arca in diluvio fluctuare."—August., *Serm.* 264, § 5, vol. v. p. 1078.

29. Deus est ex Substantia Patris ante sæcula genitus : homo ex substantia matris in sæculo natus.

30. Perfectus Deus, perfectus homo ex anima rationali et humana carne subsistens.

31. Æqualis Patri secundum Divinitatem : minor Patre secundum humanitatem.

32. Qui licet Deus sit et homo, non duo tamen, sed unus est Christus.

33. Unus autem, non conversione Divinitatis in carnem, sed adsumptione humanitatis in Deum.

29. (*ex Substantia*). Colbertin. de substantia : et infra, de substantia matris. (*Homo*). Ambros. Cod. legit, et homo est. Fortunat. et homo. Post, matris, San-germ. Cod. habet, in sæculo genitus perfectus homo.
30. (*rationali*), rationabili. Codd. Ambros. Colbert. et San-germ.

31. (*minor Patre*), minor Patri. Colb.
32. Deest *et* Colb.

33. (*in carnem*), in carne. MSS. Ambros. Colbert, San-germ. aliique plurimi, et vetusti. Habent etiam in Deo, pro, in Deum. At multi etiam Codices, cum Fortunati Cod. Ambrosiano, receptam lectionem præferunt ; quæ utique præferenda videtur. Cod. San-germ. pro *conversione* habet *conversatione*. Cod. Colbert: totam hanc pericopen sic exhibet ; Unus autem, non ex eo quod sit in carne conversa Divinitas, sed quia est in Deo adsumpta dignanter humanitas.

29. " Deus ante omnia sæcula: homo in nostro sæculo—unus Dei Filius, idemque hominis Filius."—*Ibid.*

30. " Confitemur in Christo unam esse Filii personam, ut dicamus duas esse perfectas atque integras substantias, id est, Deitatis, et humanitatis quæ ex anima continetur et corpore."—Pelag., *Symb.*, p. 275.

31. " Æqualem Patri secundum Divinitatem, minorem autem Patre secundum carnem, hoc est, secundum hominem."—August., *Epist.* 137, vol. ii. p. 406.

32. " Agnoscamus geminam substantiam Christi; Divinam scilicet qua æqualis est Patri, humanam qua major est Pater: utrumque autem simul non duo, sed unus est Christus."—August., *in Johan.*, *Tract.* 78, § 3, vol. iii. part 2, p. 699.

33. " Verbum caro factum est, a Divinitate carne suscepta, non in carnem Divinitate mutata."—August., *Enchir.*, c. 34, § 10, vol. vi. p. 209.

29. " Idem ex Patre ante sæcula genitus, idem in sæculo ex matre generatus."—Vincent., c. 19.

30. "Adversus Arium, veram et perfectam verbi Divinitatem; adversus Apollinarem, perfectam hominis in Christo defendimus veritatem."—August., *Serm.* 258, § 2, vol. v. App. p. 391.

" Perfectus Deus, perfectus homo: in Deo summa Divinitas, in homine plena humanitas: quippe quæ animam simul habeat et carnem."—Vincent., c. 19.

32. " Caro Christus, et anima Christus, et verbum Christus: nec tamen tria hæc tres Christi, sed unus Christus."—August., *in Johan.*, *Tract.* 47, § 12, vol. iii. part 2, p. 612.

33. " Nemo ergo credat Dei Filium conversum et commutatum esse in hominis Filium; sed potius credamus, et non consumpta divina, et perfecte assumpta humana substantia, manentem Dei Filium factum hominis Filium."—August., *Serm.* 187, § 3, vol. v. p. 887.

" Deus ergo hominem assumsit, homo in Deum transivit: non naturæ versibilitate, sicut Apollinaristæ dicunt, sed Dei dignatione."—Gennad., *Eccl. Dogm.*, c. 2, in August., vol. viii. p. 75.

34. Unus omnino, non confusione substantiæ, sed unitate Personæ.

35. Nam sicut anima rationalis et caro unus est homo; ita Deus et homo unus est Christus.

36. Qui passus est pro salute nostra, descendit ad inferos, tertia die resurrexit a mortuis.
37. Adscendit ad Cælos, sedet ad dexteram Patris; inde venturus judicare vivos et mortuos.

38. Ad cujus adventum omnes homines resurgere habent cum corporibus suis, et reddituri sunt de factis propriis rationem.
39. Et qui bona egerunt, ibunt in vitam æternam, qui vero mala, in ignem æternum.

---

34. (*Unus omnino*), unus Christus est. Colbert.

35. (*Nam sicut*, &c.) Totum omittit Cod. Colbertinus. Scilicet, uti credo, ne simile illud in erroris sui patrocinium arriperent Monophysitæ. (*Rationalis*), rationabilis. Ambros.

36. (*Qui passus est pro salute nostra*), qui secundum Fidem nostram passus et mortuus. Colbert.
(*ad inferos*), ad infernos. Cod. San-germ. ad inferna. Fortunat. MS. Oxon. ad inferna descendens. Cod. Colbertin.
(*tertia die*), deest in Cod. Ambros. San-germ. Cotton 1, Jacob. 1, (*resurrexit*), surrexit. Cod. Ambros. Fortunat.

37. (*sedet*), sedit. Cod. Ambr. (*Dexteram Patris*): Ita Codd. Ambros. et Fortunat. et Symb. Roman. Vet. Dexteram Patris Omnipotentis. Cod. San-germ. Dextram Omnipotentis. Cod. Brunonis, Dexteram Dei Patris sedet, sicut vobis in Symbolo traditum est. Cod. Colbert. Dexteram Dei Patris Omnipotentis. Codd. recentiores, cum excusis.

38. (*resurgere habent cum corporibus suis, et*), desunt in Cod. Ambros. Colbertinus legit; ad cujus adventum erunt omnes homines sine dubio in suis corporibus resurrecturi. Sed nihil mutamus.

39. (*egerunt*) egerint. Cod. Ambros. Totum hunc Articulum

34. " Idem Deus qui homo, et qui Deus idem homo: non confusione naturæ, sed unitate personæ."—August., *Serm.* 186, § 1, vol. v. p. 885.

35. " Sicut enim unus est homo anima rationalis et caro; sic unus est Christus Deus et homo."—August., *in Joh., Tract.* 78, § 3, vol. iii. p. 699.

36. " Descendit ad inferna, tertia die resurrexit a mortuis."—*Symb. Aquileiæ,* in Heurtley, p. 30.

37. " Ascendit ad cœlos, sedet ad dexteram Patris; inde venturus judicare vivos et mortuos."—*Symb. Roman. Vet.,* in Heurtley, p. 31.

38. " Resurrectionem carnis ita credimus, ut dicamus nos in eadem qua nunc sumus veritate membrorum esse reparandos."—Pelag., *Symb.,* p. 275.

39. " Et procedent qui bona fecerunt, in resurrectionem vitæ, qui vero mala egerunt in resurrectionem judicii."—Joh. v. 29.

34. "Unus autem, non . . . Divinitatis et humanitatis confusione sed . . . unitate personæ."—Vincent. Lir., c. 19.

36. "Quis ergo, nisi infidelis, negaverit fuisse apud inferos Christum? . . .
" Quamobrem teneamus firmissime quod fides habet fundatissima auctoritate firmatum . . . et cætera quæ de illo testatissima veritate conscripta sunt; in quibus etiam hoc est, quod apud inferos fuit."
—August., *Ep.* 164, vol. ii. pp. 574, 578.

38. "Si id resurgere dicitur quod cadit, caro ergo nostra in veritate resurget, sicut in veritate cadit. Et non secundum Origenem, immutatio corporum erit," &c.—Gennad., *Eccl. Dogmat.,* c. 6, p. 76.

39. " Post resurrectionem et judicium, non credamus restitutio-

40. Hæc est Fides Catholica, quam nisi quisque fideliter, firmiterque crediderit, salvus esse non poterit.

sic legit Colbertinus; Ut qui bona egerunt, eant in vitam æternam; qui mala in ignem æternum.
(*qui vero*), Cod. Ambros. et Cotton. 1, omittunt *vero*. Codices nonnulli legunt, et qui vero: alii, et qui mala.
40. (*quisque*), Cod. Ambros. unusquisque. Colbertinus pergit: Hæc est Fides sancta et catholica, quam omnis homo, qui ad vitam æternam pervenire desiderat, scire integre debet, et fideliter custodire.

"Ibunt hi in supplicium æternum, justi autem in vitam æternam."—Matt. xxv. 46.

40. "Cavete, dilectissimi, ne quis vos ab Ecclesiæ Catholicæ Fide ac unitate seducat. Qui enim vobis aliter Evangelizaverit præterquam quod accepistis, anathema sit."—August., *Serm.* 205, § 8, vol. v. p. 952.

nem futuram, sicut Origenes delirat, ut dæmones vel impii homines post tormenta quasi suppliciis expurgati, vel illi in angelicam qua creati sunt redeant dignitatem, vel isti justorum societate donentur."—Gennad., *ibid*, c. 9, p. 77.

40. Ὁ ταῦτα πιστεύσας ὡς ἔχει, ὡς γεγένηται, μακάριος· ὁ ταῦτα μὴ πιστεύων ἐναγὴς οὐχ ἧττον τῶν τὸν κύριον σταυρωσάντων.—Pseud. Ignat., *ad Philipp.*, c. 3, p. 118.

APPENDIX TO CHAPTER IX.

PASSAGES FROM THE ANTE-NICENE FATHERS, CONFIRMING
THE STATEMENTS OF THE ATHANASIAN CREED.

THE evidence adduced by Dr. Waterland in the preceding chapter in confirmation of the statements made in the Athanasian Creed being confined to extracts from writers of the fourth and fifth centuries, it seems desirable to complete the chain of testimony, by adding passages from the Ante-Nicene Fathers, which express, with more or less closeness, the same views as to the nature of God, and the distinction and Divinity of the three Persons in the blessed Trinity. The collection of passages is derived, in great measure, from the late Professor Blunt's "Lectures on the Right Use of the Early Fathers[a]," supplemented from Dr. Burton's "Testimonies of the Ante-Nicene Fathers to the Divinity of Christ, and to the Doctrine of the Trinity." The series begins with Ignatius, as the evidence of Clement of Rome on the subject consists in implication[b] rather than direct statement, with the exception of some passages in his second Epistle[c], which is of very doubtful authenticity.

[a] Series ii. lect. x. pp. 396—408 of second edition.
[b] c. 2, pp. 10, 12; c. 16, pp. 62, 64; c. 22, p. 98; c. 36, p. 134.
See Burton, Div. of Christ, pp. 4—12.
[c] e.g. c. 1, p. 229: Οὕτως δεῖ ἡμᾶς φρονεῖν περὶ Ἰησοῦ Χριστοῦ ὡς περὶ Θεοῦ. c. 9, p. 248: Χριστὸς ὁ Κύριος, ὁ σώσας ἡμᾶς, ὢν μὲν τὸ πρῶτον πνεῦμα, ἐγένετο σάρξ, καὶ οὕτως ἡμᾶς ἐκάλεσεν.

ARTICLES 1—3.—Irenæus, lib. iv. c. 33, § 7, p. 273. "Judicabit autem et omnes eos qui sunt extra veritatem, id est qui sunt extra ecclesiam; ipse autem a nemine judicabitur. Omnia enim ei constant: εἰς ἕνα Θεὸν παντοκράτορα, ἐξ οὗ τὰ πάντα, πίστις ὁλόκληρος· καὶ εἰς τὸν Υἱὸν τοῦ Θεοῦ Ἰησοῦν Χριστόν, τὸν Κύριον ἡμῶν, δι' οὗ τὰ πάντα, καὶ τὰς οἰκονομίας αὐτοῦ, δι' ὧν ἄνθρωπος ἐγένετο ὁ Υἱὸς τοῦ Θεοῦ, πεισμονὴ βεβαία· καὶ εἰς τὸ Πνεῦμα τοῦ Θεοῦ, qui præstat agnitionem veritatis, τὸ τὰς οἰκονομίας Πατρός τε καὶ Υἱοῦ σκηνοβατοῦν καθ' ἑκάστην γενεὰν ἐν τοῖς ἀνθρώποις, καθὼς βούλεται ὁ Πατήρ."

Cyprian, *Ep.* 73, § 14, p. 206. "Quomodo ergo quidam dicunt foris extra Ecclesiam imo et contra Ecclesiam, modo in nomine Jesu Christi, ubicumque et quomodocumque gentilem baptizatum remissionem peccatorum consequi posse, quando ipse Christus gentes baptizari jubeat in plena et adunata Trinitate."

ARTICLE 3.—Justin Martyr, *Apol.*, c. 13, pp. 50, 51.
Ἄθεοι μὲν ὡς οὐκ ἐσμέν, τὸν δημιουργὸν τοῦδε τοῦ παντὸς σεβόμενοι,—τίς σωφρόνων οὐχ ὁμολογήσει; τὸν διδάσκαλόν τε τούτων γενόμενον ἡμῖν,—Υἱὸν αὐτοῦ τοῦ ὄντως Θεοῦ μαθόντες, καὶ ἐν δευτέρᾳ χώρᾳ ἔχοντες· Πνεῦμά τε προφητικὸν ἐν τρίτῃ τάξει ὅτι μετὰ λόγου τιμῶμεν, ἀποδείξομεν.

Theophilus, *Ad Autolycum*, lib. ii. c. 15, p. 360.
Ὡσαύτως καὶ αἱ τρεῖς ἡμέραι [πρὸ] τῶν φωστήρων γεγονυῖαι τύποι εἰσὶν τῆς Τριάδος, τοῦ Θεοῦ, καὶ τοῦ λόγου αὐτοῦ, καὶ τῆς σοφίας αὐτοῦ [d].

Cyprian, *Ep.* 73, § 6, p. 200. "Dominus post resur-

[d] This passage is important, as the earliest in which the word Τριὰς is used by any of the Fathers.

rectionem discipulos suos mittens quemadmodum baptizare deberent instituit et docuit, dicens, *Data est mihi omnis potestas in cœlo et in terra. Ite ergo et docete gentes omnes, baptizantes eos in nomine Patris, et Filii, et Spiritus Sancti.* Insinuat Trinitatem, cujus sacramento gentes baptizarentur."
Dionysius Rom., *adv. Sabellium*, p. 377. Οὕτω γὰρ ἂν καὶ ἡ θεία Τριὰς, καὶ τὸ ἅγιον κήρυγμα τῆς μοναρχίας διασώζοιτο.

ARTICLES 4, 5.—Justin Martyr, *Dial. c. Tryph.*, § 128, p. 221. Καὶ ὅτι δύναμις αὕτη, ἣν καὶ Θεὸν καλεῖ ὁ προφητικὸς λόγος, ὡς διὰ πολλῶν ὡσαύτως ἀποδέδεικται, καὶ ἄγγελον, οὐ ὡς τὸ τοῦ ἡλίου φῶς ὀνόματι μόνον ἀριθμεῖται, ἀλλὰ καὶ ἀριθμῷ ἕτερόν τί ἐστι, καὶ ἐν τοῖς προειρημένοις διὰ βραχέων τὸν λόγον ἐξήτασα, εἰπὼν τὴν δύναμιν ταύτην γεγεννῆσθαι ἀπὸ τοῦ Πατρὸς δυνάμει καὶ βουλῇ αὐτοῦ, ἀλλ' οὐ κατὰ ἀποτομήν, ὡς ἀπομεριζομένης τῆς τοῦ Πατρὸς οὐσίας, ὁποῖα τὰ ἄλλα πάντα μεριζόμενα καὶ τεμνόμενα οὐ τὰ αὐτά ἐστιν ἃ καὶ πρὶν τμηθῆναι· καὶ παραδείγματος χάριν παρειλήφειν τὰ ὡς ἀπὸ πυρὸς ἀναπτόμενα πυρὰ ἕτερα ὁρῶμεν, οὐδὲν ἐλαττουμένου ἐκείνου, ἐξ οὗ ἀνάφθηαι πολλὰ δύνανται, ἀλλὰ ταὐτοῦ μένοντος.

Athenagoras, *Legat. pro Christ.*, c. 10, p. 287. Τίς οὖν οὐκ ἂν ἀπορήσαι, λέγοντας Θεὸν Πατέρα καὶ Υἱὸν Θεὸν καὶ Πνεῦμα ἅγιον, δεικνύντας αὐτῶν καὶ τὴν ἐν τῇ ἑνώσει δύναμιν καὶ τὴν ἐν τῇ τάξει διαίρεσιν, ἀκούσας ἀθέους καλουμένους;

Ib., c. 12, p. 289. Εἰδέναι . . . τίς ἡ τοῦ Παιδὸς πρὸς τὸν Πατέρα ἑνότης, τίς ἡ τοῦ Πατρὸς πρὸς τὸν Υἱὸν κοινωνία, τί τὸ Πνεῦμα, τίς ἡ τῶν τοσούτων ἕνωσις, καὶ διαίρεσιν ἑνουμένων, τοῦ Πνεύματος, τοῦ Παιδὸς, τοῦ Πατρός·

Tertullian, *adv. Praxeam*, c. 2, p. 501. "Unicum Deum non alias putat credendum, quam si ipsum eundemque et Patrem Filium et Spiritum Sanctum dicat; quasi non sic quoque unus sit omnia, dum ex uno omnia, per substantiæ scilicet unitatem, et nihilominus custodiatur œconomiæ sacramentum, quæ unitatem in trinitatem disponit, tres dirigens, Patrem et Filium et Spiritum Sanctum : tres autem non statu sed gradu ; nec substantia sed forma ; nec potestate sed specie ; unius autem substantiæ, et unius status, et unius potestatis."

Ib., cc. 11, 12, p. 506. "His itaque paucis tamen manifeste distinctio Trinitatis exponitur. Est enim ipse qui pronuntiat Spiritus, et Pater ad quem pronuntiat, et Filius de quo pronuntiat. Sic et cætera quæ nunc ad Patrem de Filio, vel ad Filium, nunc ad Filium de Patre, vel ad Patrem, nunc ad Spiritum pronuntiantur ; unamquamque personam in sua proprietate constituunt.

"Si te adhuc numerus scandalizat Trinitatis, quasi non connexæ in unitate simplici, interrogo quomodo unicus et singularis pluraliter loquitur? Faciamus hominem ad imaginem et similitudinem nostram ; cum debuerit dixisse, Faciam hominem ad imaginem et similitudinem meam, utpote unicus et singularis?"

Hippolytus, *c. Noëtum*, c. 7, vol. ii. p. 11. Ἐὰν δὲ λέγει, αὐτὸς εἶπεν, Ἐγὼ καὶ ὁ Πατὴρ ἕν ἐσμεν, ἐπιστανέτω τὸν νοῦν καὶ μανθανέτω, ὅτι οὐκ εἶπεν ὅτι Ἐγὼ καὶ ὁ Πατὴρ ἕν εἰμι, ἀλλὰ ἕν ἐσμεν. Τὸ γάρ ἐσμεν οὐκ ἐφ' ἑνὸς λέγεται, ἀλλ' ἐπὶ δύο πρόσωπα ἔδειξεν, δύναμιν δὲ μίαν.

Origen, on St. John i. 3, tom. ii. § 6, vol. iv. p. 60.

Ἔσται δέ τις καὶ τρίτος παρὰ τοὺς δύο, τόν τε διὰ τοῦ Λόγου παραδεχόμενον τὸ Πνεῦμα τὸ ἅγιον γεγονέναι, καὶ τὸν ἀγέννητον αὐτὸν εἶναι ὑπολαμβάνοντα, δογματίζων μηδὲ οὐσίαν τινα ἰδίαν ὑφεστάναι τοῦ ἁγίου Πνεύματος ἑτέραν παρὰ τὸν Πατέρα καὶ τὸν Υἱόν . . . . ἡμεῖς μέντοιγε τρεῖς ὑποστάσεις πειθόμενοι τυγχάνειν, τὸν Πατέρα, καὶ τὸν Υἱόν, καὶ τὸ ἅγιον Πνεῦμα, καὶ ἀγέννητον μηδὲν ἕτερον τοῦ Πατρὸς εἶναι πιστεύοντες, ὡς εὐσεβέστερον καὶ ἀληθὲς προσιέμεθα τὸ, πάντων διὰ τοῦ Λόγου γενομένων, τὸ ἅγιον Πνεῦμα πάντων εἶναι τιμιώτερον, καὶ τάξει πάντων τῶν ὑπὸ τοῦ Πατρὸς διὰ Χριστοῦ γεγεννημένων. Καὶ τάχα αὕτη ἐστὶν ἡ αἰτία τοῦ μὴ καὶ αὐτουιὸν χρηματίζειν τοῦ Θεοῦ, μόνου τοῦ Μονογενοῦς φύσει Υἱοῦ ἀρχῆθεν τυγχάνοντος, οὗ χρήζειν ἔοικε τὸ ἅγιον Πνεῦμα, διακονοῦντος αὐτοῦ τῇ ὑποστάσει, οὐ μόνον εἰς τὸ εἶναι, ἀλλὰ καὶ σοφὸν εἶναι καὶ λογικὸν καὶ δίκαιον, καὶ πᾶν ὁτιποτοῦν χρὴ αὐτὸ νοεῖν τυγχάνειν, κατὰ μετοχὴν τῶν προειρημένων ἡμῖν Χριστοῦ ἐπινοιῶν.

Novatian[e], *de Trinitate*, c. 21, p. 720. " Quis enim non secundam Filii post Patrem agnoscat esse personam, cum legat dictum a Patre consequenter ad Filium, *Faciamus hominem ad imaginem et similitudinem nostram.*"

Dionysius of Alexandria, *Ex Elencho et Apol.*, c. 6, p. 93. Ἓν εἰσιν, ὄντες δύο· οὕτω γὰρ καὶ ὁ Πατὴρ καὶ ὁ Υἱὸς ἓν καὶ ἐν ἀλλήλοις ἐλέχθησαν εἶναι.

Ib., c. 8, p. 94. Οἱ δὲ οὐκ ἴσασιν ὅτι μήτε ἀλλοτρίωται Πατὴρ Υἱοῦ ᾗ Πατήρ· προκαταρκτικὸν γάρ ἐστι τῆς συναφείας τὸ ὄνομα· οὔτε ὁ Υἱὸς ἀπῴκισται τοῦ Πατρός. Ἡ γὰρ Πατὴρ

---

[e] The testimony of Novatian is considered by Dr. Burton as valuable, since, though heretical in matters of discipline and practice, his opinions in matters of doctrine were always held to be sound.—Burton, " Divinity of Christ," p. 366.

προσηγορία δηλοῖ τὴν κοινωνίαν· ἔν τε ταῖς χερσὶν αὐτῶν ἐστι τὸ Πνεῦμα, μήτε τοῦ πέμποντος μήτε τοῦ φέροντος δυνάμενον στέρεσθαι. Πῶς οὖν ὁ τούτοις χρώμενος τοῖς ὀνόμασι, μεμερίσθαι ταῦτα καὶ ἀφωρίσθαι παντελῶς ἀλλήλων οἴομαι;

ARTICLE 6.—Clemens Alex., *Pædagog.*, lib. iii. c. 12, p. 311. Αἰνοῦντας εὐχαριστεῖν τῷ μόνῳ Πατρὶ καὶ Υἱῷ, Υἱῷ καὶ Πατρὶ, παιδαγωγῷ καὶ διδασκάλῳ Υἱῷ, σὺν καὶ τῷ ἁγίῳ Πνεύματι, πάντα τῷ ἑνὶ, ἐν ᾧ τὰ πάντα, δι' ὃν τὰ πάντα ἕν, δι' ὃν τὸ ἀεί.

ARTICLE 8.—Irenæus, lib. iii. c. 8, § 3, p. 183. "Quoniam autem ipse omnia fecit libere et quemadmodum voluit, ait iterum David: Deus autem noster in cœlis sursum et in terra, omnia quæcunque voluit, fecit. Altera autem sunt, quæ constituta sunt, ab eo qui constituit, et quæ facta sunt, ab eo qui fecit. Ipse enim infectus, et sine initio et sine fine et nullius indigens, ipse sibi sufficiens, et adhuc reliquis omnibus, ut sint, hoc ipsum præstans; quæ vero ab eo sunt facta initium sumpserunt. Quæcunque autem initium sumpserunt, et dissolutionem possunt percipere et subjecta sunt et indigent ejus, qui se fecit; necesse est omnimodo, ut differens vocabulum habeant apud eos etiam, qui vel modicum sensum in discernendo talia habent: ita ut is quidem, qui omnia fecerit, cum Verbo suo juste dicatur Deus et Dominus solus; quæ autem facta sunt, non jam ejusdem vocabuli participabilia esse, neque juste id vocabulum sumere debere, quod est creatoris."

Id., lib. ii. c. 13, § 8, p. 132. Speaking of the absurd doctrines of some of the Gnostics, Irenæus goes on to say, "Decentiora autem magis quam hi, qui generationem prolativi hominum verbi transferunt in Dei æternum Verbum, et prolationis initium donantes et genesin, quemadmodum et suo verbo. Et in quo distabit Dei Verbum, immo magis ipse Deus, cum sit Verbum, a verbo hominum, si eamdem habuerit ordinationem et emissionem generationis."

ARTICLE 9.—Ib., lib. iii. c. 16, § 6, p. 206. "In omnibus autem est et homo, plasmatio Dei ; et hominem ergo in semetipsum recapitulans est, invisibilis visibilis factus, et incomprehensibilis factus comprehensibilis, et impassibilis passibilis, et Verbum homo."

Clemens Alex., *Strom.*, lib. vii. c. 2, p. 831. οὐ γὰρ ἐξίσταταί ποτε τῆς αὐτοῦ περιωπῆς ὁ Υἱὸς τοῦ Θεοῦ· οὐ μεριζόμενος, οὐκ ἀποτεμνόμενος, οὐ μεταβαίνων ἐκ τόπου εἰς τόπον, πάντῃ δὲ ὢν πάντοτε, καὶ μηδαμῇ περιεχόμενος, ὅλος νοῦς, ὅλος φῶς πατρῷον, ὅλος ὀφθαλμὸς, πάντα ὁρῶν, πάντα ἀκούων, εἰδὼς πάντα.

Id., *Pedagog.*, lib. i. c. 6, p. 123. Ὦ θαύματος μυστικοῦ· εἷς μὲν ὁ τῶν ὅλων Πατήρ· εἷς δὲ καὶ ὁ τῶν ὅλων Λόγος· καὶ τὸ Πνεῦμα τὸ ἅγιον ἕν, καὶ τὸ αὐτὸ πανταχοῦ.

ARTICLE 10.—Ignatius, *Ep. ad Polycarp*, c. 3, p. 490. Τὸν ὑπὲρ καιρὸν προσδόκα, τὸν ἄχρονον, τὸν ἀόρατον, τὸν δι' ἡμᾶς ὁρατὸν, τὸν ἀψηλάφητον, τὸν ἀπαθῆ, τὸν δι' ἡμᾶς παθητὸν, τὸν κατὰ πάντα τρόπον δι' ἡμᾶς ὑπομείναντα.

Justin Martyr, *Ep. ad Diognet.*, c. 11, p. 240. Οὗτος ὁ ἀπ' ἀρχῆς, ὁ καινὸς φανείς . . . οὗτος ὁ ἀεὶ, σήμερον Υἱὸς λογισθείς.

Irenæus, lib. iv. c. 20, § 3, p. 253. "Quoniam Verbum, id est Filius, semper cum Patre erat, per multa demonstravimus. Quoniam autem et Sapientia, quæ est Spiritus, erat apud eum ante omnem constitutionem, per Salomonem ait."

Origen, *Comment. in Genes.*, tom. i. vol. ii. p. 1. Οἱ γὰρ ὁ Θεὸς Πατὴρ εἶναι ἤρξατο, κωλυόμενος ὡς οἱ γινόμενοι πατέρες ἄνθρωποι, ὑπὸ τοῦ μὴ δύνασθαί πω πατέρες εἶναι· εἰ γὰρ ἀεὶ τέλειος ὁ Θεὸς, καὶ πάρεστιν αὐτῷ δύναμις τοῦ Πατέρα αὐτὸν εἶναι, καὶ καλὸν αὐτὸν εἶναι Πατέρα τοῦ τοιούτου Υἱοῦ, τί ἀναβάλλεται, καὶ ἑαυτὸν τοῦ καλοῦ στηρίσκει, καὶ, ὡς ἔστιν εἰπεῖν, ἐξ οὗ δύναται Πατὴρ εἶναι Υἱοῦ; τὸ αὐτὸ μέντοιγε καὶ περὶ τοῦ ἁγίου Πνεύματος λεκτέον.

Id., *de Principiis*, lib. iv. § 28, p. 190. "Hoc autem ipsum quod dicimus, quia nunquam fuit quando non fuit, cum venia audiendum est. Nam et hæc ipsa nomina temporalis vocabuli significantiam gerunt, id est quando vel nunquam; supra omne autem tempus, et supra omnia sæcula, et supra omnem æternitatem intelligenda sunt ea quæ de Patre et Filio et Spiritu Sancto dicuntur. Hæc enim sola Trinitas est quæ omnem sensum intelligentiæ non solum temporalis verum etiam æternalis excedit. Cætera vero quæ sunt extra Trinitatem in sæculis et temporibus metienda sunt [f]."

ARTICLES 15—17.—Athenagoras, *Legat. pro Christ.*, c. 24, p. 302. Ὡς γὰρ Θεὸν φαμέν, καὶ Υἱὸν τὸν Λόγον αὐτοῦ καὶ Πνεῦμα ἅγιον, ἑνούμενα μὲν κατὰ δύναμιν, τὸν Πατέρα, τὸν Υἱὸν, τὸ Πνεῦμα, ὅτι νοῦς, λόγος, σοφία, Υἱὸς τοῦ Πατρὸς, καὶ ἀπόρροια, ὡς φῶς ἀπὸ πυρὸς, τὸ Πνεῦμα.

Tertullian, *adv. Prax.*, c. 13, p. 507. "Deos om-

---

[f] Passages quoted in Latin from this treatise must be taken for what they are worth, being found only in the Latin translation of Rufinus, which is not to be implicitly relied upon.—See Burton, "Divinity of Christ," pp. 284, 285.

nino non dicam, nec Dominos: sed apostolum sequar, ut si pariter nominandi fuerint Pater et Filius, Deum Patrem appellem, et Jesum Christum Dominum nominem. Solum autem Christum potero Deum dicere, sicut idem Apostolus, *Ex quibus Christus, qui est,* inquit, *Deus super omnia, benedictus in ævum omne.*"

Hippolytus, c. *Noëtum*, c. 12, vol. ii. p. 14. Οὐκοῦν ἔνσαρκον Λόγον θεωροῦμεν, Πατέρα δι' αὐτοῦ νοοῦμεν, Υἱῷ δὲ πιστεύομεν, Πνεύματι ἁγίῳ προσκυνοῦμεν.

Origen, *in Psalm.* cxxii. 2, vol. ii. p. 821. Δοῦλοι κυρίων, Πατρὸς καὶ Υἱοῦ, πνεῦμα καὶ σῶμα; παιδίσκη δὲ κυρίας τοῦ ἁγίου Πνεύματος ἡ ψυχή. Τὰ δὲ τρία Κύριος ὁ Θεὸς ἡμῶν ἐστίν· οἱ γὰρ τρεῖς τὸ ἕν εἰσιν.

Id., *in Joan.*, tom. xxxii. vol. iv. p. 429. Πρῶτον πάντων πίστευσον ὅτι εἷς ἐστιν ὁ Θεὸς ὁ τὰ πάντα κτίσας, καὶ καταρτίσας, καὶ ποιήσας ἐκ τοῦ μὴ ὄντος εἰς τὸ εἶναι τὰ πάντα. Χρὴ δὲ καὶ πιστεύειν ὅτι Κύριος Ἰησοῦς Χριστὸς, καὶ πάσῃ τῇ περὶ αὐτοῦ κατὰ τὴν θεότητα, καὶ τὴν ἀνθρωπότητα, ἀληθείᾳ· δεῖ δὲ καὶ εἰς τὸ ἅγιον πιστεύειν Πνεῦμα.

ARTICLE 19.—Tertullian, *adv. Prax.*, c. 13, p. 507. "Duos quidem definimus, Patrem et Filium, et jam tres cum Spiritu Sancto. . . . Duos tamen Deos et duos Dominos nunquam ex ore nostro proferimus; non quasi non et Pater Deus, et Filius Deus, et Spiritus Sanctus Deus, et Deus unusquisque."

ARTICLE 20.—Irenæus, lib. iii. c. 8, § 3, p. 183. "Ipse enim infectus et sine initio et sine fine et nullius indigens, ipse sibi sufficiens et adhuc reliquis omnibus, ut sint, hoc ipsum præstans."

Article 21.—Justin Martyr, *Dial.*, c. 61, p. 157. Μαρτύριον δὲ καὶ ἄλλο ὑμῖν ἀπὸ τῶν γραφῶν δώσω, ὅτι ἀρχὴν πρὸ πάντων τῶν κτισμάτων ὁ Θεὸς γεγέννηκε δύναμίν τινα ἐξ ἑαυτοῦ λογικὴν, ἥτις καὶ δόξα Κυρίου ὑπὸ τοῦ Πνεύματος τοῦ ἁγίου καλεῖται.

Ib., c. 129, p. 222. Νοεῖτε, ὦ ἀκροαταί, εἴ γε καὶ τὸν νοῦν προσέχετε, καὶ ὅτι γεγεννῆσθαι ὑπὸ τοῦ Πατρὸς τοῦτο τὸ γέννημα πρὸ πάντων ἁπλῶς τῶν κτισμάτων ὁ λόγος ἐδήλου, καὶ τὸ γεννώμενον τοῦ γεννῶντος ἀριθμῷ ἕτερόν ἐστι, πᾶς ὁστισοῦν ὁμολογήσειε.

Irenæus, lib. ii. c. 28, § 6, p. 158. "Si quis itaque nobis dixerit: Quomodo ergo Filius prolatus a Patre est? dicimus ei, quia prolationem istam, sive generationem, sive nuncupationem, sive adapertionem, aut quolibet quis nomine vocaverit generationem ejus inenarrabilem exsistentem nemo novit; non Valentinus, non Marcion, neque Saturninus, neque Basilides, neque angeli, neque archangeli, neque principes, neque potestates, nisi solus qui generavit Pater et qui natus est Filius."

Tertullian, *Apol.*, c. 21, p. 19. "Hunc ex Deo prolatum didicimus, et prolatione generatum, et idcirco Filium Dei, et Deum dictum ex unitate substantiæ."

Dionysius Alex., *ex Elench. et Apol.*, c. 13, p. 97. Ζωὴ ἐκ ζωῆς ἐγεννήθη, καὶ ὥσπερ ποταμὸς ἀπὸ πηγῆς ἔρρευσε, καὶ ἀπὸ φωτὸς ἀσβέστου λαμπρὸν φῶς ἀνήφθη.

Dionysius Rom., *adv. Sabell.*, p. 376. Πολλαχοῦ δὲ τῶν θείων λογίων γεγεννῆσθαι ἀλλ' οὐ γεγονέναι τὸν υἱὸν λεγόμενον εὕροι τις ἄν· ὑφ' ὧν καταφανῶς ἐλέγχονται τὰ ψεύδη περὶ τῆς τοῦ Κυρίου γεννήσεως ὑπολαμβάνοντες, οἱ ποίησιν αὐτοῦ τὴν θείαν καὶ ἄρρητον γέννησιν λέγειν τολμῶντες.

Article 22.—Tertullian, *adv. Prax.*, c. 4, p. 502. "Ceterum, qui Filium non aliunde deduco, sed de substantia Patris, nihil facientem sine Patris voluntate, omnem a Patre consecutum potestatem, quomodo possum de fide destruere monarchiam, quam a Patre Filio traditam in Filio servo? Hoc mihi et in tertium gradum dictum sit, quia Spiritum non aliunde puto, quam a Patre per Filium."

Ib., c. 8, p. 504. "Omne quod prodit ex aliquo, secundum sit ejus necesse est de quo prodit, non ideo tamen est separatum. Secundus autem ubi est, duo sunt. Et tertius ubi est, tres sunt. Tertius enim est Spiritus a Deo et Filio, sicut tertius a radice fructus ex fructice. Et tertius a fonte, rivus ex flumine. Et tertius a sole, apex ex radio. Nihil tamen a matrice alienatur, a qua proprietates suas ducit. Ita Trinitas per consertos et connexos gradus a Patre decurrens, et monarchiæ nihil obstrepit, et œconomiæ statum protegit."

Article 24.—Tertullian, *adv. Hermogenem*, c. 7, p. 235. "Divinitas autem gradum non habet, utpote unica."

Origen, *de Princip.*, lib. i. c. 3, § 7, vol. i. p. 63. "Ne quis sane existimet nos ex eo quod diximus Spiritum Sanctum solis sanctis præstari, Patris vero et Filii beneficia vel inoperationes pervenire ad bonos et malos, justos et injustos, prætulisse per hoc Patri et Filio Spiritum Sanctum, vel majorem ejus per hoc asserere dignitatem; quod utique valde inconsequens est. Proprietatem namque gratiæ ejus operisque descripsimus. Porro autem nihil in Trinitate majus minusve dicendum est, quum unius Divinitatis fons

Verbo ac Ratione sua teneat universa, Spiritu vero oris sui quæ digna sunt sanctificatione, sanctificet."

ARTICLE 25.—Origen, c. Celsum, lib. viii. c. 12, vol. i. p. 751. Θρησκεύομεν οὖν τὸν Πατέρα τῆς ἀληθείας, καὶ τὸν Υἱὸν τὴν ἀλήθειαν, ὄντα δύο τῇ ὑποστάσει πράγματα, ἓν δὲ τῇ ὁμονοίᾳ, καὶ τῇ συμφωνίᾳ, καὶ τῇ ταυτότητι τοῦ βουλήματος.

Tertullian, *de Oratione*, c. 10, p. 133. " Nec ab ira solummodo, sed omni omnino confusione animi libera debet esse orationis intentio, de tali spiritu emissa, qualis est Spiritus, ad quem mittitur. Neque enim agnosci poterit a Spiritu Sancto spiritus inquinatus; aut tristis a læto, aut impeditus a libero."

ARTICLE 27—29.—Justin Martyr, *Dial.*, c. 71, p. 169. Καὶ ὅτι πολλὰς γραφὰς τέλεον περιεῖλον ἀπὸ τῶν ἐξηγήσεων τῶν γεγενημένων ὑπὸ τῶν παρὰ Πτολεμαίῳ γεγενημένων πρεσβυτέρων, ἐξ ὧν διαρρήδην οὗτος αὐτὸς ὁ σταυρωθεὶς ὅτι Θεὸς καὶ ἄνθρωπος καὶ σταυρούμενος καὶ ἀποθνήσκων κεκηρυγμένος ἀποδείκνυται, εἰδέναι ὑμᾶς βούλομαι.

Ib., c. 87, p. 184. Καὶ ὁμολογήσας ταῦτα ... εἰς Χριστὸν εἰρῆσθαι, καὶ Θεὸν αὐτὸν προϋπάρχοντα λέγεις, καὶ κατὰ τὴν βουλὴν τοῦ Θεοῦ σαρκοποιηθέντα αὐτὸν λέγεις διὰ τῆς παρθένου γεγεννῆσθαι ἄνθρωπον.

Tatian, *Orat. c. Græcos*, c. 21, p. 262. Οὐ γὰρ μωραίνομεν, οὐδὲ λήρους ἀπαγγέλλομεν, Θεὸν ἐν ἀνθρώπου μορφῇ γεγονέναι καταγγέλλοντες.

Irenæus, lib. i. c. 10, § 1, p. 48. Καὶ εἰς Πνεῦμα ἅγιον, τὸ διὰ τῶν προφητῶν κεκηρυχὸς τὰς οἰκονομίας, καὶ τὰς ἐλεύσεις, καὶ τὴν ἐκ παρθένου γέννησιν, καὶ τὸ πάθος, καὶ τὴν ἔγερσιν ἐκ νεκρῶν, καὶ τὴν ἔνσαρκον εἰς τοὺς οὐρανοὺς ἀνάληψιν τοῦ ἠγαπημένου Χριστοῦ Ἰησοῦ τοῦ Κυρίου ἡμῶν, καὶ τὴν ἐκ τῶν οὐρανῶν ἐν τῇ δόξῃ τοῦ πατρὸς παρουσίαν αὐτοῦ.

Clemens Alex., *Cohort. ad Gentes*, c. 1, p. 7. Νῦν δὴ ἀπεφάνη ἀνθρώποις αὐτὸς οὗτος ὁ Λόγος, ὁ μόνος ἄμφω, Θεός τε καὶ ἄνθρωπος.

Tertullian, *de Carne Christi*, c. 5, p. 310. "Non diceretur homo Christus sine carne; nec hominis filius, sine aliquo parente homine: sicut nec Deus sine Spiritu Dei; nec Dei filius sine Deo patre."

Hippolytus, *de Antichristo*, c. 4, vol. i. p. 6. Ὁ Λόγος τοῦ Θεοῦ, ἄσαρκος ὤν, ἐνεδύσατο τὴν ἁγίαν σάρκα ἐκ τῆς ἁγίας παρθένου, ὡς νυμφίος ἱμάτιον ἐξυφάνας ἑαυτῷ ἐν τῷ σταυρικῷ πάθει, ὅπως συγκεράσας τὸ θνητὸν ἡμῶν σῶμα τῇ ἑαυτοῦ δυνάμει, καὶ μίξας τῷ ἀφθάρτῳ τὸ φθαρτὸν καὶ τὸ ἀσθενὲς τῷ ἰσχυρῷ, σώσῃ τὸν ἀπολλύμενον ἄνθρωπον.

Origen, *c. Celsum*, lib. i. c. 60, vol. i. p. 375. Φέροντες μὲν δῶρα, ἃ (ἵν᾽ οὕτως ὀνομάσω) συνθέτῳ τινὶ ἐκ Θεοῦ καὶ ἀνθρώπου θνητοῦ προσήνεγκαν σύμβολα μὲν, ὡς βασιλεῖ τὸν χρυσὸν, ὡς δὲ τεθνηξομένῳ τὴν σμύρναν, ὡς δὲ Θεῷ τὸν λιβανωτόν.

Dionys. Alex., *c. Paul. Samos.*, p. 214. Τὸν φύσει Κύριον, καὶ Λόγον τοῦ Πατρὸς, δι᾽ οὗ τὰ πάντα ἐποίησεν ὁ Πατὴρ, καὶ ὁμοούσιον τῷ Πατρὶ εἰρημένον ὑπὸ τῶν ἁγίων πατέρων [g].

ARTICLE 30.—Ignatius, *Epist. ad Smyrn.*, c. 3, p. 452. Μετὰ δὲ τὴν ἀνάστασιν συνέφαγεν αὐτοῖς καὶ συνέπιεν ὡς σαρκικὸς, καίπερ πνευματικῶς ἡνωμένος τῷ Πατρί.

[g] This passage is remarkable, not only as containing the word ὁμοούσιος, but as shewing that even then it was no new word.

Melito, *de Incarnat. Christi*, p. 121. Θεὸς γὰρ ὢν ὁμοῦ τε καὶ ἄνθρωπος τέλειος ὁ αὐτὸς, τὰς δύο αὐτοῦ οὐσίας ἐπιστώσατο ἡμῖν· τὴν μὲν Θεότητα αὐτοῦ διὰ τῶν σημείων ἐν τῇ τριετίᾳ τῇ μετὰ τὸ βάπτισμα, τὴν δὲ ἀνθρωπότητα αὐτοῦ, ἐν τοῖς τριάκοντα χρόνοις τοῖς πρὸ τοῦ βαπτίσματος· ἐν οἷς διὰ τὸ ἀτελὲς τὸ κατὰ σάρκα ἀπεκρύβη τὰ σημεῖα τῆς αὐτοῦ Θεότητος· καίπερ Θεὸς ἀληθὴς προαιώνιος ὑπάρχων.

Irenæus, lib. iii. c. 21, § 3, p. 217. " Quod autem non consentiet nequitiæ, ut eligat bonum, proprium hoc est Dei, uti non per hoc, quod manducabit butyrum et mel, nude solummodo eum hominem intelligeremus, neque rursus per nomen Emmanuel sine carne eum Deum suspicaremur."

Hippolytus, *c. Beronem et Helicem*, c. 1, vol. i. p. 226. Θεὸν ἄπειρον ὁμοῦ καὶ περιγραπτὸν ἄνθρωπον ὄντα τε καὶ νοούμενον, τὴν οὐσίαν ἑκατέρου τελείως τελείαν ἔχοντα.

Origen, *c. Celsum*, lib. iii. c. 29, vol. i. p. 465. Περὶ δὲ τοῦ Ἰησοῦ εἴποιμεν ἂν, ἐπεὶ συμφέρον ἦν τῷ τῶν ἀνθρώπων γένει παραδέξασθαι αὐτὸν ὡς υἱὸν Θεοῦ, Θεὸν ἐληλυθότα ἐν ἀνθρωπίνῃ ψυχῇ καὶ σώματι.

Dionys. Alex., *de Martyris*, c. 9, p. 39. Τὸ μέντοι ἐξουσίαν ἔχω θεῖναι τὴν ψυχήν μου καὶ ἐξουσίαν ἔχω πάλιν λαβεῖν αὐτὴν, ἐν τούτοις δηλοῖ ἑκούσιον εἶναι τὸ πάθος· καὶ ἔτι, ὡς ἄλλη μὲν ἡ τιθεμένη καὶ λαμβανομένη ψυχὴ, ἄλλη δὲ ἡ τιθεῖσα καὶ λαμβάνουσα θεότης.

Methodius, *Sympos.*, Or. 3, p. 79. Τοῦτο γὰρ εἶναι τὸν Χριστὸν, ἄνθρωπον ἀκράτῳ θεότητι καὶ τελείᾳ πεπληρωμένον, καὶ Θεὸν ἐν ἀνθρώπῳ κεχωρημένον.

ARTICLE 32.—Ignatius, *ad Ephes.*, c. 7, p. 288. Εἷς ἰατρός ἐστιν, σαρκικός τε καὶ πνευματικὸς, γεννητὸς καὶ ἀγέννητος, ἐν σαρκὶ γενόμενος Θεὸς, ἐν ἀθανάτῳ ζωῇ ἀληθινῇ, καὶ ἐκ Μαρίας καὶ ἐκ Θεοῦ, πρῶτον παθητὸς καὶ τότε ἀπαθής.

Origen, c. *Celsum*, lib. vi. c. 47, vol. i. p. 669.

Οὐκ εἰσὶ δύο ἡ ψυχὴ τοῦ Ἰησοῦ πρὸς τὸν πάσης κτίσεως πρωτότοκον Θεὸν Λόγον.

ARTICLE 33.—Tertullian, *adv. Prax.*, c. 27, p. 516.

"De hoc quærendum, quomodo Sermo caro sit factus; utrumne quasi transfiguratus in carne, an indutus carnem? Immo indutus. Ceterum, Deum immutabilem et informabilem credi necesse est, ut æternum. Transfiguratio autem interemptio est pristini. Omne enim quodcunque transfiguratur in aliud, desinit esse quod fuerat, et incipit esse quod non erat. Deus autem neque desinit esse, neque aliud potest esse."

Origen, c. *Celsum*, lib. iii. c. 41, vol. i. p. 474.

Ὅμως δὲ ἴστωσαν οἱ ἐγκαλοῦντες, ὅτι ὃν μὲν νομίζομεν, καὶ πεπείσμεθα ἀρχῆθεν εἶναι Θεὸν καὶ Υἱὸν Θεοῦ, οὗτος ὁ αὐτολόγος ἐστὶ καὶ ἡ αὐτοσοφία καὶ ἡ αὐτοαλήθεια· τὸ δὲ θνητὸν αὐτοῦ σῶμα, καὶ τὴν ἀνθρωπίνην ἐν αὐτῷ ψυχήν, τῇ πρὸς ἐκεῖνον οὐ μόνον κοινωνίᾳ, ἀλλὰ καὶ ἑνώσει καὶ ἀνακράσει, τὰ μέγιστά φαμεν προσειληφέναι, καὶ τῆς ἐκείνου θεότητος κεκοινωνηκότα εἰς Θεὸν μεταβεβηκέναι.

ARTICLE 34.—Tertullian, *adv. Prax.*, c. 27, p. 516. "Quia neque Sermo aliud quam Deus, neque caro aliud quam homo.... Videmus duplicem statum non confusum, sed conjunctum in una persona, Deum et hominem Jesum."

ARTICLE 36.—Id., *de Anima*, c. 55, p. 304. "Christus Deus, quia et homo, mortuus secundum scripturas, et sepultus secus easdem, huic quoque legi satisfecit, forma humanæ mortis apud inferos functus; nec ante ascendit in sublimiora cœlorum, quam descendit in inferiora terrarum, ut illic patriarchas et prophetas compotes sui faceret."

ARTICLE 37.—Origen, *in Psalm.* xlvii. 6, vol. ii. p. 715.

Ὥσπερ ὁ Κύριος ἐλεύσεται ἐν φωνῇ ἀγγέλου, καὶ ἐν σάλπιγγι Θεοῦ καταβήσεται ἀπ' οὐρανοῦ, οὕτως ἀνέβη ὁ Θεὸς ἐν ἀλαλαγμῷ.

CHAPTER X.

A COMMENTARY ON THE ATHANASIAN CREED[a].

1. *WHOSOEVER will be saved, before all things it is necessary that he hold the Catholic Faith.*

By the words, *before all things,* is meant *in the first place.* Faith goes before practice; and is therefore first in order, though practice may be, comparatively, more considerable, and first in value, as the end is above the means.

2. *Which Faith except every one do keep whole[b] and undefiled, without doubt he shall perish everlastingly.*

Which Faith, that is, the Catholic Faith before spoken of, which is another name for the true and right faith, as taught in Scripture; called Catholic, or Universal, as

---

[a] In the Primer of 1539, and another of 1555, where the version is made from the Latin, and joined with the Popish Service of that time, the English title of the Creed was, "The Symbole or Crede of the great Doctour Athanasius, dayly red in the Church."
In King Edward's Prayer-book, A.D. 1549, it is barely intituled, "This Confession of our Christian Faith;" and it was ordered to be song or sayed upon six feasts in the year. At the revisal of the Common Prayer, in 1552, it was appointed to be used on several feasts in the year, the whole number thirteen. But the title still continued the same till the last review under Charles the Second, when were added thereto, "commonly called the Creed of St. Athanasius:" from which time the running title has been "St. Athanasius's Creed," as before *Quicunque vult,* in our Prayer-Books.

[b] In King Edward's Prayer-books, and so down to the year 1627, *holy* was read for what is now *whole;* which, I suppose, was intended for *wholly,* as one may reasonably imagine from Queen Elizabeth's of 1561, where it is *wholy,* and from the metrical version, which plainly meant *wholly,* by *holy,* answering to *undefiledly;* and it is certain that *holy* was the ancient spelling for what we now write *wholly.*

being held by the Universal Church of Christ, against which the gates of hell shall never prevail. The meaning, then, is, that every one is obliged, under pain of damnation, to preserve, as far as in him lies, the true and right Faith, in opposition to those that endeavour to corrupt it either by taking from it or adding to it. That men shall perish eternally for unbelief, for rejecting the Faith in the lump, cannot be doubted, when it is expressly said (Mark xvi. 16), "He that believeth not shall be damned." And as to rejecting any particular branch, or Article of it, it must of consequence be a sin against the whole; against truth, and peace, and therefore damnable in its own nature, as all wilful sins are without repentance. As to the allowances to be made for invincible ignorance, prejudice, or other unavoidable infirmities, as they will be pleadable in the case of any other sin, so may they, and will they also be pleadable in this; but it was foreign to the purpose of the Creed to take notice of it in this case particularly, when it is common to all cases of like nature, and is always supposed and understood, though not specially mentioned.

3. *And the Catholic faith is this; that we worship one God in Trinity, and Trinity in Unity.*

One of the principal branches of the Catholic Faith, and which is of nearest concernment (since our worship depends upon it, and the main body of the Christian religion is bound up in it), is the doctrine of a *Trinity in Unity*, of three Persons and one God, recommended in our baptism as the object of our faith, hope, and worship. He that takes upon him to corrupt or deprave this most fundamental part of a Christian's

P

faith cannot be innocent, it being his bounden duty to maintain and preserve it, as he will answer it another day.

4. *Neither confounding the Persons, nor dividing the substance.*

Here would be no need of these particular cautions, or critical terms, in relation to this point, had men been content with the plain primitive faith in its native simplicity. But as there have been a set of men, called Sabellians, who have erroneously taught that the Father, Son, and Holy Ghost are all one Person, who was incarnate, and suffered, and rose again,—making the Father (and Holy Ghost) to have suffered, as well as the Son (from thence called Patripassians)—hence it becomes necessary to caution every pious Christian against *confounding* the persons as those men have done: and as there have been others, particularly the Arians, who have pretended, very falsely, that the three Persons are three substances, and of different kinds, divided from each other, one being before the other, existing when the other two were not, as also being present where the other two are not present; these false and dangerous tenets having been spread abroad, it is become necessary to give a caution against *dividing the substance*, as these have done, very much to the detriment of sobriety and truth.

5. *For there is one Person of the Father, another of the Son, and another of the Holy Ghost.*

The Sabellians, therefore, were extremely to blame in confounding the Persons, and running them into one, taking away the distinction of Persons plainly taught in Scripture.

6. *But the Godhead of the Father, of the Son, and of the Holy Ghost is all one, the glory equal, the majesty coeternal.*

The Arians, therefore, were equally to blame for *dividing* the *substance* and *Godhead* in the manner before hinted. To be a little more particular on this head, we may go on to open and explain this Unity of Godhead, equality of glory, and coeternity of majesty.

7. *Such as the Father is, such is the Son, and such is the Holy Ghost.*

That is, as to their substance and Godhead, there is no difference or inequality amongst them, though there is a difference in respect of some personal acts and properties, as shall be observed in its place. In real dignity and perfection they are equal and undivided, as in the instances here following.

8. *The Father uncreate, the Son uncreate, and the Holy Ghost uncreate.*

These three Persons were never brought into being by the will of another; they are no creatures, nor changeable, as creatures are; they are all infinitely removed from dependence or precarious existence, one as much as another, and every one as much as any one. They exist in the highest and most emphatical sense of existing, which is called necessary existence, opposed to contingent or precarious existence. In a word, every person must, and cannot but exist; and all must exist together, having the same unchangeable perfections.

9. *The Father incomprehensible, the Son incomprehensible, and the Holy Ghost incomprehensible.*

These words are not a just translation of the Latin

original, though containing as true and just a proposition as the Latin words do. *Immensus* signifies *omnipresent*, rather than *incomprehensible*, in the modern sense of incomprehensible. But if by *incomprehensible* be understood, not to be comprehended within any bounds, it will then answer to the Latin pretty nearly. The translator here followed the Greek copy[c], taking perhaps the Creed to be the original language wherein the Greek was written. However, some Latins have understood by *immensus*, *incomprehensible*[d], in such a sense as has been hinted.

10. *The Father eternal, the Son eternal, and the Holy Ghost eternal.*

None of the Persons ever began to be, nor shall ever cease to be; they always were, they always will be, and must be; the same yesterday, to-day, and for ever.

11. *And yet they are not three Eternals, but one Eternal.*

Some account ought to be given of this manner of speaking, because it often occurs in the Creed, and may be thought most apt to offend the malicious, or to mis-

[c] There are two printed Greek copies, which read ἀκατάληπτος. Stephens's, first printed by Bryling, and Baifius's, first printed by Genebrard: which two copies are in the main one. Our translators, in 1548, could have seen none but Bryling's, that is, Stephens's copy. The Constantinopolitan copy, published by Genebrard, reads ἄπειρος; the Palatine copy, by Felckman ἄμετρος. The Saxon, French, and old English versions, exactly follow the Latin original. As does also the Primer of 1539, set forth by John Hilsey, Bishop of Rochester; and the other later one of 1555 by Cardinal Pole. The first has *immeasurable* (where we have *incomprehensible*), the other has *without measure*.

[d] "Immensus Pater: non mole, sed potestate omnia concludente. Vel immensus, id est, incomprehensibilis."—Abælard, *in Symb. Athanas.*, p. 382. (The page is numbered 368 by mistake, but it should be 382).

lead the unwary. The way of speaking came in a little after the middle of the fourth century, and then only into the Latin Church; for the Greeks never used it, but taught the same things under a different form of expression. What Greeks and Latins both intended was, that as the three Persons are one substance and one God, so every Divine perfection and every substantial attribute belonging to any one person is common to all; and there is nothing peculiar to any one but the Divine relations. To the Father, paternity and whatever it implies or carries with it; to the Son, filiation; to the Holy Ghost, procession. In this account, eternity, immensity, omnipotence, and the like, being substantial attributes, are common to all the Three Persons; who have therefore one eternity, one immensity, one omnipotence, and so on, as one substance and one Godhead. Thus far Greeks and Latins agreed both in doctrine and expression. But the Latins, building hereupon, thought it very allowable to go a little farther (which the Greeks did not), and to express the same thing by saying of the three Persons, that they are one eternal, one immense, one omnipotent, one holy, one uncreated, &c. And this was the current language at the making, and before the making, of this Creed. The Arians were the sole occasion of introducing both kinds of expression, which must therefore be interpreted accordingly. Two things were designed by them: one, to obviate the Arian tenet, that the three Persons were differing in kind and in degree, as being of unequal perfections; the other to obviate the Arian charge, or calumny, upon the Church as making three Gods. In regard to the former, when the Catholics speak of one

Divinity, they intend equal Divinity, not Divinities differing in kind or degree; and in regard to the latter, they further mean undivided and inseparable Divinity, not many Divinities. The true meaning, then, and the full meaning of the expressions of the Creed will be very clear and obvious. The three Persons are equal in duration, and undivided too; one Eternity (one, because undivided and inseparable) is common to all, and therefore they are not *three Eternals*, but *one Eternal*.

The oldest writers who have used this way of expression are, so far as I have observed, Ambrose, Faustinus, and Austin; and their meaning in it is very plain and certain, from the places themselves where they make use of it. Fulgentius, who came not long after them, sometimes falls into the same manner of expression[e]; but sparingly, as if he either did not fully attend to it, or had some scruple about it; for his general way is to say, *not three eternal Gods, but one eternal God*[f], instead of the other in the Creed, and so

[e] "Relativa nomina Trinitatem faciunt, essentialia vero nullo modo triplicantur. Deus Pater, Deus Filius, Deus Spiritus Sanctus. Bonus Pater, bonus Filius, bonus Spiritus Sanctus. Pius Pater, pius Filius, pius Spiritus Sanctus. Justus Pater, justus Filius, justus et Spiritus Sanctus. Omnipotens Pater, omnipotens Filius, omnipotens et Spiritus Sanctus. Et tamen non dicimus nec Tres Deos, nec Tres bonos, nec Tres pios, nec Tres justos, nec Tres omnipotentes, sed unum Deum, bonum, pium, justum, omnipotentem, Patrem et Filium et Spiritum sanctum."—Fulgent., *de Trin.*, c. 2, p. 330.

[f] ".Eternus est sine initio Pater, æternus est sine initio Filius, æternus est sine initio Spiritus Sanctus: nec tamen tres Dii æterni sed unus æternus Deus."—Fulgent., *ad Ferrand.*, Epist. 14, § 6, p. 232.

"Immensus est Pater, sed immensus est Filius, et immensus est et Spiritus Sanctus: nec tamen tres Dii immensi, sed unus Deus immensus."—Fulgent., *ib.*

"Omnipotens Pater; Omnipotens Filius, omnipotens Spiritus Sanctus; nec tamen tres Dii omnipotentes, sed unus Deus omnipotens est Pater, et Filius, et Spiritus Sanctus."—Fulgent., *ib.*

in the like cases. Which, indeed, is a very insipid and dull way of expressing it, and if applied to every Article in the Athanasian Creed, would make it a very flat composition in comparison to what it is. It is true, that all at length resolves into this, that the three Persons are *not three Gods*, but *one God*. This is the ground and foundation, and the other is the superstructure. But then it is a fine and elegant, as well as a solid superstructure; improving the thought, and carrying on a train of new and distinct propositions, and not merely a jejune and sapless repetition of the same thing.

12. *As also there are not three Incomprehensibles, nor three Uncreated; but one Uncreated, and one Incomprehensible* ^g.

Not three Incomprehensibles, &c., as not differing either in kind or degree of incomprehensibility, nor yet divided in those perfections; but one Incomprehensible, and one Uncreated, one as to the kind and degree of those attributes or perfections; and one in number, too, as much as union and inseparability, infinitely close and perfect, can be conceived to make, or do really make one.

13. *So likewise the Father is Almighty, the Son Almighty, and the Holy Ghost Almighty.*

Equally Almighty every one, without any difference or inequality in kind or degree.

^g Here, again, one may perceive what copy our translators followed, namely, Bryling's Greek copy. All the other copies, Greek and Latin, place the words in a different order: "Not three uncreated, nor three incomprehensibles, but one uncreated," &c. Only the Ambrosian Latin copy reads, "Not three uncreated, nor three incomprehensibles (immense) but one incomprehensible (immense) and one uncreated."

14. *And yet they are not three Almighties, but one Almighty.*

One Omnipotence, or Almightiness, is common to all three: one in kind as being of equal extent, and equally reaching over all; and one also in number, because of the inseparable union among the three, in the inward perfection, and outward exercise, or operation.

15. *So the Father is God, the Son is God, and the Holy Ghost is God.*

The whole three Persons equally Divine, and enjoying every perfection belonging to the Godhead.

16. *And yet they are not three Gods, but one God.*

Because the Godhead or Divinity which belongs to one, belongs to all: the same in kind because of the equality, and the same in number because inseparably one.

17. *So likewise the Father is Lord, the Son Lord, and the Holy Ghost Lord.*

Having the same right of dominion, and of equal dominion; and equally exercising it when and where they please.

18. *And yet not three Lords, but one Lord.*

Because one dominion is common to all three, jointly possessing, and jointly exercising every branch of it; undividedly, and inseparably bearing supreme rule over all.

19. *For, like as we are compelled by the Christian verity to acknowledge every Person by Himself to be God and Lord; so are we forbidden by the Catholic religion to say, There be three Gods, or three Lords.*

That is to say, the whole foundation of what hath been before taught rests upon this, that the same Christian *verity*, or *truth*, laid down in Scripture, obliges us to acknowledge every Person distinctly considered to be *God* and *Lord;* and at the same time to reject the notion of *three Gods* or *three Lords:* which being so, all that has been here taught must, of course, be admitted as true, right, and just. And now, having considered the equality and union of the three sacred Persons, it may next be proper to consider their distinction, as it is set forth to us in Scripture by the several personal characters belonging to the Father, Son, and Holy Ghost.

20. *The Father is made of none, neither created nor begotten.*

Were I at liberty to make conjectural emendations, I would here read, *Pater a nullo est: neque factus, nec &c. The Father is of none: neither made, nor created, &c.* And thus the next Article (*The Son is of the Father* alone) would better answer, and the whole would be more elegant. But having met with no copy[b] to countenance such a correction, I must not pretend to it, lest it should appear like correcting the author. However, the sense is very plain and obvious. All the three negatives here predicated of the Father amount to this one, that He is absolutely of none. This is His peculiar property, His distinguishing cha-

[b] Lazarus Baifius's copy, in Genebrard, reads, ὁ πατὴρ ἀπ' οὐδενός ἐστι. But then it entirely omits ποιητὸς, which, as is plain from what follows in the Creed, ought not to be omitted. Had the copy run thus, ἀπ' οὐδενός ἐστι. οὔτε μὴν ποιητὸς. οὔτε κτιστὸς, &c., it would have answered my meaning. Indeed, the first Greek copy in Labbe's Councils (vol. ii. p. 601), and third in Montfaucon, run in such a way as I suppose: but then I take them to have been patched up from several distinct copies, at the pleasure of the editor or editors; and none of the Latin copies will warrant such a reading.

racter, to be first in order, and the Head of everything; to whom even the Son and Holy Ghost are referred, but diversely and in different manner.

21. *The Son is of the Father alone; not made, nor created, but begotten.*

The Son is here said to be of the Father alone, in contradistinction to the Holy Ghost, to be named after, who is not of the Father *alone*, but of *both*. The Greeks that struck out the words, *and of the Son*, below, and left the word *alone* here, were not aware of it. This conduct of theirs betrayed a shortness of thought, and at the same time served to shew that the Latins had not been interpolators of the Creed, but that the Greeks had been curtailers. It must, however, be owned, that the Greeks who drew up that form, which Bishop Usher printed from Junius, were wise enough to observe how this matter stood, and therefore struck out the word *alone* here, as well as *and of the Son* below.

22. *The Holy Ghost is of the Father, and of the Son; neither made, nor created, nor begotten, but proceeding.*

The peculiar and distinguishing character of the Holy Ghost is to *proceed*, and to proceed both from *Father and Son*. Indeed, the Son and Holy Ghost are both *of the Father*, but in a different manner, to us inexplicable; one by the way of generation, the other by procession, though the word Procession, in a lax sense, has been sometimes applied to either. However, to proceed *from the Father* and *the Son*, or, as the Greeks will needlessly cavil, *from the Father* by *the Son;* that is peculiar to the Holy Ghost. The Greeks and Latins have had many and tedious disputes about the Procession. One thing is observable, that though the ancients, appealed to by both parties, have often said that the Holy Ghost proceeds *from the Father*, without mentioning the *Son*, yet they never said that He proceeded from the Father *alone;* so that the modern Greeks have certainly innovated in that Article, in expression at least, if not in real sense and meaning. As to the Latins, they have this to plead, that none of the ancients ever condemned their doctrine; that many of them have expressly asserted it; that the Oriental Churches themselves rather condemn their taking upon them to add anything to a Creed formed in a general Council than the doctrine itself; that those Greek Churches that charge their doctrine as heresy, yet are forced to admit much the same thing, only in different words; and that Scripture itself is plain that the Holy Ghost proceeds at least by the Son, if not from Him, which yet amounts to the same thing.

I should here observe, that some time before the compiling of this Creed, the usual Catholic way of speaking of the Holy Ghost was to say, that He was *nec genitus, nec ingenitus*, neither *begotten* nor *unbegotten*, while this Creed, by barely denying Him to be *begotten*, seems to leave room to think that He is *unbegotten*. This raised a scruple in the minds of some here in England, concerning that part of the Creed, above 700 years ago, as we learn from Abbo Floriacensis of that time. For Gregory's *Synodicon* admitted here, as well as this Creed, had the very expression concerning the Holy Ghost, *nec ingenitus, nec genitus*. It might have been easy to end the dispute, only by distinguishing upon the equivocal meaning of the word *ingenitus*. It had been taken from the Greek, ἀγένητος, which signified not barely *unbegotten*, but absolutely *underived*: in this sense the Holy Ghost could not be said to be *ingenitus*. But if it barely means *not begotten*, it may be applied to Him, as it is in the Creed. The whole difficulty then arose only from the scantiness of the Latin tongue, in not affording a single word which should fully express the Greek ἀγένητος, "unoriginate." *Ingenitus* might tolerably do it; but the word was more commonly taken in a narrower construction. Peter Abelard has hit off the whole difficulty very clearly; whose words, therefore, I have thrown into the margin[1].

23. *So there is one Father, not three Fathers; one Son, not three Sons; one Holy Ghost, not three Holy Ghosts.*

Whether this paragraph be borrowed from St. Austin, or from an elder writer under the name of Ignatius, I know not. The foundation of it was laid in 1 Cor. viii. 6, *one God the Father*, and *one Lord Jesus Christ;* to which it was usual to add, after reciting it, *and one Holy Ghost*, to complete the whole number of the Divine Persons. The intent and purport of the words in this Creed is to set forth the distinction of the three Persons and their several offices and characters; that there is *one Father*, and that He alone is *unoriginate*, is First

[1] "Solum itaque Patrem ingenitum dicimus, hoc est, a seipso non ab alio: unde Augustinus adversus Felicianum Arrianum; Patrem ingenitum dico, quia non processit ab altero... Aliud itaque dicere est Patrem ingenitum, aliud non genitum... Spiritus vero Sanctus ipse quoque est non genitus... Nec tamen ideo est ingenitus, cum ipse ab alio sit, tam a Patre scilicet quam a Filio procedens. Solus itaque Pater ingenitus dicitur, sicut solus Filius genitus: Spiritus vero Sanctus nec genitus est, nec ingenitus, sed, ut dictum est, non genitus."—Abælard., *Introd. ad Theolog.*, lib. i. c. 6, p. 983.

Person, is Head, &c., and neither the Son nor Holy Ghost have any share in these titles or characters to make three Unoriginates, three Heads, &c. That there is *one Son,* and He alone *begotten,* and afterwards *incarnate,* &c., which characters and offices belong not to the other two, but are distinct and appropriate to one. And there is *one Holy Ghost,* whose character is to *proceed,* and whose office is to sanctify, which character and office are not to be ascribed in the same sense to the other two; for that would be confounding the personal characters and offices, and making *three Holy Ghosts* instead of one.

24. *And in this Trinity, none is afore or after other, none is greater or less than another; but the whole three Persons are coeternal together and coequal.*

The compiler of the Creed now returns to the equality and unity of the Persons; that he may at length sum and throw into a short compass what he had said upon the Trinity before he should pass on to the other great Article, the Incarnation. When it is said, *none is afore or after other,* we are not to understand it of order; for the Father is first, the Son second, and the Holy Ghost third in order. Neither are we to understand it of office; for the Father is supreme in office, while the Son and Holy Ghost condescend to inferior offices. But we are to understand it, as the Creed itself explains it, of duration, and of dignity; in which respect none is *afore or after,* none *greater* or *less,* but the whole *three Persons coeternal* and *coequal.*

25. *So that in all things, as is aforesaid, the Unity in Trinity, and the Trinity in Unity is to be worshipped.*

In all things (per omnia) as is aforesaid. One of the

Greek copies tacks these words to the former Article, making them run thus: *coequal in all things, as aforesaid*. Another Greek copy reads them thus: *coequal in all things; so that in all things, as is now said*, &c. Both interpret the *all things* of the coequality in *all things*. And, indeed, Venantius Fortunatus, in his Comment, long before, seems to have understood, *per omnia*, in the same way, to signify that the Son is what the Father is, in all essential or substantial perfections. And it is favoured both by what goes before and after; for, from speaking of the *coeternity* and *coequality*, the author proceeds to say, *so that* in all things, as aforesaid, *the Unity in Trinity, and the Trinity in Unity is to be worshipped*; namely, on account of their perfect coeternity and coequality: to which he subjoins, *He therefore that will be saved, &c.* Wherefore I incline to the moderate opinion of those who think that the author here does not lay the stress upon every little nicety of explication [k] before given, but upon the main doctrine of a coequal and coeternal Trinity; which is the very construction given by Hincmar 900 years ago, or nearly [l]. And Wickliff's comment upon the same

[k] Le Quien's ingenious and handsome reflection upon the conduct of Pope Gregory the Ninth's legates, may deserve a recital here:—
"Quamquam non possum quin ingenue fatear Nuncios Apostolicos consultius facturos fuisse, si ab ejusmodi sententia pronuntianda sibi temperassent; *Qui credit Spiritum Sanctum non procedere ex Filio, in via perditionis est:* tunc quippe temporis Ecclesia Catholica in nulla Synodo Generali hoc de capite judicium definitorium tulerat."—Panopl., contr. Schism. Græcor., sæc. xiii. c. 1, § 23, p. 360.

[l] "Et in hac Trinitate nihil est prius, nihil posterius; nihil majus, aut minus; sed totæ tres Personæ coæternæ sibi sunt et coæquales: ita ut per omnia, et unitas Deitatis in Trinitate Personarum, et Trinitas Personarum in unitate Deitatis veneranda est."
—Hincm., *de non Trina Deitate*, vol. i. c. 17, p. 540.

passage, when put into a modern dress, may appear not contemptible: "And so we conclude here, as is before said, that there is both an Unity of Godhead, and a Trinity of Persons; and that the Trinity in this Unity is to be worshipped above all things; and whosoever will be saved must thus think of the Trinity, if not thus explicitly (or in every particular), yet thus in the general, or implicitly."

26. *He therefore that will be saved, must thus think of the Trinity.*

Thus, as consisting of three Persons, coeternal and coequal, and all one God; distinct enough to be three, united enough to be one; distinct without division, united without confusion.

27. *Furthermore, it is necessary to everlasting salvation, that he also believe rightly* [m] *the Incarnation of our Lord Jesus Christ.*

Much depends upon our having true and just sentiments of the *Incarnation*, in which the whole œconomy of our salvation is nearly concerned. To corrupt and deprave this doctrine is to defeat and frustrate, in a great measure, the Gospel of Christ, which bringeth salvation: wherefore it is of great moment, of everlasting concernment to us, not to be guilty of doing it ourselves, nor to take part with those that do.

28. *For the right faith is, that we believe and confess that our Lord Jesus Christ, the Son of God, is God and Man.*

There have been heretics who would not allow that our Saviour Christ was Man, but in such a sense as

---

[m] Ὀρθῶς πιστεύσῃ. So Bryling's Greek copy. The Latin copies have, *Fideliter credat.* Some Greek copies read, πιστῶς, or βεβαίως, though two, besides Bryling's, have also ὀρθῶς.

a shadow, or a picture of a man, may be called a man; and there have been others who would not allow that Christ is God but in such a sense as any creature whatever might be called, or may be made a God. But all good Christians have ever abhorred those vile tenets, and conformably to Scripture, rightly and justly interpreted, have believed and confessed that Christ is both really God and really Man, one God-man.

29. *God, of the substance of the Father, begotten before the worlds; and Man, of the substance of His Mother, born in the world.*

We are forced to be thus particular and expressive in the wording of this Article, because of the many wiles, equivocations, and disguises of those who endeavour to corrupt the faith. The Arians make of Christ a created God, and call Him God on account only of His office, and not of His nature or unchangeable substance. For this reason, we are obliged to be particular in expressing His *substance*, as being not frail, mutable, perishing, as the substance of creatures is, but eternal and unchangeable, and all one with the Father's. On the other hand, the Apollinarians and other heretics have pretended either that Christ had no human body at all, or that He brought it with Him from heaven, and took it not of the Virgin-Mother. We are therefore forced to be particular in this profession, that He was Man *of the substance of His Mother:* which, though it be not taught in express words, yet is very plainly the sense and meaning of Holy Scripture on this Article; and was never questioned till conceited men came to pervert the true doctrine of Sacred Writ by false glosses and comments of their own.

30. *Perfect God and perfect Man; of a reasonable soul and human flesh subsisting.*

Here, again, the perverseness of heretics has made it necessary to guard the Faith by strong and expressive words that cannot easily be eluded. Christ is *perfect God*, not such a nominal imperfect God as Arians and Photinians pretend. He is, moreover, *perfect Man*, which it is necessary to insist upon against the Apollinarians, who pretended that He had a human body only, without any rational soul, imagining the Logos to have supplied the place of the rational or *reasonable* soul: whereas, in reality, He had both *soul* and *body*, as all men have, and was therefore *perfect Man*.

31. *Equal to the Father, as touching His Godhead: and inferior to the Father, as touching His Manhood.*

Which needs no comment.

32. *Who, although He be God and Man, yet He is not two, but one Christ.*

This is said to guard against calumny and misconstruction; for, because the Church asserted two natures in Christ, whereby He is both *perfect God* and *perfect Man*, the Apollinarians, having an hypothesis of their own to serve, pretended that this was making two Christs, a Divine Christ, as to one nature, and a human Christ in the other: which was a vain thought, since both the natures joined in the one *God-man* make still but *one Christ*, both God and man.

33. *One, not by conversion of the Godhead into flesh, but by taking of the manhood into God.*

The Apollinarian way of making one Christ, by confounding the two natures in one, and by subjecting the Godhead to change, is here condemned. There is no need of running these injudicious and absurd lengths for solving the difficulty how the two natures make one Christ: He did not change His Divine nature, or convert it into flesh, though He be said to have been *made flesh;* He took flesh upon Him, He assumed human nature, took man into an union with God, and thus was He *one Christ.*

34. *One altogether, not by confusion of substance, but by unity of Person.*

We are thus forced to distinguish with the utmost nicety and accuracy, to obviate the cavils and pretences of heretics. Christ, then, is *one altogether,* entirely one, though his two natures remain distinct. He is not one by confounding or mingling two natures or substances into one nature or substance (as the Apollinarians pretended), but by uniting them both in *one person;* one I, one He, one Christ, as Scripture everywhere represents.

35. *For as the reasonable soul and flesh is one Man; so God and Man is one Christ.*

That is to say, there are two very distinct and different substances in man, a body and a soul: one material, the other immaterial; one mortal, the other immortal; and both these substances, nevertheless, make up but *one man.* Not by confounding or mingling those two different substances (for they are entirely distinct and different, and will ever remain so), but by uniting them in *one Person.* Even so may the two distinct natures, Divine and human, in Christ make *one person;* and this is really and truly the case in fact.

36. *Who suffered for our salvation, descended into Hell, rose again the third day from the dead.*

The author, having finished his explication of the great Article of *God incarnate*, now goes on to other parts of the Creed, such as were commonly inserted in the Creeds before. The Article of *The Descent into Hell* had not, indeed, at this time come into the Roman, otherwise called the Apostles' Creed; but it had been inserted in the Creed of Aquileia, and had been all along the standing doctrine of the Church. I shall leave it, as our Church has left it, without any particular interpretation, referring the reader to those who have commented on the Apostles' Creed, and particularly to the much-admired author of the history of it, who hath exhausted the subject.

37. *He ascended into Heaven, He sitteth on the right hand of the Father, God Almighty, from whence He shall come to judge the quick and the dead.*

These are all so many Articles of the Roman Creed, and probably taken from it; excepting only that the words, *God Almighty*, appear not in the most ancient manuscripts; and, very probably, were not originally in this Creed any more than in the ancient Roman.

38. *At whose coming all men shall rise again with their bodies, and shall give account for their own works.*

Here are two very expressive phrases, *all men*, all that have died, or shall die, to obviate the false opinion of a partial resurrection; and *with their bodies*, to obviate the notion of those who either thought that the soul only should continue for ever, while the body should be left to perish, or that the resurrection-body should be quite of another matter, form, or kind, than what our bodies are here. I have hinted, in my Latin notes above, that some words are wanting in the Ambrosian manuscript; and I may here observe farther, that in the words of the Creed, as they commonly run, there is not all the accuracy that might have been; for *all men* shall not rise, but only all that *die*. However, it seems that about that time there was some variety of sentiments in respect of that Article, as we may learn from Gennadius[n]; which was owing to the different reading of 1 Cor. xv. 51, from whence, probably, arose some variation in the copies of this Creed. See Pearson on the Apostles' Creed, Article 7, p. 532.

39. *And they that have done good shall go into life everlasting, and they that have done evil into everlasting fire.*

This is the express doctrine of Scripture, and appears almost in the same words, John v. 28, Matt. xxv. 46, to say nothing of many other texts to the same effect. Yet this Article, or rather these two Articles, had not gained admittance into the Apostles' Creed so early as the fourth century, the latter of them not at all. But, I suppose, the opinion said to have been started by Origen, that wicked men, and even devils, after a certain revolution, should have their release and

[n] "Omnium hominum erit resurrectio: si omnium erit, ergo omnes moriuntur, ut mors ab Adam ducta omnibus filiis ejus dominetur, et maneat illud privilegium in Domino, quod de eo specialiter dicitur: non dabis Sanctum tuum videre corruptionem. .... Hanc rationem, maxima patrum turba tridente, suscepimus. Verum qui sunt et alii, æque Catholici et eruditi viri, qui credunt, anima in corpore manente, mutandos ad incorruptionem et immortalitatem eos qui in Adventu Domini vivi invenicndi sunt, et hoc eis reputari pro resurrectione ex mortuis, quod mortalitatem immutatione deponant, non morte; quolibet quis a quiescat modo, non est hæreticus, nisi ex contentione hæreticus fiat. Sufficit enim in Ecclesiæ lege, carnis resurrectionem credere futuram de morte."
—Gennad., *Eccles. Dogm.*, c. 7, pp. 76, 77.

restoration, might make it the more necessary, or convenient at least, to insert these Articles in the Creeds, and to express the punishment of the damned by the words *eternal fire:* for the Origenists, at that time, denied both the eternity of the fire and also its reality, as appears from Orosius in St. Austin °.

40. *This is the Catholic Faith, which except a man believe faithfully*ᴾ, *he cannot be saved.*

This is to be understood, like all other such general propositions, with proper reserves and qualifying constructions. As, for instance, if, after laying down a system of Christian morality, it be said, *This is the Christian practice, which except a man faithfully observe and follow, he cannot be saved,* it would be no more than right and just thus to say: But no one could be supposed hereby to exclude any such merciful abatements or allowances as shall be made for men's particular circumstances, weaknesses, frailties, ignorance, inability, or the like; or for their sincere intentions, and honest desires of knowing and doing the whole will of God; accompanied with a general repentance of their sins, and a firm reliance upon God's mercy, through the sole merits of Christ Jesus. There can be no doubt, however, but that men are accountable for their Faith, as

---

° " Ignem sane æternum, quo peccatores puniantur, neque esse ignem verum, neque æternum prædicaverunt, dicentes dictum esse ignem propriæ conscientiæ punitionem, æternum autem, juxta etymologiam Græcam, non esse perpetuum," &c.—Epist. Orosii ad Augusl., in August., vol. viii. p. 609.

ᴾ Πιστῶς πιστε ση. So Bryling's copy, which our translators followed.

The Latin copies have, "fideliter, firmiterque crediderit." And the other Greek copies, Πιστῶς τε καὶ βεβαίως πιστεύσῃ. Or, ἐκ πίστεως βεβαίως πιστεύσῃ.

well as for their practice; and especially if they take upon them to instruct and direct others, trusting to their own strength and parts, against the united judgment and verdict of whole Churches, ancient and modern.

CHAPTER XI.

THE CHURCH OF ENGLAND VINDICATED, BOTH AS TO THE RECEIVING AND RETAINING THE ATHANASIAN CREED.

THERE would be no occasion for this chapter, had not a late Author[a] of name and character, out of his abundant zeal to promote Arianism, taken upon him to disparage this excellent form of Faith; nay, and to apply, with some earnestness, to the governors of our Church to get it laid aside. He thinks " it may well deserve the most serious and deliberate consideration of the governors of the Church, whether it would not be more advantageous to the true interest of the Christian religion to retain only those more indisputable forms[a];" that is, to have this wholly taken away, or at least not imposed in our Articles or Liturgy. Then he subjoins his reasons: which, because they may be presumed to be the closest and strongest that can be offered on that side, and because they have hitherto stood without any particular confutation on one hand, or retractation on the other, I shall here take upon me to answer them as briefly as may be.

OBJECTION I.

The first is, that this Creed is confessed not to be Athanasius's, but the composition of an uncertain obscure author, written in one of the darkest and most ignorant ages of the Church, having never appeared till

[a] Clarke's Script. Doctr., first edit., pp. 446, 447.

about the year 800, nor been received in the Church till so very late as about the year 1000.

Answ. As to the false facts contained in this Article, I need only refer to the preceding sheets. As to the Creed being none of Athanasius's, which is certainly true, it is to be considered that our Church receives it not upon the authority of its compiler, nor determines anything about its age or author; but we receive it because the truth of the doctrines contained in it may be proved by most certain warrants of Holy Scripture, as is expressly said in our Eighth Article. I may add, that the early and general reception of this Creed by Greeks and Latins, by all the Western Churches, not only before, but since the Reformation, must needs give it a much greater authority and weight than the single name of Athanasius could do, were it ever so justly to be set to it. Athanasius has left some Creeds and Confessions, undoubtedly his, which yet never have obtained the esteem and reputation that this hath done: because none of them are really of the same intrinsic value, nor capable of doing the like service in the Christian Churches. The use of it is, to be a standing fence and preservative against the wiles and equivocations of most kinds of heretics. This was well understood by Luther, when he called it "a bulwark to the Apostles' Creed[b];" much to the same purpose with what has been above cited from Ludolphus Saxo[c]. And it

[b] "Athanasii scilicet Symbolum est paulo prolixius, et ad confutandos Arianos hæreticos, aliquanto uberius declarat, et illustrat Articulum alterum de Divinitate Christi Jesu . . . estque hoc velut propugnaculum primi illius Apostolici Symboli."—Luther., *de Trib. Symbol.*, vol. vii. p. 139.

[c] Thus also Alexander of Hales, 100 years before Ludolphus. "Causa multiplicationis Symbolorum fuit triplex: Instructio Fidei,

was this and the like considerations that have all along made it be of such high esteem among all the Reformed Churches, from the days of their great leader.

OBJECTION II.

The second reason assigned for laying this form aside is, that it is so worded as that many of the common people cannot but be too apt to understand it in a sense favouring either Sabellianism or Tritheism.

Answ. This objection is not particularly levelled against this Creed, but against all Creeds containing the doctrine of a Coeternal Trinity in Unity. It is therefore an objection rather against the Faith of the Church (which those gentlemen endeavour constantly to run down, under the notion of Sabellianism, or Tritheism), than against this particular form of expressing it.

I may further add, that the common people will be in no danger of running either into Sabellianism or Tritheism if they attend to the Creed itself (which fully obviates and confutes both those heresies), instead of listening to those who first industriously labour to deceive them into a false construction of the Creed, and then complain of the common people's being too apt to misunderstand it. This is not ingenuous, nor upright dealing with the common people.

OBJECTION III.

A third reason is, that there are in this Creed many phrases which . . . may seem to give unbelievers a need-

veritatis explanatio, erroris exclusio. . . . Erroris exclusio, propter hæreses multiplices pullulantes, causa fuit Symboli Athanasii, quod cantatur in prima."—Alexand. Alens., Part iii., q. 82; Membr. 2, vol. i p. 279, (p. 541); Johan. Januensis in his *Catholicon* (An. 1286), under *Symbolum*, says the same thing. (See above, p. 37.)

less advantage of objecting against religion; and among believers themselves cannot but to the vulgar have too much the appearance of contradictions; and sometimes (especially the damnatory clauses) have given offence to the piousest and most learned men, insomuch as to have been the principal reason of Mr. Chillingworth's refusing to subscribe the XXXIX. Articles.

Answ. As to unbelievers, and their objections, the Church has been always able and willing to answer them; sorry at the same time to find, that any who call themselves Christians should join with the unbelievers in the same trifling objections, thereby giving the unbelievers a very needless advantage and the most pernicious encouragement. As to vulgar believers, they suspect no contradictions, till some, who think themselves above the vulgar, labour to create such a suspicion in them. Leave the vulgar to their better guides and their true orthodox pastors, without endeavouring to corrupt or seduce them, and then all will be safe and easy.

As to Mr. Chillingworth, he had for a while, it is owned, some scruples upon him about the Fourth Commandment as appertaining to Christians, and about the damnatory clauses in the Athanasian Creed, and therefore refused to subscribe for a time. This was in the year 1635. But within three years after, upon more mature consideration, he happily got over his difficulties, and subscribed, July the 20th, in the year 1638, as stands upon record in the office of Sarum, where he was instituted Chancellor of the Church[d].

[d] "Ego Gulielmus Chillingworth, Clericus, in Artibus Magister, ad Cancellariatum Ecclesiæ Cathedralis Beatæ Mariæ Sarum, una

OBJECTION IV.

A fourth reason offered, not for laying aside this Creed, I suppose, but for the governors taking it into consideration, is, that the Preface to the Book of Common Prayer declares that particular forms of Divine Worship, and rites and ceremonies appointed to be used therein, being things in their own nature indifferent and alterable, may, upon the various exigency of times and occasions, be changed or altered.

ANSW. No doubt but the Church may, if it be thought proper or expedient, throw out all the Creeds out of her daily service, or Articles, and retain one only, in the office of Baptism, as formerly. But, I suppose, the authors of the Preface to the Book of Common Prayer had no thought of excluding any of the three Creeds amongst their alterable forms of worship, or rites and ceremonies: nor will the revival of Arianism be ever looked upon as one of those exigencies of times that shall make it expedient to part with our Creeds, but a reason rather for retaining them the more firmly, or even for taking them in again, had any of them ever been unhappily thrown out.

OBJECTION V.

A further reason pleaded is, that Scripture alone is sufficient; that the primitive Church was very cautious about multiplying Creeds; that the Council of

cum Præbenda de Brinworth, alias Bricklesworth, in comitatu Northampton Petriburgensis diœceseos in eadem Ecclesia fundata, et eidem Cancellariatui annexa, admittendus et instituendus, omnibus hisce Articulis, et singulis in eisdem contentis volens et ex animo subscribo, et consensum meum eisdem præbeo, vicesimo die Julii, 1638."—Gulielmus Chillingworth. (Extract from the Register of the Church of Salisbury, inserted in the preface to the ninth edition of the Works of Chillingworth.)

Ephesus forbade, under the penalty of an anathema, any other Creed after that of Nice to be proposed or received in the Church.

ANSW. The whole design and end of Creeds is to preserve the rule of faith, as contained in the Holy Scriptures, and not in the false glosses and corrupt inventions of men[e]. And when endeavours are used to poison those fountains of truth by ill comments and forced constructions, preservatives must be thought on to keep the fountain pure and the faith sound and whole.

As to the primitive Churches, their constant way was to enlarge their Creeds in proportion to the growth of heresies, that so every corruption arising to the faith of Christ might have an immediate remedy; without which prudent and wise caution the faith would have been lost in a little time through the wiles and artifices of subtle intriguing men.

The Council of Ephesus made no order against new Creeds, that is, Creeds still more and more enlarged, if there should be occasion, but against a new Faith (ἑτέραν πίστιν)[f], a Faith different from and repugnant to that of Nice, such as was offered by the Nestorians in that Council. This is the literal construction and real intended meaning of that decree of the Ephesine Council[g]; though, had they intended it against the receiv-

---

[e] Οὐ γὰρ ὡς ἔδοξεν ἀνθρώποις συνετέθη τὰ τῆς πίστεως· ἀλλ' ἐκ πάσης γραφῆς τὰ καιριώτατα συλλεχθέντα μίαν ἀναπληροῖ τὴν τῆς πίστεως διδασκαλίαν.—Cyrill., *Catech.*, v. c. 12, p. 78.

[f] Ἑτέραν πίστιν μηδενὶ ἐξεῖναι προφέρειν ἤγουν συγγράφειν ἢ συντιθέναι, παρὰ τὴν ὁρισθεῖσαν παρὰ τῶν ἁγίων πατέρων τῶν ἐν τῇ Νικαέων συναχθέντων πόλει.—Conc. Ephes., Can. 7, in Routh's *Opusc.*, vol. ii. p. 8.

[g] Le Quien, *Panopl. c. Schism. Græc.*, sæc. xi. c. 2, § 9, &c., p. 230; *Dissertat. Damascen.*, p. 14, &c.

ing any other form but the Nicene, all that follows from it is, that they thought no more necessary at that time, or that definitions in Councils (as in the Council of Chalcedon afterwards), or condemnation of heretical tenets might suffice, leaving the Baptismal Creed (all Creeds were such at that time) just as was before. However, the practice of the Church afterwards, in multiplying Creeds as need required, at the same time that they acknowledged the Ephesine Council, shews fully how they understood it. Nay, the constant reception of the Constantinopolitan Creed (which is the Nicene interpolated, and yet was never understood to be excluded by the Ephesine Canon) shews plainly the sense of the Synod in that matter. It is to be noted, that the Ephesine Council by Nicene Creed meant the Nicene strictly so called [h], and which had already been interpolated by the Constantinopolitan Council.

Objection VI.

Another plea offered is, that, in the year 1689, many wise and good prelates of our own (commissioned to review and correct our Liturgy) unanimously agreed that the use of the Athanasian Creed should no longer be imposed.

Answ. There may be reason to question the truth of this report. There are two accounts which I have seen of this matter; one of Dr. Nichols, the other of Dr. Calamy, which he received of a friend. Dr. Nichols's account runs thus:—"Athanasius's Creed being disliked by many, because of the damnatory clauses, it was left to the minister's choice either to use it, or to

[h] Vid. Le Quien, ib., p. 231; *Dissert. Damascen.*, p. 18.

change it for the Apostles' Creed[i]." Dr. Calamy's account is thus:—"About the Athanasian Creed, they came at last to this conclusion: that least the wholly rejecting it should by unreasonable persons be imputed to them as Socinianism, a Rubric shall be made, setting forth, or declaring the curses denounced therein not to be restrained to every particular Article, but intended against those that deny the substance of the Christian religion in general [k]." Now, from these two accounts compared, it may be reasonable to believe that those wise and good prelates had once drawn up a scheme to be debated and canvassed, in which scheme it was proposed to leave every minister at liberty with respect to the Athanasian Creed; but, upon more mature consideration, they came at last to this conclusion, to impose the Creed as before, and to qualify the seeming harshness of the damnatory clauses by a softening Rubric. They were therefore at length unanimously agreed still to retain and impose this Creed, quite contrary to the objector's Report. And, indeed, it must have appeared very astonishing in the eyes of all the reformed Churches, Lutheran and Calvinist (who have the greatest veneration for this Creed), to have seen it

[i] Nicholsii, *Apparat. ad Defens. Eccl. Angl.*, p. 95.
[k] Calamy's Life of Baxter, vol. i. p. 455.
In a Postscript to his second edition, Dr. Waterland gives the rubric, of which he had procured a copy, at full length, as follows: "Upon these Feasts, *Christmas Day, Easter Day, Ascension Day, Whit-sunday, Trinity Sunday*, and upon *All Saints*, shall be said at Morning Prayer, by the minister and people standing, instead of the Creed, commonly called the Apostles' Creed, this Confession of our Christian Faith, commonly called the Creed of St. Athanasius, the Articles of which ought to be received and believed as being agreeable to the Holy Scriptures. And the condemning clauses are to be understood as relating only to those who obstinately deny the substance of the Christian Faith."

wholly rejected by the English clergy, when there had been no precedent before of any one Church in Christendom that had done the like. All that ever received it have constantly retained it, and still retain it. It is further to be considered, that what those very worthy prelates at that time intended sprung from a just and becoming tenderness towards the Dissenters, because of their long scruples against the damnatory clauses; but there is not the same reason at this day. The wiser and more moderate part of the Dissenting Ministers[1] seem very well reconciled to the damnatory clauses, modestly expounded; as Dr. Wallis particularly has expounded them, justly and truly, as well as modestly. And I am confident the soberer Dissenters would not, at this time, wish to see so excellent and so useful a form of faith laid aside, only to serve the interests of our new Arians. However, since the damnatory clauses were the main difficulty, a better way might have been contrived than was then thought on; namely, to have preserved the whole Creed except those clauses which are separable from it. But the best of all, as I humbly

---

[1] "This Creed, by whomsoever framed, hath been long received in the Church, and looked on as agreeable to the Scriptures, and an excellent explication of the Christian Faith. Constantinople, Rome, and the Reformed Churches have owned it.... Our pious and excellent Mr. Baxter, in his Method of Theol., p. 123, speaks thus of it: 'In a word, the damnatory sentences excepted, or modestly expounded (such a modest Explication of the Damnatory Clauses see in Dr. Wallis*, &c.), I embrace the Creed, commonly called Athanasius's, as the best explication of the Trinity. And in vol. ii. of his Works†, p. 132, says he, I unfeignedly account the doctrine of the Trinity the sum and kernel of the Christian religion, as exprest in our Baptism, and Athanasius his Creed the best explication of it I ever read.' "—Doctrine of the Trinity Stated, &c., by some London Ministers, pp. 62, 63.

* Wallis, Explication of the Athanasian Creed, pp. 2, 3.
† Baxter, the Reasons of the Christian Religion, part ii. c. 10.

conceive, is what has prevailed, and still obtains, to let it stand as before, since the damnatory clauses have been often and sufficiently vindicated by the reformed Churches abroad [m] as well as by our own here.

OBJECTION VII.

It is pleaded farther, mostly in the words of Bishop Taylor [n], that the Apostles' Creed is the Rule of Faith; that this only is necessary to Baptism; that what was once sufficient to bring men to heaven must be so now; that there is no occasion for being so minute and particular in the matter of Creeds; with more to the like purpose.

ANSW. 1. Dr. Taylor goes upon a false supposition, that the Creed called the Apostles' was compiled by the Apostles.

2. He has another false presumption, appearing all the way in his reasonings on this head, that the Apostles' Creed has been always the same that it is now: whereas learned men know that it was not brought to its present entire form till after the year 600 [o]; is nothing

---

[m] Tentzelius, a Lutheran, is very smart upon this head, against the Arminians, for their objecting to the damnatory sentences.

"Verum injuste, atque impudenter accusant initium Symboli, quod pridem vindicarunt nostrates Theologi: Danuhawerus in *Stylo Vindice*, p. 200; Hulsemannus *de Auxiliis Gratiæ*, p. 218; Kromayerus *in Theologia Positivo Polemica*, pp. 98, 99; and *in Scrutinio Religionum*, p. 205, aliique passim."—Tentzel., p. 110. To these which Tentzelius has mentioned, I may add David Pareus (a Calvinist), in his Comment upon this Creed, published at the end of Ursinus's Catechism, A.D. 1634, by Philip Pareus.

[n] Taylor, Liberty of Prophesying, §§ 1, 10, 11, vol. v. p. 373.

[o] I know not whether the words, *Maker of Heaven and Earth*, can be proved by any certain authority to have come into that Creed before the eighth century; for after the best searches I have been hitherto able to make, I can find no copy (to be depended upon) higher than that time, which has that clause.

else but the Baptismal Creed of one particular Church, the Church of Rome, and designedly short for the ease of those who were to repeat it at Baptism. Now, when we are told of the Apostles' Creed containing all that is necessary to salvation, and no more than is necessary, we would gladly know whether it be meant of the old short Roman Creed [p], or of the present one considerably larger: and if they intend the old one, why application is not made to our governors to lay the new one aside, or to curtail and reduce it to its primitive size, by leaving out the Belief, or profession of God's being Creator of heaven and earth, and of Christ's being dead, and of His descent into hell, and of the Church being Catholic, and of the communion of saints, and life everlasting, as unnecessary Articles of Faith. For why may not that suffice now which was once sufficient? or how can anything be necessary at this day that was not so from the beginning?

3. To set this whole matter right, it ought to be considered that Creeds were never intended to contain, as it were, a certain quantity of faith as necessary to bring men to heaven, and no more than is necessary. Were this the case, all Creeds ought precisely to have consisted of an equal number of Articles, and the same

[p] The old Roman (or Apostles') Creed was no more than this, as may be seen in Bishop Usher, *de Symbol.*, pp. 8, 10, (6, 9).

"I believe in God the Father Almighty: And in Jesus Christ His only Son our Lord; who was born of the Holy Ghost and the Virgin Mary; crucified under Pontius Pilate, and buried, rose again the third day from the dead, ascended into heaven, sitteth at the right hand of the Father, from whence He shall come to judge the quick and dead. And in the Holy Ghost, the holy Church, the remission of sins, the resurrection of the body. Amen."

See also Heurtley, *de Fide et Symbolo,* p. 31; where, however, the third Article is given, "Qui natus est d Spiritu Sancto ex Maria Virgine."

R

individual Articles: whereas there are no two Creeds anywhere to be found which answer to such exactness. A plain argument that the Church, in forming of Creeds, early and late, went upon no such view, but upon quite another principle. The design of all was, to keep up, as strictly as possible, the whole *compages*, or fabric of the Christian Faith, as it stands in Scripture[q]. And if any part came to be attacked, they were then to bend all their cares to succour and relieve that part, in order still to secure the whole. Some few of the main stamina, or chief lines, were taken care of from the first, and made up the first Creeds: particularly the doctrine of the Trinity, briefly hinted, and scarce anything more, because the form of baptism led to it. As to other Articles, or larger explications of this, they came in occasionally, according as this or that part of the Christian Faith seemed most to be endangered, and to require present relief. And as this varied in several countries or Churches (some being more disturbed than others, and some with one kind of heresy, others with another), so the Creeds likewise varied; some insisting particularly upon this Article, others upon that, as need required, and all still endeavouring to keep up and maintain one whole and entire system of the Christian Faith, according to the true and full meaning of Sacred Writ. There is nothing more in it than the very nature and circumstance of the thing necessarily leads to. I may illustrate the case a little farther by

[q] Ἐπειδὴ γὰρ οὐ πάντες δύνανται τὰς γραφὰς ἀναγινώσκειν, ἀλλὰ τοὺς μὲν ἰδιωτεία, τοὺς δὲ ἀσχολία τις ἐμποδίζει πρὸς τὴν γνῶσιν· ὑπὲρ τοῦ μὴ τὴν ψυχὴν ἐξ ἀμαθίας ἀπολέσθαι, ἐν ὀλίγοις τοῖς στίχοις τὸ πᾶν δόγμα τῆς πίστεως περιλαμβάνομεν.—Cyril. Catech., v. c. 12, p. 78.

an easy parallel between matters of faith and matters of practice. The sum of Christian practice is contained in two brief rules,—to love God, and to love one's neighbour, which comprehend all. No one needs more than this; nor, indeed, can there be anything more. But then a perverse man may possibly understand by God, not the true God, the God of Jews and Christians, but some other of his own devising, or such as has been received by pagans or heretics; and he may understand by neighbour, one of his own country only, or tribe, or sect, or family. Well, then, to obviate any such method of undermining Christian practice, it will be necessary to be a little more particular than barely to lay down in brief to love God and one's neighbour: we must add, the true God, the God of Jews and Christians, that very God and none else: and as to neighbour, we must insist upon it, that it means not this or that sect, tribe, party, &c., but all mankind. And now our rule of practice begins to extend and enlarge itself beyond its primitive simplicity, but not without reason. To proceed a little farther: mistakes and perverse sentiments may arise in the interpreting the word *love*, so as thereby to evacuate and frustrate the primary and fundamental rule; to correct and remove which it may be necessary still farther to enlarge the rule of practice, and to branch it out into many other particulars, which to mention would be needless. Now, if such a method as this will of course be necessary to preserve the essentials of practice, let it not be thought strange if the like has been made use of to preserve the essentials of faith. There is the same reason and the like occasion for both; and if due care be taken in both to make all the branches hang naturally upon the primary and fundamental rules, and to adopt no foreign ones, as belonging thereunto when they really do not, then there is nothing in this whole affair but a just and prudent care about what most of all deserves it, and such as will be indispensably required in every faithful minister or steward of the mysteries of God. To return to our point in hand : as more and more of the sacred truths, in process of time, came to be opposed, or brought in question, so Creeds have been enlarged in proportion, and an explicit profession of more and more Articles required of every candidate for baptism. And because this was not security sufficient, since many might forget, or not know, or not attend to what they had professed in their baptism (by themselves or by their sureties), it was found highly expedient and necessary to insert one or more Creeds in the standing and daily offices of the Church, to remind people of that Faith which they had solemnly engaged to maintain, and to guard the unwary against the wily attempts of heretics to pervert them. This is the plain and true account of Creeds, and of their use in the Christian Churches. And therefore, if any man would talk sense against the use of this or that Creed in any Church, he ought to shew either that it contains such truths as no man ever did, or, in all probability, never will oppose (which will be a good argument to prove the Creed superfluous), or that it contains Articles which are not true, or are at best doubtful, which will be a good argument to prove such a Creed hurtful. Now, as to the Athanasian form, it will hardly be thought superfluous, so long as there are any Arians, Photinians,

Sabellians, Macedonians, Apollinarians, Nestorians, or Eutychians, in this part of the world; and as to its being hurtful, that may then be proved when it can be shewn that any of those forementioned heresies were no heresies, or have not been justly condemned.

If it be pleaded that the vulgar, knowing little of any of those heresies, will therefore know as little of what the Creed means, and so to them it may be at least dry and insipid, if not wholly useless; to this I answer, that there no kinds of heretics but hope to make the vulgar understand their tenets respectively, and to draw them aside from the received Faith of the Church; and therefore it behoves the pastors of the Church to have a standing form, to guard the people against any such attempts. The vulgar will understand, in the general, and as far as is ordinarily to them necessary, the main doctrines of a Trinity in unity, and of God incarnate; and as to particular explications, whenever they have occasion to look farther, they will find the true ones laid down in this Creed, which will be useful to prevent their being imposed upon at any time with false ones. If they never have occasion to go farther than generals, there is no hurt done to them by abundant caution: if they have, here is a direction ready for them, to prevent mistakes. It is not pretended that all are capable of seeing through every nicety, or of perceiving the full intent and aim of every part of this form, and what it alludes to. But, as many as are capable of being set wrong in any one branch (by the subtlety of seducers), are as capable of being kept right by this rule given them; and they will as easily understand one side of the question as they will the other. The Christian Churches throughout the world, ever since the multiplication of heresies, have thought it necessary to guard their people by some such forms as these in standing use amongst them. The Oriental Churches, which receive not this Creed into their constant offices, yet more than supply the want of it, either by other the like Creeds[r], or by their solemn stated prayers in their liturgies, wherein they express their faith as fully and particularly (or more so[s]) as this Creed does: and they are not so much afraid of puzzling and perplexing the vulgar by doing it, as they are of betraying and exposing them to the attempts of seducers should they not do it. For which reason also they frequently direct their prayers to God the Son, as well as to God the Father; being in that case more solicitous than the Latin Churches have been, because they have been oftener disturbed by Arians and other impugners of Christ's divinity[t].

Upon the whole, I look upon it as exceeding useful, and even necessary, for every Church to have some such form as this, or something equivalent, open and common to all its members, that none may be led astray for want of proper caution and previous instruction in what so nearly concerns the whole structure and fabric

---

[r] See the Creed of the Armenians in Ricaut, p. 411, &c.
[s] See Ludolphus *Histor. Æthiop.*, lib. iii. c. 5; and Renaudot's *Orient. Liturg.*, passim.
[t] "Nam cum omnes Orationes Latini Canonis, ex vetustissima traditione, ad Deum Patrem dirigantur; in Oriente plures ad Filium: nempe, quia magis conflictata est Arianorum, et aliorum qui ejus Divinitatem impugnabant, contentionibus Orientalis, quam Occidentalis Ecclesia."—Renaudot, *ad Liturg. Copt. S. Basil.*, vol. i. p. 262.

of the Christian Faith ᵘ. As to this particular form, it has so long prevailed, and has so well answered the use intended, that, all things considered, there can be no sufficient reason for changing any part of it, much less for laying the whole aside. There are several other Creeds, very good ones (though somewhat larger), which, had they been made choice of for common use, might possibly have done as well. The Creeds, I mean, (of which there is a great number) drawn up after the Council of Chalcedon, and purposely contrived to obviate all the heresies that ever had infested the Christian Church. But those that dislike this Creed would much more dislike the other, as being still more particular and explicit in regard to the Nestorian, Eutychian, and Monothelite heresies, and equally full and clear for the doctrine of the Trinity.

To conclude: as long as there shall be any men left to oppose the doctrines which this Creed contains, so long will it be expedient, and even necessary, to continue the use of it, in order to preserve the rest; and, I suppose, when we have none remaining to find fault with the doctrines, there will be none to object against the use of the Creed, or so much as to wish to have it laid aside.

ᵘ To this purpose speaks Johannes Pappus, in the name of the Lutheran Churches, commenting on the Augsburg Confession:—
"Semper in Ecclesia Scriptorum quorundam publicorum usus fuit, quibus doctrinæ Divinitus revelatæ de certis capitibus summa comprehenderetur, et contra hæreticos, aliosque adversarios defenderetur. Talia scripta, licet perbrevia, sunt Symbola illa totius Ecclesiæ, omnium hominum consensu recepta, Apostolicum, Nicænum, Athanasianum."—Joan. Papp., *Comm. in Confess. August.*, fol. 2.

I take this upon the credit of Nic. Serarius, who quotes the passage from Pappus. Serar., *in Symb. Athanas.*, Opusc. Theol., vol. ii. p. 9.

APPENDIX.

CHAPTER III.

A.D. 570. I intimated above (p. 45) that Fortunatus's Comment upon the Athanasian Creed, though before published, might deserve a second publication, and be made much more correct than it appears in Muratorius's second tome of *Anecdota*.

I have made frequent use of it in the preceding sheets; and now my design, in reprinting it, is to let the reader see what the Comment is which I so frequently refer to, that so he may judge for himself whether it really be what I suppose, and I think with good reason, A Comment of the Sixth Century, and justly ascribed to Fortunatus. I have endeavoured to make it as correct as possible, by such helps as I could anywhere procure, which are as follow:—

1. The printed copy of it, published by Muratorius, from a manuscript of the Ambrosian Library, about 600 years old.

2. A manuscript copy from Oxford, found among Franciscus Junius's MSS. (No. 25), which appears, by the character, to be about 800 years old. As it is older than Muratorius's, so is it also more faithful; and though it has a great many faults, both in the orthography and syntax, owing either to the ignorance of

the age or of the copyist, yet it does not appear to have been interpolated like the other, or to have been industriously altered in any part.

3. Besides those two copies of the entire Comment, I have had some assistance from such parcels of it as are to be met with in writers that have borrowed from it. Bruno's Comment furnishes us with some parts which he had taken into his own. But there is, among the supposititious works ascribed to St. Austin, a treatise intituled, *Sermo de Symbolo*[a], which has several scattered fragments of this very Comment in it. The whole treatise is a farrago, or collection from several other writers, as Ruffinus, Cæsarius, Pope Gregory I., and Ivo Carnotensis. By the last mentioned, one may be assured that the collection is not older than the close of the eleventh century; it may be later. It will be serviceable, however, so far as it goes, for restoring the true readings where our copies are corrupt, which is the use I make of it.

Nothing now remains but to lay before the learned reader Fortunatus's Comment in its native language, and therewith to close up our inquiries concerning the Athanasian Creed.

The Various Lections, all that are properly such, are carefully noted at the bottom of the page, that so the reader may judge whether the text be what it should be, or correct it, if it appears otherwise. But I should hint, that there are several little variations in the Oxford manuscript, which I take no notice of, as not being properly Various Lections.

1. Such as are merely orthographical: as a permu-

[a] August., vol. vi. App., p. 278.

tation of letters, using *d* for *t*, in *capud* and *reliquid*, for *caput* and *reliquit;* *e* for *i*, in *Trea* for *Tria;* and *i* for *e*, in *calit* for *calet*, and the like: *o* for *u* in *servolis*, *p* for *b* in *optenit* for *obtinet;* *v* consonant for *b*, in *enarravit* for *enarrabit*, though such as this last is might be noted among Various Lections in cases more disputable.

To this head may be referred some antique and now obsolete spellings: *inmensus* for *immensus*, *inmortalis* for *immortalis*, *inlesus* for *illæsus*, *conlocavit* for *collocavit*, *dinoscitur* for *dignoscitur*, and the like.

2. Active terminations of verbs for passive: as *finire* for *finiri*, *cogitare* for *cogitari;* though these may be referred to the former head, being only changing the letter *i* for the letter *e*. *Dominat* for *dominatur* I take notice of among the Various Lections.

3. Faults in the formation of verbs: as *abstuleret* for *tolleret*, *vivendos* for *viventes;* to which may be added *morsit* for *momordit*, having been long out of use.

4. Manifest faults in concord: as *humani carnis* for *humanæ*, *eodem captivitate* for *eadem*. But where there can be any doubt of the construction, I mark such among the Various Lections, leaving the reader to judge of them.

These and other the like niceties are generally neglected in editions of authors, it being both needless and endless to note them. But I was willing to hint something of them in this place, because they may be of use to scholars for the making a judgment of the value of a manuscript; and sometimes of the time or place; as also of the manner how a copy was taken, whether by the ear or by the eye, from word of mouth, or merely from a writing laid before the copyist. Besides that, if we can distinguish in the present case, as perhaps a good critic may, the particularities of the author from those of his transcribers, they may possibly afford some additional argument for the ascertaining the author of the Comment.

EXPOSITIO FIDEI CATHOLICÆ FORTUNATI[a].

SCRIPTA anno circiter 570. *Quicunque vult salvus esse*[b], *ante omnia opus est ut teneat Catholicam Fidem : Quam nisi quisque integram, inviolatamque servaverit, absque dubio in æternum peribit*[c]. Fides dicitur credulitas, sive credentia[d]. [Primo ergo omnium Fides necessaria est, sicut Apostolica docet auctoritas dicens ; *sine Fide impossibile est placere Deo*. Constat enim neminem ad veram pervenire posse beatitudinem, nisi Deo placeat ; et Deo neminem placere posse, nisi per Fidem. Fides namque est bonorum omnium fundamentum, Fides humanæ salutis initium. Sine hac nemo ad filiorum Dei potest consortium pervenire ; quia sine ipsa nec in hoc seculo quisquam justificationis consequitur gratiam, nec in futuro vitam possidebit æternam. Et si quis heic non ambulaverit per fidem, non perveniet ad speciem beatam Domini nostri Jesu Christi[e]]. Catholica universalis dicitur, id

---

[a] Ita se habet titulus in Codice Muratorii. Aliter in Oxoniensi, viz. *Expositio in Fide Catholica :* pro *in Fidem Catholicam*, ex corrupta loquendi ratione apud scriptores ætatis mediæ.

[b] Esse salvus. Cod. Murat.

[c] Posterior hæc Symboli Clausula, incipiens a Quam nisi, non habetur in Cod. Oxoniensi.

[d] Ita Cod. Oxon. Prima hæc pericope deest in Murator. Conf. *Brun. in Symb.*

[e] Quæ uncinulis includuntur, non comparent in MS. Oxoniensi. Nec enim Fortunati videntur esse, sed Alcuini potius ; apud quem eadem fere verbatim leguntur (*De Fid. Trin.*, lib. i. c. 2, p. 1257. 1707]). Alcuinus vero maximam partem mutuatus est a Fulgentio,

est, recta, quam Ecclesia universa [f] tenere debet. Ecclesia [g] congregatio dicitur Christianorum, sive conventus populorum. [Non enim, sicut conventicula haereticorum, in aliquibus regionum partibus coarctatur, sed per totum terrarum orbem dilatata diffunditur [h].]

Ut unum Deum in Trinitate, et Trinitatem in unitate veneremur. Et credamus, et colamus, et confiteamur. [Trinitatem in Personis, unitatem in substantia. Hanc quoque Trinitatem Personarum, atque unitatem naturae Propheta Esaias revelatam sibi non tacuit, cum se dicit Seraphim vidisse clamantia, Sanctus, Sanctus, Sanctus, Dominus Deus Sabaoth. Ubi prorsus in eo quod dicitur tertio Sanctus, Personarum Trinitatem; in eo vero quod semel dicimus Dominus Deus Sabaoth, divinae naturae cognoscimus unitatem [i].]

Neque confundentes personas. Ut Sabellius errat, qui ipsum dicit esse Patrem in Persona quem et Filium, ipsum et Spiritum Sanctum. Non ergo confundentes Personas,

(*De Fid. ad Petrum. Prolog.*, p. 500). Sed varia exemplaria varie sententiam claudunt. Fulgentius legit, Non perveniet ad speciem; nec quicquam ultra. Alcuinus, Non perveniet ad speciem beatae visionis Domini nostri Jesu Christi. Ab utrisque abit Lectio Muratorii.

[f] *Universa Ecclesia.* Cod. Mur. et Brunonis.

[g] Cod. Muratorii habet quippe, post Ecclesia: quam vocularm, utpote ineptam, saltem otiosam, expunximus, Fide Cod. Oxoniensis. Conf. Brunon. in hoc loco.

[h] Uncis hic inclusa non habentur in Codice Oxoniensi. Verba nimirum sunt, non Fortunati, sed Isidori Hispal. Orig., lib. viii. c. 1, p. 64. Alio proinde charactere imprimenda curavimus.

[i] Quae uncis comprehensa hic legere est, non comparent in Codice Oxoniensi. Verba sunt Alcuini (*de Trin.*, lib. i. c. 3, p. 1259 [709]), in quo eadem plane, similique ordine invenias. Sunt porro eadem, uno vocabulo dempto, apud Fulgentium (*de Fid. ad Petrum*, c. i. § 5, p. 503), ordine etiam tantum non eodem. Verba autem illa introductoria (viz. Trinitatem in Personis, unitatem in substantia); non leguntur in Fulgentio, nec quidem in Alcuino. Interpolator ipse, uti videtur, ex proprio illa penu deprompta praemisit caeteris, connexionis forte aliqualis conservandae gratia.

quia tres omnino Personæ sunt[k]. Est enim gignens, genitus, et[l] procedens. Gignens est Pater, qui genuit Filium; Filius est genitus, quem genuit Pater; Spiritus Sanctus est procedens, quia a Patre et Filio procedit. Pater et Filius coæterni sibi sunt et coæquales; et cooperatores, sicut scriptum est; verbo Domini Cœli firmati[m] sunt, id est, a Filio Dei creati, Spiritu[n] oris ejus, omnis virtus eorum. Ubi sub singulari numero, Spiritus[o] ejus, dicit[p], [unitatem substantiæ Deitatis ostendit; ubi sub plurali numero, omnis virtus eorum dicit[q]], Trinitatem Personarum aperte demonstrat, quia tres unum sunt, et unum tres.

Neque substantiam separantes. Ut Arius garrit, qui sicut tres personas esse dicit, sic et tres substantias esse mentitur[r]. Filium dicit minorem quam Patrem, et creaturam esse; Spiritum Sanctum adhuc minorem quam Filium, et Patri et Filio cum esse administratorem[s] adserit. Non ergo substantiam separantes, quia totæ tres Personæ in substantia Deitatis[t] unum sunt.

[k] Tres Personæ omniuo sunt. Murat.
[l] Deest 'et' in Cod. Oxon.
[m] Formati. Cod. Oxon. Vid. Symb. Damasi dictum (apud Hieronym., vol. v. p. 122) unde hæc 'Noster,' mutatis mutandis desumpsisse videtur.
[n] Spiritus. Cod. Oxon.
[o] Leg. 'Spiritu,' uterque vero codex habet 'Spiritus.'
[p] Dicitur. Cod. Murat.
[q] Lacunam in Muratorio manifestam (quippe cum desint ea verba uncis inclusa) ex Codice Oxoniensi supplevimus. Scilicet, vox 'dicit' proxime recurrens librarii oculos (uti fit) fefellit.
[r] Ita clare, Cod. Oxon. Aliter Muratorius ex vitioso Codice; Quia tres Personas esse dicit, si et tres substantias esse mentitur. Sensus impeditus, aut nullus.
[s] Et Patris et Filii eum administratorem esse adserit. Cod. Murat. Conf. Brunon.
[t] Divinitatis. Cod. Oxon.

Alia est enim Persona Patris. Quia Pater ingenitus est, eo quod a nullo est genitus. Alia Persona Filii, quia Filius a Patre solo est ᵘ genitus. Alia Spiritus Sancti, quia a Patre et Filio Spiritus Sanctus ᵛ procedens est.

Sed Patris et Filii et Spiritus Sancti una est Divinitas. Id est, Deitas. Æqualis gloria : id est, claritas. Coæterna majestas: majestas gloria est, claritas, sive potestas ˣ.

Qualis Pater, talis Filius, talis et Spiritus Sanctus. Id est, in Deitate, et Omnipotentia.

Increatus Pater, inereatus Filius, increatus et Spiritus Sanctus. Id est, a nullo creatus ʸ.

Immensus Pater, immensus Filius, immensus et Spiritus Sanctus. Non est mensurabilis in sua natura, quia inlocalis est ᶻ, incircumscriptus, ubique totus, ubique præsens, ubique potens.

Æternus Pater, æternus Filius, æternus et Spiritus Sanctus. Id est, non tres æterni, sed in tribus Personis unus Deus æternus, qui sine initio, et sine fine æternus permanet.

Similiter omnipotens Pater, omnipotens Filius, omnipotens et Spiritus Sanctus. Omnipotens dicitur, eo quod omnia potest, et omnium obtinet potestatem ᵃ.

ᵘ A Patre est solo. Cod. Oxon.

ᵛ Desunt 'Spiritus Sanctus' in Cod. Murat. quæ tamen retinuimus, tum fide Cod. Oxoniensis, tum quia in antecedentibus 'Pater,' et 'Filius' bis ponuntur, sicut et hic 'Sp. Sanctus.'

ˣ Cod. Oxoniensis legit 'claritatis, sive potestas.'

ʸ Cod. Oxoniensis legit 'creati.'

ᶻ Muratorii exemplar insertum habet 'et,' quod delendum esse censui, cum absit a Codice Oxon. et otiosum videatur.

ᵃ Fortunatus, in sua *Exposit. Symb. Apostolici,* hæc habet; Omnipotens vero dicitur, eo quod omnia possit, et omnium obtinet

Ergo, si omnia potest, quid est quod non potest? Hoc non potest, quod Omnipotenti non competit posse [b]. Falli non potest [quia veritas est; infirmari non potest], quia sanitas est [c]; mori non potest, quia immortalis vita est; finiri non potest, quia infinitus et perennis est.

Ita, Deus Pater, Deus Filius, Deus et Spiritus Sanctus. [Deus nomen est potestatis, non proprietatis [d].] Proprium nomen est Patris Pater; et proprium nomen est [e] Filii Filius; et proprium nomen est Spiritus Sancti Spiritus Sanctus.

Ita, Dominus Pater, Dominus Filius, Dominus et Spiritus Sanctus. Dominus dicitur, eo quod omnia dominat, et omnium est dominus dominator [f].

Quia sicut singillatim (id est, sicut distinctim [g])

---

[a] 'potentatum.' ed. Basil. 'obtineat potestatem.' ed. Lugd. Præluserat Ruffinus, *in Symbolum*.

[b] S. Bruno, hunc opinor locum præ oculis habens, his verbis utitur: Ergo, si omnia potest, quid est quod non potest? Hoc non potest, quod non convenit omnipotenti posse.—Brun., *in Symb. Athanas.*, p. 346.

[c] Muratorius sententiam mancam, vitiatamque exhibet: Falli non potest, quia Sanctus est; omissis intermediis. Scilicet, vocabulum proxime repetitum describentis oculum delusit: et ne nullus inde eliceretur sensus, pro Sanitas substitutum est Sanctus. Hæc porro sibimet adoptavit S. Bruno, pauculis mutatis, vel interjectis, ad hunc modum: Falli non potest, quia veritas et sapientia est: ægrotari aut infirmari non potest, quia Sanitas est; mori non potest, quia immortalis est; finiri non potest, quia influitus et perennis est.

[d] Deest hæc clausula in Codice Murator.: sed confer Symbolum Damasi dictum, quod Gregorii Bætici creditur, apud August., vol. v. App., p. 387. Item apud Hieronym., vol. v. p. 122.

[e] Deest est. Murator. Conf. Brun.

[f] Dominat, pro Dominatur, et cum accusativo, ex vitiata inferioris ævi Latinitate, vel ex scribæ imperitia. Aliter codex Muratorii, ex Isidori Orig. (lib. vii. c. 1, p. 53). Dominus dicitur, eo quod dominetur creaturæ cunctæ, vel quod creatura omnis Dominatui ejus deserviat.

[g] Distinctum. Oxon. Distincte. Murat.

unamquamque Personam et Deum[h] *et Dominum confiteri Christiana veritate compellimur.* Quia si me interrogaveris quid sit[i] Pater, ego respondebo; Deus, et Dominus. Similiter, si me interrogaveris[k] quid sit[l] Filius, ego dicam; Deus, et Dominus. Et si dicis[m], quid est Spiritus Sanctus? Ego dico[n]; Deus, et Dominus. Et in his tribus Personis, non tres Deos, nec tres Dominos, sed in[o] his tribus, sicut jam supra dictum est[p], unum Deum, et unum Dominum confiteor.

Unus ergo Pater, non tres Patres. Id est, quia[q] Pater semper Pater, nec aliquando Filius. Unus Filius, non tres Filii: id est, quia Filius semper Filius, nec aliquando Pater. Unus Spiritus Sanctus, non tres Spiritus Sancti: id est, quia Spiritus Sanctus semper est[r] Spiritus Sanctus, nec aliquando Filius, aut Pater. Hæc est proprietas Personarum.

Et in hac Trinitate nihil prius, aut posterius. Quia sicut nunquam Filius sine Patre, sic nunquam fuit Pater sine Filio, sic et nunquam fuit Pater et Filius sine Spi-

---

[h] Deest 'et.' Cod. Murator.
[i] Quid est. Murator. Eandem sententiam expressit S. Bruno, his verbis; Quia si me interrogaveris quid est Pater, ego respondeo; Deus, et Dominus.
[k] Et si me rogaveris. Cod. Oxon.
[l] Est. Murator. Locum sic exhibet S. Bruno; Similiter, si interrogaveris quid est Filius, ego dico, Deus et Dominus.
[m] Dicas. Murator.
[n] Dicam. Murator. Apud Brunonem sic legitur; Et si dicis, quid est Spiritus Sanctus? Ego respondeo; Deus, et Dominus.
[o] Deest 'in.' Oxon.
[p] Supra dixi. Cod. Oxon. Sed Brunonis lectio Muratorii lectionem confirmat.
[q] Codex Oxon. pro 'quia' habet 'qui,' in hoc loco, et in duobus proxime sequentibus. Utrumlibet elegeris, eodem fere res redit.
[r] In Cod. Oxon. deest 'est.'

S

ritu Sancto[a]. Coæterna ergo Trinitas, et inseparabilis unitas, sine initio et sine fine[t].

Nihil majus, aut minus. Æqualitatem Personarum dicit, quia Trinitatis[u] æqualis est, et una Deitas[v], Apostolo docente[x], et dicente: per ea, quæ facta sunt, intellecta conspiciuntur; et per Creaturam Creator intelligitur, secundum has comparationes, et alias quamplures. Sol, Candor, et Calor, et tria sunt vocabula, et tria unum[y]. Quod candet, hoc calet, et quod calet, hoc candet: tria hæc vocabula res una esse dignoscitur[z]. Ita[a] Pater et Filius et Spiritus Sanctus, tres Personæ in Deitate, substantia[b] unum sunt; et individua unitas recte creditur. Item de terrenis, Vena, Fons, Fluvius, tria sunt[c] vocabula, et tria unum[d] in sua natura. Ita trium Personarum, Patris et

---

[a] Paulo aliter huncce locum expressit auctor Sermonis, inter Augustini opera (vol. vi. App., p. 281): Quia sicut nunquam pater sine Filio, nec Filius sine Patre; sic et nunquam fuit Pater, et Filius sine Spiritu Sancto. Sed nihil mutandum contra fidem exemplarium.

[t] In Appendice prædicta, sic legitur: Coæterna ergo est Sancta Trinitas, &c.

[u] Sancta Trinitas. Append.

[v] Una est Deitas. Append. Una Deitatis. Oxon. male.

[x] In Cod. Oxoniensi, desunt illa 'docente et.' Sed Append. lectionem Muratorii tuetur, alio tamen verborum ordine; 'dicente, atque docente.'

[y] Ita Muratorius cum Appendice prædicta. Aliter MS. Oxon., viz., Tria sunt nomina, et res una; quæ eodem recidunt.

[z] In Appendice sic se habent; Tria hæc vocabula res una cognoscitur.

[a] 'Et' post 'ita.' Oxon.

[b] Codices habent 'Substantiæ' (quod tamen in Appendice prædicta omittitur prorsus), et comma interponunt post 'Personæ.' Prava interpunctio corrigenda est, et levicula mutatione legendum 'substantia:' quod et vidit et monuit vir quidam amicissimus simul et perspicacissimus.

[c] Appendix legit 'hæc,' non 'sunt.' Oxon. 'tria itemque sunt.'

[d] Oxoniensis, 'res una.' Append. cum Muratorio, 'unum.'

Filii et Spiritus Sancti, substantia et Deitas unum est [e].

Est ergo Fides recta, ut credamus et confiteamur, quia Dominus noster Jesus Christus [f]. Jesus Hebraice, Latine Salvator dicitur. [Christus Græce, Latine unctus vocatur. Jesus ergo dicitur [g]] eo quod salvat populum: Christus, eo quod Spiritu Sancto Divinitus sit [h] delibutus, sicut in ipsius Christi [i] Persona Esaias ait; Spiritus Domini super me, propter quod unxit me, &c. Ita et Psalmista de Christo Domino dicit [k], Unxit te Deus, Deus tuus, oleo lætitiæ præ consortibus tuis.

Dei Filius, Deus pariter et homo est. Filius a felicitate parentum dicitur: homo ab humo dicitur; id est, de humo [l] factus est.

Deus est [m] *ex substantia Patris ante sæcula genitus.* Id est, Deus de Deo, lumen de lumine, splendor de splendore, fortis de forti, virtus de virtute, vita de vita, æternitas de æternitate: per omnia, idem [n] quod Pater in Divina substantia hoc est et [o] Filius. Deus enim [p]

[e] Ita Murat. et Append. Oxoniensis legit, Substantia, Deitas una est.
[f] Oxoniensis adjicit, Dei Filius et homo est. Inepte hoc loco, quod ex sequentibus patebit.
[g] Muratorii Codex omittit verba illa intermedia, uncis inclusa. Scilicet, illud 'dicitur' proxime repetitum amanuensi hic iterum fraudi fuit.
[h] 'Divinitus sit' desunt in Cod. Oxon.
[i] Deest 'Christi.' Murator.
[k] Oxoniensis breviter, Item in Psalmo, unxit, &c. Notandum porro, quod quædam habet Fortunatus noster, in commentario suo in *Symbol. Apostol.* hisce jam proxime descriptis perquam similia. Confer etiam Ruffin. in *Symbol.*, c. 6, inter Oper. Hieronym., vol. v. p. 131; et in Heurtl. *de Fide*, &c., p. 110.
[l] De humo terræ. Murator.
[m] Non habetur 'est' in Murat.
[n] Pro 'idem,' 'id est,' Murator.
[o] Deest 'et' Cod. Oxon. His quoque gemina fere habes in *Exposit. in Symbol. Apostolicum.*
[p] Deest 'enim' Cod. Oxon; confer Symb. Damasi dictum.

Pater Deum Filium genuit, non voluntate, neque necessitate, sed natura. Nec quæratur quomodo genuit Filium [q], quod et angeli nesciunt, prophetis est incognitum: unde [r] eximius Propheta Esaias dicit; generationem ejus quis enarrabit? Ac si diceret [s], angelorum nullus, prophetarum nemo [t]. Nec inenarrabilis, et inæstimabilis Deus [u] a servulis suis discutiendus est, sed fideliter credendus [v], et pariter diligendus.

Et homo [x] ex substantia matris, in sæculo natus. Dei Filius, Verbum Patris [y], caro factum. Non [z] quod Divinitas mutasset Deitatem, sed adsumpsit humanitatem. Hoc est, Verbum caro factum est, ex utero Virginis veram humanam carnem traxit. Et de utero Virginali verus homo, sicut et verus Deus, est in sæculo natus, salva virginitatis gratia [a]; quia mater, quæ genuit, Virgo ante partum, et Virgo post partem permansit [b].

In sæculo. Id est, in isto sexto miliario, in quo nunc sumus [sæcula enim generationibus constant, et inde sæcula, quod se sequantur; abeuntibus enim aliis, alia

[q] Quomodo genitus sit, quod Angeli .... Oxon. At Muratorii lectioni astipulatur Appendix *ad Augustin.*, vol. vi. p. 279; et Fortunatus ipse, *Expos. in Symb. Apostol.*, p. 1151.
[r] Unde et isdem. Cod. Murat. conf. Fortunat. *in Symb. Apostolicum.*
[s] Muratorius habet 'dixisset.'
[t] Angelorum nemo, Prophetarum nullus. Cod. Oxon.
[u] Deest 'Deus.' Oxon.
[v] Confer Fortunat. *in Symb. Apostol.* et *Append.*, apud August., p. 279, et Ruffin. *Symb.*
[x] Homo est. Cod. Oxon.
[y] Dei Filius, Verbum caro: Murat. Dei Filius Verbo Patris caro: Cod. Oxon. Ex utrisque veram, opinor, lectionem restituimus.
[z] Et non. Cod. Murator. Expunximus illud 'et,' fide Codicis Oxon.
[a] 'Salva virginitatis gratia' desunt in Cod. Oxoniensi.
[b] Ita Cod. Oxon. Muratorius, Quia mater genuit, et virgo mansit ante partum, et post partum.

succedunt[c]]. "Deus et homo Christus Jesus, unus Dei Filius et ipse Virginis Filius. Quia dum Deitas in utero Virginis humanitatem adsumpsit, et cum ea per portam Virginis integram, et illæsam, nascendo mundum ingressus est Virginis Filius; et hominem (leg. homo) quem adsumsit, id (leg. idem) est Dei Filium (leg. Filius) sicut jam supra diximus; et Deitas et humanitas in Christo; et Dei Patris pariter et Virginis Matris Filius."

Perfectus Deus, perfectus homo. Id est, verus Deus, et verus homo[d]. Ex anima rationali: et non ut Apollinaris[e] hæreticus dixit primum, quasi Deitas pro anima fuisset in carne Christi; postea, cum per evangelicam auctoritatem fuisset[f] convictus, dixit: Habuit quidem animam quæ vivificavit corpus, sed non rationalem. E contrario[g], dicit qui Catholice sentit; Ex anima rationali et humana carne subsistens[h]: id est, plenus homo, atque perfectus.

[c] Non comparent in Codice Oxoniensi. Verba sunt Isidor. Orig., lib. v. c. 38, p. 42. Quæ sequuntur proxime, Deus et homo, &c., usque ad Matris Filius, desunt omnia in Codice Muratorii: ex Oxoniensi solo descripta dedimus. Videntur mihi Fortunati re vera esse, sed Librarii culpa (ut alia multa) mirum in modum vitiata; quæ quidem ex conjectura aliquatenus corrigere volui, ut *Syntaxis* saltem sibi constet, donec certiora, et meliora ex Codicibus (si forte supersint aliqui) eruantur. Cæterum, ut Fortunato nostro hæc ascribam, illud suadet maxime, quod in expositione sua in *Symbolum Apostolicum* gemina fere habet de porta Virginis, eisdemque ibi nonnullis phrasibus utitur quibus hic usus est. Confer *Symbolum Ruffini,* a quo solenne est nostro (quippe qui et ipse Aquileiæ olim Doctrina Christiana initiatus fuerat) tum verba, tum sententias mutuari.

[d] Deest hæc clausula in Cod. Oxon. ob vocabulum repetitum.

[e] Paulinaris, Cod. Oxon. Lectio nata ex sermone simplici et plebeio.

[f] Fuit, Cod. Oxon.

[g] Et e contrario iste dicit: Murat. Delevimus illa 'et,' atque 'iste,' quæ sententiam turbant, fide Codicis Oxoniensis.

[h] Subsistit, Cod. Oxon.

Æqualis Patri secundum Divinitatem; minor Patre secundum Humanitatem. Id est, secundum formam servi quam adsumere dignatus est.

Qui licet[i] *Deus sit et homo, non duo tamen, sed unus est Christus.* Id est, duæ substantiæ in Christo, Deitas et humanitas, non duæ personæ, sed una est persona [k].

Unus autem, non conversione Divinitatis in carnem[l], *sed adsumptione humanitatis in Deum*[l]. Id est: non quod Divinitas, quæ incommutabilis est, sit conversa in carnem [m], sed ideo unus, eo quod humanitatem adsumpsit, cœpit [n] esse quod non [o] erat, et non amisit quod erat; cœpit esse homo [p] quod antea non fuerat, non amisit Deitatem quæ incommutabilis in æternum permanet [q].

Unus omnino, non confusione substantiæ, sed unitate Personæ. Id est; Divinitas incommutabilis [r] cum homine, quem adsumere dignata [s] est, sicut scriptum est; Verbum tuum, Domine, in æternum permanet. Id est, Divinitas cum humanitate; ut diximus duas substantias unam Personam [t] esse in Christo; ut sicut ante ad-

---

[i] 'Certe,' loco τοῦ 'licet.' Cod. Oxon.
[k] 'Est Persona' desunt in Cod. Oxon.
[l] Cod. Oxoniensis habet, 'Carne,' et 'Deo :' errore, uti credo, pervetusto, multisque et antiquissimis exemplaribus communi. Quod si Verbis in Commentario immediate sequentibus (ex Muratorii lectione) steterimus, Fortunatus ipse nobis auctor erit, ut et Deum, et carnem, pro genuina lectione habeamus.
[m] Quæ immutabilis et inconvertibilis est, Caro; sed, &c. Cod. Oxon.
[n] Incipit. Cod. Oxon.
[o] Deest 'non' Cod. Murat. male.
[p] Deest 'homo' in Cod. Oxon. perperam, item, 'incipit,' pro 'cœpit.'
[q] Muratorius legit, Quia incommutabilis in æternum permanet: Cod. Oxoniensis, Quæ immutabilis in æternum permansit. Ex utrisque tertiam lectionem confecimus; quæ, opinor, cæteris et venustior est, et aptior.
[r] Immutabilis. Cod. Oxon.   [s] Dignatus. Cod. Oxon.
[t] 'Personam' perperam omittit Cod. Oxoniensis.

sumptionem [carnis, æterna fuit Trinitas, ita post adsumptionem ᵘ] humanæ naturæ, vera maneat Trinitas; ne propter adsumptionem humanæ carnis dicatur esse quaternitas, quod absit a fidelium cordibus, vel sensibus, dici, aut cogitari, cum, ita ᵛ ut supradictum est et Unitas in Trinitate, et Trinitas in Unitate veneranda sit.

Nam sicut anima rationalis, et caro unus est homo; ita Deus, et Homo unus est Christus. Etsi Deus ˣ, Dei Filius, nostram luteam et mortalem carnem, nostræ redemptionis conditionem ʸ adsumpserit, se tamen nullatenus ᶻ inquinavit, neque naturam Deitatis mutavit. Quia si sol, aut ignis aliquid immundum tetigerit, quod tangit purgat, et se nullatenus coinquinat: ita Deitas Sarcinam quoque ᵃ nostræ humanitatis adsumpsit, se nequaquam coinquinavit, sed nostram naturam carnis ᵇ,

ᵘ Desunt in Codice Oxoniensi: prætermissa scilicet festinantis Librarii incuria, ob vocem iteratam.
ᵛ Pro 'cum ita,' habet Cod. Oxon. 'nisi ita.'
ˣ Murator. Cod. omittit 'Deus.'
ʸ Cod. Oxoniensis, Nostri Redemptionis conditionis adsumpsit. Nescio an melius Muratorius; Nostram luteam, et mortalem carnem nostræ conditionis adsumpscrit. Sed levi mutatione, recte incedunt omnia. Conditio, apud Scriptores quinti et sexti sæculi, est servile onus, opusve.
ᶻ Cod. Oxon. legit 'Se nullatenus.' Murator. : Sed tamen se nullatenus. Noster vero in *Exposit. in Symb. Apostol.* in simili causa, hac utitur phrasi, se tamen non inquinat.
ᵃ Oxoniensis habet, Deitas sarcinamque nostræ humanitatis adsumpsit, se nequaquam, &c. Muratorius hoc modo; Deitas sarcinam, quam ex nostra humanitate adsumpsit, nequaquam coinquinavit. Lectio frigida prorsus, et inepta. Juvat huc conferre quæ Fortunatus noster *ad Symb. Apost.* in eandem sententiam breviter dictavit, p. 1152.
"Quod vero Deus majestatis de Maria in carne natus est, non est sordidatus nascendo de Virgine, qui non fuit pollutus hominem condens de pulvere. Denique sol, aut ignis, si lutum inspiciat, quod tetigerit purgat, et se tamen non inquinat." Conf. Ruffin. *Symb.*, (p. 133), c. 9, p. 113.
ᵇ Nostræ naturæ carnem. Murat.

quam adsumpsit, purgavit, et a maculis, et sordibus peccatorum, ac vitiorum expiavit: sicut Esaias ait; ipse infirmitates nostras accepit, et ægrotationes portavit. Ad hoc secundum humanitatem natus est, ut infirmitates nostras acciperet, et ægrotationes portaret: non quod ipse infirmitates, vel ægrotationes in se haberet, quia salus mundi est; sed ut eas a nobis tolleret, dum suæ sacræ passionis gratia, et sacramento[c], chirographo adempto, redemptionem pariter et salutem animarum nobis condonaret.

Qui passus est pro salute nostra. Id est, secundum id quod pati potuit: quod est, secundum humanam naturam; nam secundum divinitatem, Dei Filius impassibilis est.

Descendit ad inferos[d]. Ut[e] protoplastum Adam[f], et patriarchas, et prophetas, et omnes justos, qui pro originali peccato ibidem detinebantur, liberaret; et de[g] vinculis ipsius[h] peccati absolutos, de eadem captivitate, et[i] infernali[k] loco, suo sanguine redemptos, ad supernam patriam, et ad perpetuæ vitæ gaudia revocaret. Reliqui[l], qui supra originale peccatum[m] principalia crimina[n] commiserunt, ut adserit Scriptura, in pœnali

[c] Muratorius legit; Dum suæ sacræ passionis gratiam, et sacramenta: nullo sensu. Oxoniensis, Dum suæ sacræ passionis gratiæ (pro gratia) ac sacramento.
[d] Ad inferna. Cod. Oxon. Q. annon vetustissima hæc fuerit lectio *in Symbolo Athanasiano,* sicut in *Apostolico?*
[e] 'Qui,' loco τοῦ 'ut.' Cod. Oxon. At *Sermo de Symbolo,* in Append. *ad August.* (vol. vi. p. 281), legit, cum Muratorio, 'ut.'
[f] Adam Protoplastum. Append.
[g] Et ut de. Append.
[h] 'Ipsius' deest. Append.
[i] Deest 'et,' Cod. Oxon.
[k] Inferni. Append.
[l] Muratorius habet 'vero,' post 'reliqui.' Oxon. non agnoscit, nec Append.
[m] Ita legitur in Appendice. Oxoniensis, supra originale peccato: Muratorius, supra originali peccato.
[n] Principalem culpam. Append.

Tartaro remanserunt: sicut in persona Christi dictum est per prophetam; Ero mors tua, O Mors; id est, morte sua Christus humani generis inimicam mortem interfecit, et vitam dedit. Ero morsus tuus, inferne. Partim [o] momordit infernum, pro parte eorum quos liberavit: partem reliquit, pro parte eorum qui pro principalibus criminibus in tormentis remanserunt.

Surrexit a mortuis primogenitus mortuorum. Et alibi Apostolus dicit; ipse primogenitus,ex multis fratribus. Id est, primus a mortuis resurrexit. Et multa corpora [p] sanctorum dormientium cum eo surrexerunt, sicut evangelica auctoritas [q] dicit: sed ipse, qui caput est, prius, deinde qui [r] membra sunt continuo.

Postea ascendit ad cœlos. Sicut Psalmista ait; ascendit [s] in altum, captivam duxit captivitatem, id est, humanam naturam, quæ prius sub peccato venundata fuit, et captivata; eamque redemptam captivam [t] duxit in cælestem altitudinem: et ad cœlestis Patriæ [u] Regnum sempiternum, ubi antea non fuerat, eam [v] collocavit, in gloriam sempiternam.

Sedet ad dexteram Patris. Id est, prosperitatem paternam, et in [x] eo honore, quod [y] Deus est.

[o] Muratorius, et Oxoniensis, in utroque loco, 'Partem:' Appendix, in utroque, 'Partim.' Media mihi lectio maxime arridet.
[p] Deest 'corpora' in Cod. Oxon.
[q] In evangelica autoritate. Cod. Oxon.
[r] Quæ membra. Cod. Oxon.
[s] Ascendens. Murator.
[t] Conf. *Tractatum Anonymi de Essentia Divinitatis,* apud Hieronym., vol. v. p. 120; et apud Augustin., vol. viii. App., p. 69; et Isid. Hisp. *de Resurr. Dom.,* c. 56, p. 577 (p 560), ed. Paris.
[u] Cælestem Patriam. Cod. Oxon.
[v] 'Et' pro 'eam.' Murator.
[x] 'In' deest. Cod. Oxon.
[y] Mallem 'quo,' si per Codices liceret; sed et 'quod,' adverbialiter hic positum pro 'quia,' sensum non incommodum præ se ferre videtur.

Inde venturus[z] *judicare vivos et mortuos.* Vivos dicit eos quos tunc adventus Dominicus in corpore viventes invenerit [et mortuos, jam ante sepultos. Et aliter dicit[a]]; vivos justos, et mortuos peccatores[b].

Ad cujus adventum omnes homines resurgere habent cum corporibus suis; et reddituri sunt de factis propriis rationem: et qui bona egerunt, ibunt in vitam æternam; qui vero mala, in ignem æternum. Hæc est Fides Catholica, quam nisi quisque fideliter, firmiterque crediderit, salvus esse non poterit.

[z] Venturus est. Murator.
[a] Quantum hic uncis includitur, omittit Codex Oxoniensis. Delusus est forsitan librarius per binas literulas 'it' bis positas: vel, simili errore deceptus, integram lineam præterierit, dum in proxime sequentem oculos conjecerat.
[b] Operæ pretium est pauca hic subjicere, quæ noster habet in expositione sua in *Symb. Apostolicum,* "judicaturus vivos, et mortuos. Aliqui dicunt vivos, justos; mortuos vero injustos: aut certe, vivos, quos in corpore invenerit adventus Dominicus, et mortuos, jam sepultos. Nos tamen intelligamus vivos et mortuos, hoc est animas et corpora pariter judicanda."—Conf. Ruffin. *Symb.*, c. 33, p. 135 (p. 140); Method. apud *Phot. Codic.* 234, p. 932; Isid. Pelus., *Epist.* 222, lib. i. p. 64; Pseud. Ambros. *de Trin.,* c. 15, vol. ii. App., p. 331.

INDEX OF AUTHORS AND EDITIONS.

N.B. The titles of works that are referred to by Waterland, but have not had the references verified for this edition, are printed in italics. In all cases where the edition referred to is different from that used by Waterland himself, the original reference has been retained within brackets in the notes.

ABÆLARDUS, Petrus (4th century). Opera, 4to. Paris, 1616.
Abbo Floriacensis (10th century). Liber Apologeticus; in Gallandi's Bibliotheca Patrum, vol. xiv., p. 137, &c.
Adalbertus (9th century). Profession of Faith; in Harduin, vol. v., p. 1445.
Æneas Parisiensis (9th century). Liber adversus Græcos; in d'Achery's Spicilegium, vol. i., p. 113, &c.
Agobardus Lugdunensis (9th century). Opera. 2 vols., 8vo. Paris, 1666.
Alcuinus, Albinus Flaccus (8th century). De Fide S. Trinitatis; in De la Bigne's Bibliotheca Patrum, vol. iii., p. 1255, &c.
Alexander de Ales (13th century). Tabulæ quæstionum. 4 vols., 4to. Paris, 1516.
Alexander Natalis (17th century). Historia Ecclesiastica. 8 vols., fol. Paris, 1699.
Allatius Leo (17th century). De Ecclesiæ Occidentalis atque Orientalis perpetua consensione. 4to. Colon, 1648.
    Græcia Orthodoxa. 2 vols., 4to. Romæ, 1652.
    Syntagma de Symbolo S. Athanasii.
Alstedius, Joannes Henricus (17th century). Thesaurus Chronologiæ. 8vo. Herbip. Nass., 1624.
Ambrosius Mediolanensis (4th century). 2 vols., fol. Paris, 1686—1690.
Antelmius, Josephus (17th century). Nova de Symbolo Athanasiano Disquisitio. 8vo. Paris, 1693.
    De veris operibus Leonis Magni. Paris, 1669.
Antonius, Nicolaus (17th century). Bibliotheca Hispana Vetus. 2 vols., fol. Matriti, 1788.
Aquinas, Thomas (13th century). Opera, 17 vols., fol. Venetiis, 1593, 1594.

Arnoldus Lubecensis (12 century). Chronicon Slavorum; in continuation of Helmoldi's Chronicon. 4to. Lubeck, 1659.
Ashwell, George (17th century). Fides Apostolica. 8vo. Oxford, 1653.
Athanasius (4th century). Opera, Gr. et Lat. P. Nannii. 2 vols., fol. Heidelb., 1601.
—— Opera Omnia : opera et studio Monachorum Ordinis S. Benedicti. 2 vols., fol. Paris, 1679—1700.
Athenagoras (2nd century). Legatio pro Christianis: in the same volume with Justin Martyr.
Augustinus Hipponensis (5th century). Opera. 11 vols, fol. Paris, 1679—1700.
Avitus Viennensis (5th and 6th centuries). Opera; in Sirmondi Opera, vol. ii., p. 1, &c.

Bachiarius (5th century). Fides; in Muratori's Anecdota, vol. ii., p. 9, &c.
Balbus Januensis, Joannes (13th century). Catholicon Magnum. Fol. Rothomagi, 1506.
Bale, Joannes (15th century). Scriptorum Illustrium Majoris Brytanniæ Catalogus. 2 vols. in 1, fol. Basil, 1557—1559.
Baronius, Cæsar (16th century). Annales Ecclesiastici. 12 vols., fol. Romæ, Antverpiæ, Coloniæ, 1596—1624.
Baxter, Richard (17th century). Methodus Theologiæ Christianæ. Fol. Lond., 1681.
—— Practical Works. 4 vols., fol. Lond., 1707.
—— Life of: see Calamy.
Beleth, John (12th century). Divinorum Officiorum Rationale ; in the same volume with Durandus on the same subject.
Berno Augiensis (11th century). Epistola inedita; in Mabillon de Cursu Gallicano, p. 396.
Beveridge, William (17th century). Works. 9 vols., 8vo. Lond., 1824.
Bibliotheca Patrum, per Margarinum de la Bigne. 9 vols., fol. Paris, 1589.
Bibliotheca Maxima Veterum Patrum. 27 vols., fol. Lugd., 1677.
Bibliotheca Veterum Patrum, cura et studio Andreæ Gallandi. 14 vols., fol. Venet., 1765—1781.
Bingham, Joseph (18th century). Origines Ecclesiasticæ. 8 vols., 8vo. London, 1834.
Bona, Joannes (17th century). Opera. 4to. Antverpiæ, 1677.
Bruno Herbipolensis (11th century). Commentarii in totum Psalterium, et in Cantica Vet. et N. Testamenti. 4to. Norimberg, 1494.
—— Also in Bibliotheca Maxima Patrum, vol. xviii., p. 65, &c.

Cabasutius, Joannes (17th century). Notitia Ecclesiastica. Fol. Lugd., 1685.
Cæsarius Arelatensis (6th century). Sermo de Symboli Fide et Bonis Moribus; in Augustine, vol. v., App., p. 399.
Calamy, Edmund (18th century). Abridgement of Baxter's History of his Life and Times. 2 vols., 8vo. Lond., 1713.
Calecas, Manuel (14th century). Contra Græcorum Errores; in Bibliotheca Maxima Patrum, vol. xxvi., p. 382, &c.
——— De Principiis Fidei Catholicæ, in Combefis' Auctarium Novissimum, Part ii., p. 182, &c.
Calvisius, Seth (17th century). Opus Chronologicum. 4to. Francf., 1629.
Cantilupe, Walter de (13th century). Synodical Constitutions; in Spelman's Concilia, vol. ii., p. 240, &c.
Carranza, F. Barth. (16th century). Summa Conciliorum. 12mo. Lugd., 1587.
Catalogus Librorum MSS. in Bibliotheca C.C.C. in Cantabrigia. Fol. Lond., 1722.
Cave, William (17th century). Lives of the Fathers. 2 vols., fol. Lond., 1683.
——— Historia Literaria. 2 vols., fol. Lond., 1688.
Chillingworth, William (17th century). Works. Ninth edition. Fol. Lond., 1727.
Clarke, Samuel (17th and 18th centuries). The Scripture Doctrine of the Trinity; in vol. iv. of his collected works. 4 vols., fol. Lond., 1738.
——— The same. First edition. 8vo. Lond., 1712.
Clemens Alexandrinus (3rd century). Opera. 2 vols., fol. Oxon., 1715.
Clemens Romanus (1st century). Epistolæ; in Jacobson's Patres Apostolici.
Collier, Jeremy (17th and 18th centuries). An Ecclesiastical History of Great Britain. 2 vols., fol. Lond., 1708.
Combefis, François (17th century). Bibliothecæ Græcorum Patrum Auctarium Novissimum. Fol. Par., 1672.
Comber, Thomas (17th century). Companion to the Temple. Fol. Lond., 1684.
Covel, John (17th and 18th centuries). Some Account of the Present Greek Church. Fol. Cambridge, 1722.
Councils: see Carranza, Harduin, Labbe, Ruelius, Spelman.
Coxe, Henry Octavius (19th century). Catalogus Codicum MSS. in Collegiis Aulisque Oxoniensibus. 2 vols., 4to. Oxon., 1852.
——————— Catalogus Codicum MSS. Bibliothecæ Bodleianæ. 2 vols. in 3, 4to. Oxon., 1853—1858.
Cudworth, Ralph (17th century). The True Intellectual System of the Universe. Fol. Lond., 1678.

Cyparissiota, Joannes Sapiens (14th century). Expositio materiararia eorum quæ de Deo a theologis dicuntur. 8vo. Romæ, 1581. Quoted by Waterland from Bibl. Max. PP. Vol. xxi.
Cyprianus (3rd century). Opera. Fol. Paris, 1726.
Cyrillus Hierosolymitanus (4th century). Opera. Fol. Paris, 1720.

D'Achery, John Lucas (17th century). Acta Sanctorum ordinis S. Benedicti; collegit J. L. D'Achery, et cum eo in lucem edidit J. Mabillon. 9 vols., fol. Venet., 1733.
—————— Spicilegium, sive Collectio veterum aliquot Scriptorum. 3 vols., fol. Paris, 1723.
Damascenus, Joannes (8th century). Opera omnia, studio P. M. Le Quien. 2 vols., fol. Venet., 1748.
Denebert (8th century). Professio Fidei, in Textus Roffensis, p. 252.
Dodwell, Henry (17th and 18th centuries). A Discourse concerning the Use of Incense in Divine Offices. 8vo. Lond., 1711.
Dupin: see Pinn.
Durandus, Gulielmus (13th century). Rationale Divinorum Officiorum. 8vo. Antverp., 1576.
Durellus, Joannes (17th century). Ecclesiæ Anglicanæ Vindiciæ. 4to. Lond., 1669.
Dionysius Alexandrinus (3rd century). Opera. Fol. Paris, 1796.
Dionysius Romanus (3rd century). Fragmentum adv. Sabellianos; in Routh's Rel. Sacr. Vol. iii., p. 371, &c.

Epiphanius (4th century). Opera omnia, ex recensione et cum notis Petavii. 2 vols., fol. Paris, 1662.

Fabricius, John Albert (18th century). Bibliotheca Græca. 14 vols., 4to. Hamburg, 1716—1728.
Faustinus Presbyter (4th century). De Trinitate, sive de Fide, contra Arianos; in Bibl. Max. PP., vol. v., p. 637, &c.
Fleckman. Variarum lectionum congeries; appended to Nannius' edition of Athanasius.
Fortunatus Venantius (6th century). Expositio Fidei Catholicæ, printed in this book.
—————— In Symbolum Apostolicum Expositio, in Bibl. Max. PP., vol. x., p. 520, &c.
Fulgentius Ruspensis (6th century). Opera. 4to. Paris, 1643.

Gallandi: see Bibliotheca Patrum.
Gavauti, Bartholomew (17th century). Commentaria in Rubricas Missalis et Breviarii Romani. 2 vols., fol. Romæ, 1628.
Genebrard, Gilbert (16th century). In Athanasii Symbolum

Commentarium; printed at the end of his edition of the Latin Psalter. 8vo. Lugd., 1607.

Gennadius Massiliensis (5th century). De Ecclesiasticis Dogmatibus; in S. Augustine's Works, vol. viii., p. 75, &c.
——————————— Illustrium Virorum Catalogus; in S. Jerome's Works, vol. v., p. 26, &c.

Grabe, John Ernest (17th century). Vetus Testamentum, ex versione LXX. Interpretum. 4 vols., fol. Oxon., 1709.

Gregorius Nazianzenus (4th century). Opera omnia. 2 vols., fol. Paris, 1609—1611.

Gregorius Nyssenus (4th century). Quoted from Harduin, vol. iii., p. 106.

Gualdo Corbeiensis (11th century). Vita Anscharii; in Lambecius' Origines Hamburgenses, p. 322.

Gundling, Wolfgang (17th century). Notæ in Eustratii Johannidis Zialowski Delineationem Ecclesiæ Græcæ. 8vo. Norib., 1680.

Hampole, Ricardus (14th century). Symboli Apostolici et Athanasii enarratio; in Bibl. Max. PP., vol. xxvi., p. 624, &c.

Harduin, Joannes (18th century). Conciliorum collectio regia maxima. 11 vols., fol. Paris, 1715.

Harris, John (18th century). A Compleat Collection of Voyages and Travels. 2 vols., fol. Lond., 1705.

Hatto, or Ahyto of Basil (9th century). Capitulare; in Harduin's Councils, vol. ii., p. 1241.

Heidegger, John Henry (17th century). Dissertationes Selectæ, Sacram Theologiam illustrantes. 3 vols., 4to. Tiguri, 1674—1690.

Helvicus, Christopher (17th century). Theatrum Historicum et Chronologicum. Fol. Oxon., 1651.

Heurtley, Carolus A. (19th century). De Fide et Symbolo. 12mo. Oxon., 1869.

Hickes, George (17th and 18th centuries). A Collection of Sermons. 2 vols., 8vo. Lond., 1713.
——————————— Linguarum Vett. Septentrionalium Thesaurus. 3 vols., fol. Oxon., 1703—1705.

Hieronymus, Eusebius (4th century). Opera. 5 vols., fol. Paris, 1693—1706.

Higden, Ranulphus (14th century). Polychronicon, with translation by John Trevisa. New edition. By Babington Churchill. 2 vols., 8vo. Lond., 1865.

Hilarius Arelatensis (5th century). Vita S. Honorati Arelatensis; in Leo's Works, vol. i., p. 752, &c.

Hildegardis (12th century). Ad Sorores suas Explicatio Symboli S. Athanasii; in Bibl. Max. PP., vol. xxv., p. 535, &c.

Hincmarus Remensis (9th century). Opera. 2 vols., fol. Paris, 1645.
Hippolytus Portuensis (3rd century). Opera. 2 vols., fol. Hamburg, 1716.
Hody, Humphrey (17th and 18th centuries). De Bibliorum Textibus Originalibus. Fol. Oxon., 1705.
Honoratus Massiliensis (5th century). Vita S. Hilarii, in vol. i. of Leo's works.
Honorius Augustodunensis (12th century). Gemma Animæ, sive de Diversis Officiis et Antiquo Ritu Missarum; in Bibl. Max. PP., vol. xx., p. 963, &c.
Hugo a Sancto Victore (12th century). Opera. 3 vols., fol. Paris, 1526.

Ignatius Theophorus (2nd century). Opera vera et supposititia; in Coteler's Patres Apostolici. 2 vols., fol. Antverp., 1698.
——————— Epistolæ Septem genuinæ; in Jacobson's Patres Apostolici.
Irenæus (2nd century). Opera. Fol. Paris, 1710.
Isidorus Hispalensis (7th century). Opera omnia. Fol. Colon., 1617.
Isidorus Pelusiota (5th century). Epistolarum libri quinque. Fol. Paris, 1638.

Jacobson, W. (19th century). Patrum Apostolicorum quæ supersunt. 2 vols., 8vo. Oxon., 1863.
Joannes Antiochenus (5th century). Epistola ad S. Cyrillum Alexandrinum; in Routh's Opuscula, vol. ii., p. 203, &c.
Joannes Januensis: see Balbus.
Justinus Martyr (2nd century). Opera. Fol. Paris, 1712.

Kirkham, Walter de (13th century). Constitutiones; in Spelman's Concilia, vol. ii., p. 292, &c.

Labbe, Philip (17th century). Concilia Sacrosancta. 17 vols., fol. 1671.
——————— De Scriptoribus Ecclesiasticis Dissertatio. 2 vols., 8vo. Paris, 1660.
Lambecius, Petrus (17th century). Commentarium de Bibliotheca Vindobonensi; octo libris, fol. Vindobonæ, 1665—1679.
——————— Origines Hamburgenses. 4to. Hamburg, 1652.
Langbaine, Gerard. (17th century). Letter to Usher; in Usher's Letters, p. 513.
Le Cointe, Carolus (17th century). Annales Ecclesiastici Francorum. 8 vols., fol. Paris, 1665—1683.

Le Long, James (18th century). Bibliotheca Sacra. 2 vols., fol. Paris, 1723.
Leo Magnus (5th century). Opera post Paschalii Quesnelli recensionem exacta. 2 vols., fol. Paris, 1675.
Leporius Monachus (5th century). Libellus emendationis, sive satisfactionis, confessionem fidei Catholicæ continens; in Bibl. Max. PP. Vol. vii., p. 1, &c.
Lepusculus, Sebastian (16th century). Collection of documents in Munster's "Historiarum Josephi (Gorionidis) Compendium." 8vo. Basil, 1559.
Le Quien, Michael (18th century). Dissertationes Damascenicæ ; in vol. i. of his edition of Joannes Damascenus.
——— Panoplia contra Schisma Græcorum. 4to. Paris, 1718. Published under the pseudonym of Stephanus de Altimura.
L'Estrange, Hamon (17th century). The Alliance of Divine Offices. Fol. Lond., 1659.
Ludolphus, Job (17th century). Historia Ethiopica. Fol. Francf., 1681.
Ludolphus Saxo (14th century). Vita Christi. Fol. Paris, 1534.
Luther, Martin (16th century). Opera Latina. 7 vols., fol. Witenborg., 1550—1572.

Mabillon, John (16th and 17th centuries). Acta Sanctorum ; see d'Achery.
——— De Liturgia Gallicana; et de Cursu Gallicano. 4to. Paris, 1685.
——— De Re Diplomatica. Fol. Paris, 1681—1704.
Marcus Ephesius (15th century). Disputations at the Council of Florence; in Harduin, vol. ix.; quoted also in Silv. Sguropulos, p. 150.
Martene, Edmund (18th century). De Antiquis Ecclesiæ Ritibus. 3 vols., 4to. Rothomagi, 1700—1702.
Melito (2nd century). Fragmenta; in Routh's Reliquiæ Sacræ, vol. v., p. 113, &c.
Methodius Patavensis (3rd century). De Resurrectione; in Photius' Bibliotheca, codex 234.
——— Convivium decem virginum; in Combefis' Auctarium Novissimum, p. 64, &c.
Metrophanes Critopulos. Confessio Catholicæ et Apostolicæ in Oriente Ecclesiæ. Gr. et Lat. ed. J. Horneius. 4to. Helmstadt, 1661.
Montfaucon, Bernard de (17th and 18th centuries). Diarium Italicum. 4to. Paris, 1702.
——— Diatribe in Symbolum Quicunque; in the Benedictine edition of S. Athanasius, vol. ii., p. 719, &c.

T

Muratori, Ludovicus Antonius (17th and 18th centuries). Anecdota ex Ambrosianæ Bibliothecæ codicibus. 2 vols., fol. Mediolani, 1697.

Nesselius, Daniel (17th century). Catalogus Codicum MSS. Græcorum necnon linguarum Orientalium bibliothecæ Cæsareæ Vindobonensis. 6 vols., fol. Vindob., 1690.
Nicholls, *William* (17*th and* 18*th centuries*). *Defensio Ecclesiæ Anglicanæ.* 12*mo. Lond.*, 1707.
Novatianus (3rd century). Tractatus de Trinitate; in the same volume with Tertullian.

Olivet, Monks of Mount. Quoted by Le Quien in his Dissertationes Damascenicæ.
Origen (3rd century). 4 vols., fol. Paris, 1733—1759.
Orosius, Paulus (5th century). Epistola ad Augustinum; in Augustine's works, vol. viii., p. 609.
Osoma Petrus de (15*th century*). *Commentaria in Symbolum Quicunque vult, &c. 4to. Paris,* 1478.
Otto Frisingensis (12th century). Chronicon. Fol. Basil., 1569.
Oudin, Casimir (17th and 18th centuries). Commentarius de Scriptoribus Ecclesiæ antiquis. 3 vols., fol. Lips., 1722.

Pagi, Antonius (17th century). Critica Historico-Chronologica in Annales Baronii. Fol. Paris, 1689.
Papebrochius, Daniel (17th and 18th centuries). Responsio ad Exhibitionem Errorum; quoted in Muratori's Anecdota, vol. ii., p. 223.
Pappus, Joannes. Commentary on the Confession of Augsburg; quoted in Scrarius, Opuscula, vol. ii. p. 9.
Pareus, David (16*th and* 17*th centuries*). *Symbolum B. Athanasii, notis breviter declaratum.*
Paululus, Robertus (12th century). Quoted in Hugo a Sancto Victore, vol. iii. p. 223.
Pearson, John (17th century). An Exposition of the Creed; revised and corrected by the Rev. E. Burton. Fourth edition. 8vo. Oxford, 1857.
    Waterland quotes from the third edition, fol., Lond., 1669, the latest in Pearson's lifetime.
Pelagius (6th century). Symboli explanatio; in Jerome's works. vol. v., p. 123, &c.
Petavius, Dionysius (17th century). Opus de theologicis Dogmatibus. 6 vols., fol. Antverp., 1700.

Philastrius Brixiensis (4th century). Liber de Hæresibus; in Bibl. Max. PP., vol. v., p. 706, &c.
Photius (9th century). Bibliotheca. Fol. Rothomagi, 1653.
Pinn, Lewis Ellis du (17th and 18th centuries). Nouvelle Bibliothèque des auteurs Ecclesiastiques; translated by William Wotton. 6 vols., fol. Lond., 1692—1699.
Pjusiadenus, Joannes (15th century). De differentiis inter Græcos et Latinos; in Allatius Leo's Græcia Orthodoxa. Quoted by Waterland from Combefis' Auctarium, p. 297.
Prayer-Book, various editions.
Primer of John, Bishop of Rochester. 8vo. Lond., 1539.
────── of Cardinal Pole. 1555.
Prosper Aquitanensis (5th century). Epistola ad Augustinum, in Augustine's works, vol. ii., p. 825.

Quesnel, Pasquier (17th and 18th centuries). Dissertationes, in his edition of Leo, vol. ii., p. 399, &c.
────────── Observationes in breviarium chori monasterii Montis Casini; in his edition of the Pœnitentiale of Theodorus. 4to. Paris, 1676.

Ratherius Veronensis (10th century). Synodica Epistola; in Harduin's Councils, vol. vi., p. 787, &c.
Ratram, or Bertram, of Corbey (9th century). Contra opposita Græcorum; in d'Achery's Spicilegium, vol. i., p. 63, &c.
Regino Prumensis (9th and 10th centuries). De Ecclesiasticis Disciplinis et Religione Christiana. 8vo., Paris, 1671.
Rembertus (9th century). Vita Anscharii; in Lambecius' Orig. Hamburg., p. 167, &c.
Renaudot, Eusebius (18th century). Liturgiarum Orientalium Collectio. 2 vols., 4to. Paris, 1715, 1716.
Ricaut, Paul (17th century). The Present State of the Greek and Armenian Churches. 8vo. Lond., 1679.
Riculphus (9th century). Constitutiones; in Harduin's Councils, vol. vi., p. 415.
Routh, Martin Joseph (19th century). Scriptorum Ecclesiasticorum Opuscula. 2 vols., 8vo. Oxon., 1840.
────────── Reliquiæ Sacræ. 5 vols., 8vo. Oxon., 1846.
Ruelius, Johan Ludwig (17th century). Concilia illustrata. 4 vols., 4to. Norib., 1675.
Ruffinus (4th century). Commentarius in Symbolum Apostolorum; in Heurtley's De Fide et Symbolo, p. 101, &c.

Sandius, Christophorus (17th century). Nucleus Historiæ Ecclesiasticæ. 4to. Colon., 1676.

Serarius, Nicolas (16th century). Opuscula Theologica. 2 vols., fol. Mogunt., 1610.
Simon Tornacensis (13th century). Expositio Symboli; quoted in Oudin's Commentary, vol. iii., p. 30.
Sirmond, James (16th and 17th centuries). Opera varia. 3 vols. fol. Paris, 1696.
Smith, Thomas (17th century). Catalogus Librorum MSS. Bibliothecæ Cottonianæ. Fol. Oxon., 1696.
—————— An Account of the Greek Church. 8vo. Lond., 1680.
Spelman, Sir Henry (17th century). Concilia, Decreta, Leges, Constitutiones, iu Re Ecclesiarum Orbis Britannici. Vol. ii., fol. Lond., 1664.
Spondanus, Henry (17th century). Annales Ecclesiastici, ex xii. tomis Cæs. Baronii in epitomen redacti. Fol. Mogunt., 1623.
Suicer, John Caspar (17th century). Thesaurus Ecclesiasticus e Patribus Græcis. 2 vols., fol. Amstelod., 1672.
Sylvester Sguropulos (15th century). Historia Concilii Florentini. Fol. Hagæ Comitis, 1660.

Tatianus (2nd century). Oratio adversus Græcos; in the same volume with Justin Martyr.
Taylor, Jeremy, (17th century). Works. 10 vols., 8vo. Lond., 1861.
Tentzelius, Ernestus (17th century). Exercitationes Selectæ. 2 vols., 4to. Lips., 1692.
—————— Judicia eruditorum de Symbolo Athanasiano studiose collecta. Gothæ, 1687.
Tertullianus (2nd century). Opera. Fol. Paris, 1695.
Textus Roffensis, Ernulphi episcopi ut vulgo fertur. 8vo. Oxon., 1720.
Theodulphus Aurelianensis (9th century). De Spiritu Sancto; in Sirmond's Opera Varia. Vol. ii., p. 695, &c.
Tillemont, Lewis Seb. Le Nau de (17th century). Mémoires pour servir à l'histoire ecclesiastique des six premiers siècles. 10 vols., fol. Brux., 1732.

Usher, James (17th century). Historia dogmatica. 4to. Lond., 1690.
—————— De Symbolo. 4to. Lond., 1647.
—————— De Græca LXX. Interpretum editione Syntagma. 4to. Lond., 1655.
—————— Letters. Fol. Lond., 1686.

Vincentius Lirinensis (5th century). Adversus prophanas Hæresewm Novationes libellus. 8vo. Colon., 1600.

Vossius, Gerard John (17th century). Opera. 6 vols., fol. Amstelod., 1701.

Wall, William (18th century). History of Infant Baptism. 4 vols., 8vo. Oxford, 1844.

Wallis, John (17th century). An Explication and Vindication of the Athanasian Creed. 4to. Lond., 1691.

Wanley, Humphrey (18th century). Librorum Vett. Septentrionalium Catalogus. Fol. Oxon., 1705; being vol. iii. of Hickes' Thesaurus.

Wharton, Henry (17th century). Auctarium Historiæ Dogmaticæ Jacobi Usseri. 4to. Lond., 1689; at the end of Usher's Historia Dogmatica.

———— Appendix ad Historiam Literariam Gul. Cave. Fol. Lond., 1689; at the end of vol. i. of Cave's Historia Literaria.

Wotton, William (18th century). Linguarum vett. Septentrionalium Thesauri, auctore G. Hickesio, conspectus brevis. 8vo. Lond., 1708.

Zialowski : see Gundling.

AN INDEX OF MANUSCRIPTS.

Ambrosian I., Athanasian Creed, pp. 72, 120, 176, &c., 215.
Ambrosian II., Anonymous Comments on the Creed, 64.
Ambrosian III., Fortunatus' Comment, 15, 43, 249—266.

Baiffius, Greek Copy of the Creed, 102, 106.
Balliol, Oxon., Bruno's Comment, 51.
Basil, Brnuo's and Hampole's Comment, 54.
Bennet, Camb. (N. X.), Athanasian Creed, 76, 178, 184.
Bennet (I. 1),Wickliff's Comment, 61.
Bennet (K. 10), Athanasian Creed, 79.
Bennet (N. O. V.), Athanasian Creed, 77, 86.
Bennet (N. 15), Gregory's Psalter, 67.
Bodleian (E. 6, 11), Neckham's Comment, 53.
Bodleian (E. 7, 8), Neckham's Comment, 53.
Bodleian (Junius 25), Fortunatus' Comment, 45, 248—266.
Bodleian (Laud, E. 71), Bruno's Comment, 50.
Bodleian (Laud, H. 61), Bruno's Comment, 50.
Bodleian (1205), Athanasian Creed, 81.
Bryling, Greek Copy of the Creed, 102, 215.

C.C.C.C., see Bennet.
Cambridge, Athanasian Creed, 79, 123.
Cassinensis, Athanasian Creed, 80.
Colbert I., Athanasian Creed, 71, 74, 148, 184—190.
Colbert II., Athanasian Creed, 77.
Constantinopolitan, Greek copy of the Creed, 102, 106.
Cotton I., Athanasian Creed in Athelstan's Psalter, 70, 73, 86, 109.
Cotton II., (Vitell., E. 18), Athanasian Creed, 78.
Cotton III., (Vespasian, A.), Athanasian Creed, 60, 70, 79.
Cotton IV., (Nero, C. 4), Gallican Version, 94.

Dionysian, see Baiffius.

Emanuel, Camb., Wickliff's Bible, 58.

Felckman's Greek copy of the Creed, 101.
Friars Minors, Latino-Gallican Creed, quoted by Montfaucon, 80, 81.

Germain de Prez, Bruno's Comment, 51, 52.
Germains', St., Athanasian Creed, 75, 177, &c.
Gotha, Bruno's with Hampole's Comment, 54.

Harleian I., Athanasian Creed, 78, 86.
Harleian II., Athanasian Creed, 80.
Harleian III., Bruno's Comment, 51.
Harleian IV., Triple Psalter, 89.
Hilarian, Athanasian Creed, 82.

James', St., I., Hampole's Comment, 61.
James', St., II., Athanasian Creed, 77, 94, 124.
James', St., III., Athanasian Creed, 80.
John's, St., Camb., I., Triple Psalter, 80, 89.
John's, St., Camb., II., Wickliff's Comment, 57.
John's, St., Oxon., Bruno's Comment, 50.

Lambeth, Athanasian Creed, 78, 86, 94.
Leipsic, Bruno's with Hampole's Comment, 54.

Magd., Camb., I., Wickliff's New Testament, 59.
Magd., Camb., II., Athanasian Creed, 96.
Magd., Oxon., Hampole's Comment, 55.
Merton, Oxon., Bruno's Comment, 50.

Norfolk I., Athanasian Creed, 78.
Norfolk II., Athanasian Creed, 80.
Norfolk III., Athanasian Creed, 80, 94.
Norfolk IV., English Gospels, 58.

Palatine, Greek copy of the Creed, 101, 107.
Paris I., Athanasian Creed, 75.
Paris II., Greek copy of the Creed, 102.
Patrick Young, Greek copy of the Creed, 103.

Sarum, Saxon Version of the Creed, 95.
Sydney, Camb., Hampole's Comment on the Psalms, English, 62.

Thuanus, Athanasian Creed, 81.
Trêves, Athanasian Creed, 71, 148.
Trin. Coll., Camb., I., Athanasian Creed, 93.
Trin. Coll., Camb., II., Bruno's Comment, 50, 52, 89, 93.
Trin. Coll., Camb., III. Hampole's Comment on the Psalms, 52.
Trin. Coll., Camb., IV., Rhythmus Anglicus, 38.
Trin. Coll., Camb., V., Wickliff's Comment, 61.

Usher I., Athanasian Creed, 67.
Usher II., Book of Hymns, 103.

Vienna I., Athanasian Creed, 75, 117, 119.
Vienna II., Greek Creed, 99.
Vienna III., Greek Creed, 100.
Vienna IV., German Version, 94, 116.

Wurtzburgh, Bruno's Comment, 49, 86.

York, Bruno's Comment, 51, 52.

AN INDEX OF AUTHORITIES.

ABÆLARDUS, 52, 65, 212, 220.
Abbo, 31, 96, 117, 219.
Adalbertus, 30.
Adrian 1., 26, 87, 117, 119.
Æneas Parisiensis, 7, 29, 98.
Agobardus, 27.
Alcuinus, 252, 253.
Alexander Alensis, 35, 54, 232.
Alexander 1V., 121.
Alexander Natalis, 16, 67, 114.
Allatius Leo, 8, 34, 135.
Alstedius, 114.
Ambrose, 104, 142, 151, 153, 154, 181, 185, 214.
Ambrose, Pseudo, 266.
Amerbachius, 92.
Anastasius I., 16, 81, 170.
Anastasius II., 146.
Anastasius of Antioch, 81.
Anscharius, 27, 116, 117.
Antelmius, 14, 33, 71, 82, 149, 158, 162, 163, 164.
Antonius, Nicol., 64.
Apollinarians, 225, 226, 245, 261.
Aquinas, 37, 122, 163.
Arians, 210, 211, 213, 224, 225, 235, 239, 244, 246, 254.
Arnoldus, 33.
Ashwell, S.
Athanasius, 32, 151, 232.
Athanasius of Spire, 10, 170.
Athelard, 118.
Athenagoras, 194.
Augustine, 20, 54, 84, 142—145, 147, 154, 155, 160, 164, 168, 173, 177—191, 214, 249, 256, 258, 260, 264, 265.
Augustine of Canterbury, 87.
Aurelius, 161.

Avitus Viennensis, 111, 159, 171.

Bacchiarius, 120, 182.
Bacon, Roger, 88.
Baiffius, 102, 106, 212, 217.
Baldensal, 39.
Bale, 60.
Baluzius, 25, 27.
Baronius, 9, 14, 113, 126.
Baxter, 239.
Beleth, 34.
Benedict, 122.
Berno Augiensis, 89.
Beveridge, 12.
Bingham, 16, 24.
Blunt, 192.
Bona, 7, 33, 81, 86—88, 112, 119, 121, 125, 129.
Boniface, 25, 81, 170.
Bruno, 47, 48, 54, 56, 182, 188, 249, 252—257.
Brunswick, Abbot of, 28.
Bryling, Nicol., 102, 105, 212, 214, 223, 229.
Burton, 192, 196, 199.

Cabasutius, 13, 24.
Cæsarius, 159, 171, 249.
Calamy, 236, 237, 238.
Caleca, Manuel, 35, 97, 99, 100, 125, 126, 171.
Calvin, 127, 238.
Calvisius, 113.
Cantilupe, Walter de, 36.
Carranza, 64.
Carrillus, 64.
Carthusians, 81.
Cassian, 157.
Cave, 11, 17.

AN INDEX OF AUTHORITIES. 281

Caxton, 60.
Cazanovius, 127.
Charles the Great, 26, 75, 109, 117, 119, 122.
Chillingworth, 234.
Clarke, 17, 179.
Claudianus, 147.
Clemens Alex., 197, 198, 204.
Clemens Romanus, 192.
Cochleus, 48, 49.
Collier, 60.
Combefis, 39, 40, 97, 126, 143, 171.
Comber, 12, 67.
Covel, 134.
Coverdale, 87.
Councils, viz.—
    Autun, A.D. 670. 13, 21, 46, 109, 110.
    Chalcedon, A.D. 451. 144, 145, 148, 237, 247.
    Ephesus, A.D. 431. 156, 236, 237.
    Exeter, A.D. 1287. 38.
    Florence, A.D. 1439. 136.
    Frankfort, A.D. 794. 25, 116.
    Gentilly, A.D. 767. 97.
    Spain, A.D. 447. 7.
    Toledo, III., A.D. 589. 112.
    Toledo, IV., A.D. 633. 111, 112, 113.
    Turribius, A.D. 447. 145.
Coxe, 50, 51, 55.
Creeds, viz.—
    Apostolic, passim.
    Athanasian, passim.
    Aquileian, 189, 227.
    Of Constantinople, passim.
    Of Damasus, 254, 256, 259.
    Of Epiphanius, 140, 152.
    Of Pelagius, 179, 185, 187, 189.
    Romanum Vetus, 189, 241.
Cudworth, 10.
Cyparissiota, 40, 104.
Cyprian, 193.
Cyril of Alexandria, 156.
Cyril of Jerusalem, 236, 242.
Cyril, missionary in Servia, 130.

Damasus, 85, 154, 254, 256, 259.

Danhawerus, 240.
Denebertus, 118.
Dionysius Alex., 196, 201, 204.
Dionysius of Milan, 104.
Dionysius Rom., 194, 201.
Dionysius of Sienna, 106.
Dodwell, 112.
Douza, 125.
Dudithius, 11.
Dupin, 13, 24.
Duranto, 38.
Durell, 88.

Epiphanius, 140, 152, 183.
Ethelbald, 68.
Euphronius, 46.
Eusebius, 39, 104, 170.
Eutyches, 144—147, 245, 247.

Fabricius, 9, 15, 24, 34, 105, 108.
Faustinus, 142, 179, 181, 214.
Felckmann, 83, 101, 107, 212.
Felix III., 145.
Feller, 55.
Flavian, 145, 147.
Fortunatus, 15, 43, 44, 110, 158, 170, 176, 182, 184, 186, 188, 222, 248—266.
Frassenius, 121.
Fulgentius, 146, 214, 252, 253.

Gaudentius, 20.
Gavantus, 114.
Genebrard, 102, 103, 105, 106, 107, 123, 127, 131, 212, 217.
Gennadius, 54, 120, 163, 187, 189, 191, 228.
Gorrham, 57.
Grabe, 73.
Gregory Bœticus, 256.
Gregory I., 67, 87, 249.
Gregory IX., legates of, 6, 11, 36, 66, 222.
Gregory Nazianzen, 20, 142, 147, 152, 153, 177.
Gregory Nyssen, 151.
Gregory of Tours, 46, 86, 112, 122.
Gualdo, 32.

Gundling, 11, 101, 103, 106, 126.
Hampole, 54, 61.
Harduin, 21, 24, 27, 30, 36, 136, 151.
Harris, 128, 129.
Hatto, 27, 116, 125.
Heath, 87.
Heidegger, 11.
Helvicus, 114.
Hermantius, 24.
Heurtley, 152, 241, 259.
Hickes, 68, 96, 134.
Higden, 58.
Hilary of Arles, 163—170.
Hilary of Poictiers, 82, 167, 170.
Hildegarde, 52.
Hilsey, 212.
Hincmar, 7, 22, 28, 47, 91, 93, 109, 163, 222.
Hippolytus, 195, 200, 204, 205.
Hody, 84, 86—89, 122.
Honoratus of Arles, 165.
Honoratus of Marseilles, 163, 166.
Honorius, 32.
Hormisdas, 146.
Hugo de S. Victor, 34.
Hulsemannus, 240.
Hydruntinus, Nicol., 34, 98, 99, 133.

Ignatius, 192, 198, 204.
Ignatius, Pseudo, 183, 191.
Irenæus, 193, 197, 198, 200, 201, 203, 205.
Isidorus Hispalensis, 9, 20, 253, 256, 261, 265.
Isidorus Pelusiota, 266.
Ivo Carnotensis, 249.

Januensis Johannes, 37, 55, 57, 233.
Jerome, 84—88, 151, 154, 256, 259, 265.
John of Antioch, 156.
John II., 146.
Julianus, 100.
Julius, 39, 100, 140.
Justin, 193, 194, 196, 201, 203.

Justinian, 146.
Kirkham, 37.
Kromayer, 240.
Labbe, 10, 24, 107, 113, 217.
Lambecius, 29, 32, 38, 79, 94, 117, 179, 185.
Langbaine, 57.
Le Cointe, 24.
Le Lando, 24.
Le Long, 48, 49, 58, 85, 89, 91, 94.
Leo I., 10, 145, 151, 157.
Leo III., 27, 122.
Leodegarius, 21, 23.
Leporius, 156, 160, 161.
Lepusculus, 106.
Le Quien, 15, 27, 67, 111, 123, 148, 149, 150, 151, 159, 222, 236, 237.
L'Estrange, 8, 67.
Liberius, 40, 140.
Livius, 163.
Ludolphus, Job, 127, 136, 246.
Ludolphus Saxo, 38, 232.
Lupus, 46.
Luther, 232, 238.
Lyra, 57.

Mabillon, 75, 86, 89, 112, 115, 117.
Macedonians, 245.
Marcus Ephesius, 136.
Martene, 134.
Martianay, 85, 86.
Meletius, 125.
Melito, 205.
Methodius, 205, 266.
Methodius, a Servian missionary, 130.
Metrophanes, 133.
Monothelites, 247.
Montfaucon, 14, 20, 24, 51, 67, 71, 73, 74, 75, 77, 80, 82, 83, 87, 93, 94, 97, 102, 103, 114, 149, 160, 217.
Muratori, 15, 21, 24, 43, 44, 64, 65, 67, 72, 115, 126, 160, 182, 248—266.

Neander, 105, 106.

Neckham, 53.
Nesselius, 100.
Nestorius, 149, &c., 245, 247.
Nichols, 237.
Nisselius, 108.
Nithardus, 93.
Novatian, 196.

Olivet, Monks of Mt., 27, 119, 122.
Origen, 86, 195, 199, 200, 202—207, 228.
Orosius, 229.
Osma, 63.
Otfridus, 94, 116.
Otho, 33, 38.
Oudin, 18, 23, 24, 29, 53, 57, 58, 115, 159.

Pagi, 13, 24, 80, 109, 110.
Papebrochius, 21.
Pappus, 247.
Parous, 46.
Patripassians, 210.
Paululus, 34.
Pearson, 9, 228.
Pelagius I., 146.
Pelagius, Monk, 154.
Petavius, 6, 148, 151.
Petrus de Harentals, 57.
Philastrius, 179.
Photinians, 225, 244.
Photius, 266.
Pius V., 86, 87.
Planudes, 100.
Plusiadenus, 40.
Pole, Cardinal, 96, 212.
Primers, 208, 212.
Prosper, 164.
Psalters, 83, &c.

Quesnel, 10, 24, 80, 82, 109, 110, 114, 163.

Ratherius, 30, 118, 120.
Ratram, 7, 29, 98.
Ravennius, 163.
Regino, 24.
Rembertus, 29, 117.
Renaudot, 126, 129, 246.
Ricaut, 136, 246.

Riculphus, 30.
Rotharius, 120.
Routh, 157, 236.
Ruelius, 9.
Ruffinus, 249, 256, 259, 260, 261, 263, 266.

Sabellians, 210, 233, 245, 253.
Sandius, 10.
Serrarius, 106, 247.
Simon, 53.
Sirmondus, 23, 24, 26, 28, 158, 159.
Smith, 73, 78, 79, 126.
Spelman, 36, 37, 38.
Spondanus, 126.
Stephens, 102, 105, 106, 212.
Strabo, 86.
Suicer, 136.
Sylvester Sguropulos, 136.

Tatian, 203.
Taylor, 8, 240.
Tentzel, 8, 13, 24, 29, 34, 54, 67, 68, 83, 94, 108, 129, 133, 240.
Tertullian, 194, 199, 200—204, 206.
Textus Roffensis, 118.
Thecaras, 132.
Theodoret, 154.
Theodulphus, 12, 26, 158.
Theophilus, 193.
Tillemont, 14, 24, 67, 71, 114.
Tonstall, 87.
Trevisa, 58, 60.

Ullerston, 56.
Usher, 7, 49, 58, 67—73, 92, 103, 104, 107, 129, 132, 218, 241.

Vigilius, Pope, 112.
Vigilius Tapsensis, 10, 12, 17, 82, 148, 149, 170.
Vincentius Lirinensis, 14, 145, 147, 157, 162, 164, 170, 171, 173, 177, 179, 187, 189.
Voss, 5, 25, 83, 125, 127.

Wall, 154, 155.
Wallis, 239.
Wanley, 50, 69, 77—79, 93, 94, 124.
Wharton, 58, 61, 92—94.
Wicliff, 57, 96, 223.
Wilkins, 95.

Willehad, 117, 119.
Wotton, 78, 95.

Young, 103.

Zialowski, 11.

Printed by James Parker and Co., Crown-yard, Oxford.

A SELECTION FROM
THE PUBLICATIONS OF
MESSRS. JAS. PARKER AND CO.

NEW BOOKS.

Studia Sacra:
COMMENTARIES ON THE INTRODUCTORY VERSES of St. John's Gospel, and on a portion of St. Paul's Epistle to the Romans; with other Theological Papers by the late Rev. JOHN KEBLE, M.A. 8vo., cloth, 10s. 6d.

Occasional Papers and Reviews,
On Sir Walter Scott, Poetry, and Sacred Poetry, Bishop Warburton, Rev. John Miller, Exeter Synod, Judicial Committee of Privy Council, Parochial Work, the Lord's Supper, Solomon, the Jewish Nation. By the late Rev. JOHN KEBLE, Author of "The Christian Year." 532 pp., with two Facsimiles from Common-place Book, Demy 8vo., cloth extra, 12s.

"They are prefaced by two letters of deep interest from Dr. NEWMAN and Dr. PUSEY. There is something extremely touching in the reunion, as it were, of the three old friends and fellow-labourers."—*Guardian.*

The First Prayer-book of Edward VI.
Compared with the Successive Revisions of the Book of Common Prayer. Together with a Concordance and Index to the Rubrics in the several Editions. Crown 8vo., cloth, 12s.

AN INTRODUCTION TO THE HISTORY OF THE Successive Revisions of the Book of Common Prayer. Crown 8vo., pp. xxxii., 532, cloth, 12s.

The History of Confirmation.
By WILLIAM JACKSON, M.A., Queen's College, Oxford; Vicar of Heathfield, Sussex. Crown 8vo., cloth, 4s.

The Awaking Soul,
As sketched in the 130th Psalm. Addresses delivered at St. Peter's, Eaton-square, on the Tuesdays in Lent, 1877, by E. R. WILBERFORCE, M.A., Vicar of Seaforth, Liverpool; and Sub-Almoner to the Queen. Crown 8vo., limp cloth, 2s. 6d.

Stories from the Old Testament.
With Four Illustrations. Square crown 8vo., 4s.

Adams's Historical Tales.
TALES ILLUSTRATING CHURCH HISTORY. ENGLAND: Mediæval Period. By the Rev. H. C. ADAMS, Vicar of Dry Sandford; Author of "Wilton of Cuthbert's," "Schoolboy Honour," &c. With four Illustrations on Wood. Fcap. 8vo., cloth, 5s.

JAMES PARKER AND CO., OXFORD AND LONDON.

Offices of the Old Catholic Prayer-book.

A CATHOLIC RITUAL, published according to the Decrees of the First Two Synods of the Old Catholics of the German Empire. Done into English and compared with the Offices of the Roman and Old German Rituals. By the Rev. F. E. WARREN, B.D., Fellow of St. John's College, Oxford. Crown 8vo., cl., 3s. 6d.

The Founder of Norwich Cathedral.

The LIFE, LETTERS, and SERMONS of BISHOP HERBERT DE LOSINGA (b. circ. A.D. 1050, d. 1119), the LETTERS (as translated by the Editors) being incorporated into the LIFE, and the SERMONS being now first edited from a MS. in the possession of the University of Cambridge, and accompanied with an English Translation and English Notes. By EDWARD MEYRICK GOULBURN, D.D., Dean of Norwich, and HENRY SYMONDS, M.A., Rector of Tivetshall, and late Precentor of Norwich Cathedral. 2 vols. 8vo., cloth, 24s. [*Shortly.*

The Archæology of Rome.

THE ARCHÆOLOGY OF ROME. By JOHN HENRY PARKER, C.B.
9. THE TOMBS IN AND NEAR ROME, with the Columbaria and the Painted Tombs on the Via Latina, with 24 Plates.
10. MYTHOLOGY IN FUNEREAL SCULPTURE, and Early Christian Sculpture, with Sixteen Plates.
The above two Parts in one Vol. Medium 8vo, cl., 15s.
12. THE CATACOMBS, OR ANCIENT CEMETERIES OF ROME, with Twenty-four Plates and Plans. Medium 8vo., cloth, 15s.

The Catholic Doctrine of the Sacrifice and Participation of the Holy Eucharist.

By GEORGE TREVOR, M.A., D.D., Canon of York; Rector of Beeford. Second Edition, Revised and Enlarged. Crown 8vo., cloth, 10s. 6d.

The Annals of England:

AN EPITOME OF ENGLISH HISTORY, from Contemporary Writers, the Rolls of Parliament, and other Public Records. A LIBRARY EDITION, revised and enlarged, with additional Woodcuts. 8vo., cloth, 12s.

THE SCHOOL EDITION of THE ANNALS of ENGLAND. In Five Half-crown Parts. 1. Britons, Romans, Saxons, Normans. 2. The Plantagenets. 3. The Tudors. 4. The Stuarts. 5. The Restoration, to the Death of Queen Anne. Fcap. 8vo., cloth.

The Exile from Paradise.

Translated by the Author of the "Life of S. Teresa." Fcap., cloth, 1s. 6d.

JAMES PARKER AND CO.

Daniel the Prophet.

Nine Lectures delivered in the Divinity School, Oxford. With a Short Preface in Answer to Dr. Rowland Williams. By E. B. PUSEY, D.D., Regius Professor of Hebrew, and Canon of Christ Church. *Seventh Thousand.* 8vo., 10s. 6d.

The Minor Prophets;

With a Commentary Explanatory and Practical, and Introductions to the Several Books. By the Rev. E. B. PUSEY, D.D., &c. 4to., cloth, price £1 11s. 6d.

The Fifty-third Chapter of Isaiah,

According to the Jewish Interpreters. I. Texts edited from Printed Books, and MSS., by AD. NEUBAUER. Price 18s. II. Translations by S. R. DRIVER and AD. NEUBAUER. With an Introduction to the Translations by the Rev. E. B. PUSEY, Regius Professor of Hebrew, Oxford. Post 8vo., cloth, 12s.

The Prophecies of Isaiah.

Their Authenticity and Messianic Interpretation Vindicated, in a Course of Sermons preached before the University of Oxford. By the Very Rev. R. PAYNE SMITH, D.D., Dean of Canterbury. 8vo., cloth, 10s. 6d.

A Plain Commentary on the Book of Psalms

(Prayer-book Version), chiefly grounded on the Fathers. For the Use of Families. 2 vols., Fcap. 8vo., cloth, 10s. 6d.

The Psalter and the Gospel.

The Life, Sufferings, and Triumph of our Blessed Lord, revealed in the Book of Psalms. Fcap. 8vo., cloth, 2s.

A Summary of the Evidences for the Bible.

By the Rev. T. S. ACKLAND, M.A., late Fellow of Clare Hall, Cambridge; Incumbent of Pollington cum Balne, Yorkshire. 24mo., cloth, 3s.

Godet's Biblical Studies

ON THE OLD TESTAMENT. Edited by the Hon. and Rev. W. H. LYTTELTON, Rector of Hagley, and Honorary Canon of Worcester. Fcap. 8vo. cloth, price 6s.

Catena Aurea.

A Commentary on the Four Gospels, collected out of the Works of the Fathers by S. THOMAS AQUINAS. Uniform with the Library of the Fathers. A Re-issue, complete in 6 vols., cloth, £2 2s.

A Plain Commentary on the Four Holy Gospels,

Intended chiefly for Devotional Reading. By the Very Rev. J. W. BURGON, B.D., Dean of Chichester. New Edition. 4 vols., Fcap. 8vo., limp cloth, £1 1s.

The Last Twelve Verses of the Gospel according to S. Mark

Vindicated against Recent Critical Objectors and Established, by the Very Rev. J. W. BURGON, B.D., Dean of Chichester. With Facsimiles of Codex ℵ and Codex L. 8vo., cloth, 12s.

The Gospels from a Rabbinical Point of View,

Shewing the perfect Harmony of the Four Evangelists on the subject of our Lord's Last Supper, and the Bearing of the Laws and Customs of the Jews at the time of our Lord's coming on the Language of the Gospels. By the Rev. G. WILDON PIERITZ, M.A. Crown 8vo., limp cloth, 3s.

Christianity as Taught by S. Paul.

By WILLIAM J. IRONS, D.D., of Queen's College, Oxford; Prebendary of S. Paul's; being the BAMPTON LECTURES for the Year 1870, with an Appendix of the CONTINUOUS SENSE of S. Paul's Epistles; with Notes and Metalegomena, 8vo., with Map, Second Edition, with New Preface, cloth, 9s.

S. Paul's Epistles to the Ephesians and Philippians.

A Practical and Exegetical Commentary. Edited by the late Rev. HENRY NEWLAND. 8vo., cloth, 7s. 6d.

A History of the Church,

From the Edict of Milan, A.D. 313, to the Council of Chalcedon, A.D. 451. By WILLIAM BRIGHT, D.D., Regius Professor of Ecclesiastical History, and Canon of Christ Church, Oxford. Second Edition. Post 8vo., 10s. 6d.

The Age of the Martyrs;

Or, The First Three Centuries of the Work of the Church of our Lord and Saviour Jesus Christ. By the late JOHN DAVID JENKINS, B.D., Fellow of Jesus College, Oxford; Canon of Pieter Maritzburg. Cr. 8vo., cl., reduced to 3s. 6d.

The Councils of the Church,

From the Council of Jerusalem, A.D. 51, to the Council of Constantinople, A.D. 381; chiefly as to their Constitution, but also as to their Objects and History. By E. B. PUSEY, D.D. 8vo., cloth, 6s.

The Ecclesiastical History of the First Three Centuries,

From the Crucifixion of Jesus Christ to the year 313. By the late Rev. Dr. BURTON. Fourth Edition. 8vo., cloth, 12s.

A Brief History of the Christian Church,

From the First Century to the Reformation. By the Rev. J. S. BARTLETT. Fcap. 8vo., cloth, 2s. 6d.

Manual of Ecclesiastical History,

From the First to the Twelfth Century inclusive. By the Rev. E. S. FFOULKES, M.A. 8vo., cloth, 6s.

A History of the English Church,

From its Foundation to the Reign of Queen Mary. By MARY CHARLOTTE STAPLEY. Third Edition, revised, with a Recommendatory Notice by DEAN HOOK. Crown 8vo., cloth, 5s.

Bede's Ecclesiastical History of the English Nation.

A New Translation by the Rev. L. GIDLEY, M.A., Chaplain of St. Nicholas', Salisbury. Crown 8vo., cloth, 6s.

The Principles of Divine Service;

Or, An Inquiry concerning the True Manner of Understanding and Using the Order for Morning and Evening Prayer, and for the Administration of the Holy Communion in the English Church. By the late Ven. PHILIP FREEMAN, M.A., Archdeacon of Exeter, &c. 2 vols. 8vo., cloth, 16s.

A History of the Book of Common Prayer,

And other Authorized Books, from the Reformation; with an Account of the State of Religion in England from 1640 to 1660. By the Rev. THOMAS LATHBURY, M.A. Second Edition, with an Index. 8vo., cloth, 10s. 6d.

Catechetical Lessons on the Book of Common Prayer,

Illustrating the Prayer-book, from its Title-page to the end of the Collects, Epistles, and Gospels. Designed to aid the Clergy in Public Catechising. By the Rev. Dr. FRANCIS HESSEY, Incumbent of St. Barnabas, Kensington, Fcap. 8vo., cloth, 6s.

A Short Explanation of the Nicene Creed,

For the Use of Persons beginning the Study of Theology. By the late A. P. FORBES, D.C.L., Bishop of Brechin. Second Edition, Crown 8vo., cloth, 6s.

An Explanation of the Thirty-Nine Articles.

By the late A. P. FORBES, D.C.L., Bishop of Brechin. With an Epistle Dedicatory to the Rev. E. B. PUSEY, D.D. Second Edition, in one vol., Post 8vo., 12s.

Addresses to the Candidates for Ordination on the Questions in the Ordination Service.

By the late SAMUEL WILBERFORCE, LORD BISHOP OF WINCHESTER. Fifth Thousand. Crown 8vo., cloth, 6s.

A Commentary on the Epistles and Gospels in the Book of Common Prayer.

Extracted from Writings of the Fathers of the Holy Catholic Church, anterior to the Division of the East and West. With an Introductory Notice by the DEAN OF ST. PAUL'S. 2 vols., Crown 8vo., cloth, 15s.

Sunday-School Exercises,

Collected and Revised from Manuscripts of Burghclere School-children, under the teaching of the Rev. W. B. BARTER, late Rector of Highclere and Burghclere; Edited by his Son-in-law, the BISHOP OF ST. ANDREW'S. Second Edition, Crown 8vo., cloth, 5s.

On Eucharistical Adoration.

With Considerations suggested by a Pastoral Letter on the Doctrine of the Most Holy Eucharist. By the late Rev. JOHN KEBLE, M.A., Vicar of Hursley. 24mo., sewed, 2s.

The Administration of the Holy Spirit

IN THE BODY OF CHRIST. The Bampton Lectures for 1868. By the Right Rev. the LORD BISHOP OF SALISBURY. Second Edition. Crown 8vo., 7s. 6d.

Sayings ascribed to our Lord

By the Fathers and other Primitive Writers, and Incidents in His Life narrated by them, otherwise than found in Scripture. By JOHN THEODORE DODD, B.A., late Junior Student of Christ Church. Crown 8vo., cloth, 3s.

The Pastoral Rule of S. Gregory.
Sancti Gregorii Papæ Regulæ Pastoralis Liber, ad JOHANNEM, Episcopum Civitatis Ravennæ. With an English Translation. By the Rev. H. R. BRAMLEY, M.A., Fellow of Magdalen College, Oxford. Fcap. 8vo., cloth, 6s.

The Canons of the Church.
The Definitions of the Catholic Faith and Canons of Discipline of the First Four General Councils of the Universal Church. In Greek and English. Fcap. 8vo., cloth, 2s. 6d.

The English Canons.
The Constitutions and Canons Ecclesiastical of the Church of England, referred to their Original Sources, and Illustrated with Explanatory Notes, by MACKENZIE E. C. WALCOTT, B.D., F.S.A., Præcentor and Prebendary of Chichester. Fcap. 8vo., cloth, 4s.

Vincentius Lirinensis
For the Antiquity and Universality of the Catholic Faith against the Profane Novelties of all Heretics. Latin and English. New Edition, Fcap. 8vo. [*Nearly ready.*
Translation only. 18mo., 1s. 6d.

De Fide et Symbolo:
Documenta quædam nec non Aliquorum SS. Patrum Tractatus. Edidit CAROLUS A. HEURTLEY, S.T.P., Dom. Margaretæ Prælector, et Ædis Christi Canonicus. Fcap. 8vo., cloth, 4s. 6d.

The Athanasian Creed.
A Critical History of the Athanasian Creed, by the Rev. DANIEL WATERLAND, D.D. Fcap. 8vo., cloth, 5s.

St. Cyril, Archbishop of Alexandria.
The Three Epistles (ad Nestorium, ii., iii., et ad Joan Antioch). A Revised Text, with an old Latin Version and an English Translation. Edited by P. E. PUSEY, M.A. 8vo., in wrapper, 3s.

S. Aurelius Augustinus,
EPISCOPUS HIPPONENSIS,
De Catechizandis Rudibus, de Fide Rerum quæ non videntur, de Utilitate Credendi. In Usum Juniorum. Edidit C. MARRIOTT, S.T.B., olim Coll. Oriel. Socius. A New Edition, Fcap. 8vo., cloth, 3s. 6d.

Cur Deus Homo,
Or Why God was made Man; by ST. ANSELM. Translated into English, with an Introduction, &c. Fcap. 8vo., 2s. 6d.
Latin and English Edition *nearly ready.*

The Book of Ratramn
The Priest and Monk of Corbey, commonly called Bertram, on the Body and Blood of the Lord. (Latin and English.) To which is added AN APPENDIX, containing the Saxon Homily of Ælfric. Fcap. 8vo. [*Nearly ready.*

NEW AND CHEAPER ISSUE
OF
The Library of the Fathers
OF THE HOLY CATHOLIC CHURCH, ANTERIOR TO THE DIVISION OF THE EAST AND WEST.

Translated by Members of the English Church.

Already Issued.

St. Athanasius against the Arians. 1 vol., 10s. 6d.
——————— Historical Tracts } 10s. 6d.
——————— Festal Epistles }
St. Augustine's Confessions, with Notes, 6s.
——————— Sermons on the New Testament. 2 vols., 15s.
——————— Homilies on the Psalms. 6 vols., £2 2s.
——————— on the Gospel and First Epistle of St. John. 2 vols., 15s.
——————— Practical Treatises. 6s.
St. Chrysostom's Homilies on the Gospel of St. Matthew. 3 vols., £1 1s.
——————— Homilies on the Gospel of St. John. 2 vols., 14s.
——————— Homilies on the Acts of the Apostles. 2 vols., 12s.
——————— to the People of Antioch. 7s. 6d.
——————— Homilies on St. Paul's Epistle to the Romans. 1 vol., 6s.
——————— The Hebrews. One Vol., cloth, 7s.
St. Cyprian's Treatises and Epistles, with the Treatises of St. Pacian. 10s.
St. Cyril (Bishop of Jerusalem), Catechetical Lectures on the Creed and Sacraments. 7s.
St. Cyril (Archbishop of Alexandria), Commentary upon the Gospel of St. John. Vol. I. 8s.
St. Ephrem's Rhythms on the Nativity, and on Faith. 8s. 6d.
St. Gregory the Great, Morals on the Book of Job. 4 vols., £1 11s. 6d.
St. Irenæus, the Works of. 8s.
St. Justin the Martyr. Works now extant. 6s.
Tertullian's Apologetical and Practical Treatises. 9s.

The following may still be had in the original bindings:—

St. Chrysostom's Homilies on St. Paul's Epistles to the Corinthians. 2 vols., 18s.
——————— Timothy, Titus, and Philemon. 1 vol., 7s. 6d.

Works of the Standard English Divines,
PUBLISHED IN THE LIBRARY OF ANGLO-CATHOLIC THEOLOGY,

At the following prices in Cloth.

Andrewes' (Bp.) Complete Works. 11 vols., 8vo., £3 7s.
    The Sermons. (Separate.) 5 vols., £1 15s.

Beveridge's (Bp.) Complete Works. 12 vols., 8vo., £1 4s.
    The English Theological Works. 10 vols., £3 10s.

Bramhall's (Abp.) Works, with Life and Letters, &c. 5 vols., 8vo., £1 15s.

Bull's (Bp.) Harmony on Justification. 2 vols., 8vo., 10s.
——————— **Defence of the Nicene Creed.** 2 vols., 10s.
——————— **Judgment of the Catholic Church.** 5s.

Cosin's (Bp.) Works Complete. 5 vols., 8vo., £1 10s.

Crakanthorp's Defensio Ecclesiæ Anglicanæ. 8vo., 7s.

Frank's Sermons. 2 vols., 8vo., 10s.

Forbes' Considerationes Modestæ. 2 vols., 8vo., 12s.

Gunning's Paschal, or Lent Fast. 8vo., 6s.

Hammond's Practical Catechism. 8vo., 5s.
——————— **Miscellaneous Theological Works.** 5s.
——————— **Thirty-one Sermons.** 2 Parts. 10s.

Hickes's Two Treatises on the Christian Priesthood. 3 vols., 8vo., 15s.

Johnson's (John) Theological Works. 2 vols., 8vo., 10s.
——————— **English Canons.** 2 vols., 12s.

Laud's (Abp.) Complete Works. 7 vols., (9 Parts,) 8vo., £2 17s.

L'Estrange's Alliance of Divine Offices. 8vo., 6s.

Marshall's Penitential Discipline. 8vo., 4s.

Nicholson's (Bp.) Exposition of the Catechism. (This volume cannot be sold separate from the complete set.)

Overall's (Bp.) Convocation-book of 1606. 8vo., 5s.

Pearson's (Bp.) Vindiciæ Epistolarum S. Ignatii. 2 vols., 8vo., 10s.

Thorndike's (Herbert) Theological Works Complete. 6 vols., (10 Parts,) 8vo., £2 10s.

Wilson's (Bp.) Works Complete. With **Life,** by Rev. J. Keble. 7 vols., (8 Parts,) 8vo., £3 3s.

The Catechist's Manual;
With an Introduction by the late SAMUEL WILBERFORCE, LORD BISHOP OF WINCHESTER. 5th Thousand. Cr. 8vo., limp cl., 5s.

The Confirmation Class-book:
Notes for Lessons, with APPENDIX, containing Questions and Summaries for the Use of the Candidates. By EDWARD M. HOLMES, LL.B., Author of the "Catechist's Manual." Fcap. 8vo., limp cloth, 2s. 6d.

THE QUESTIONS, separate, 4 sets, in wrapper, 1s.
THE SUMMARIES, separate, 4 sets, in wrapper, 1s.

The Church's Work in our Large Towns.
By GEORGE HUNTINGTON, M.A., Rector of Tenby, and Domestic Chaplain of the Rt. Hon. the Earl of Crawford and Balcarres. Second Edit., revised and enlarged. Cr. 8vo., cl. 3s. 6d.

The Church and the School:
Containing Practical Hints on the Work of a Clergyman. By H. W. BELLAIRS, M.A., One of Her Majesty's Inspectors of Schools. Cheap re-issue, Crown 8vo., limp cloth, 2s. 6d.

Notes of Seven Years' Work in a Country Parish.
By R. F. WILSON, M.A., Prebendary of Sarum, and Examining Chaplain to the Bishop of Salisbury. Fcap. 8vo., cloth, 4s.

A Manual of Pastoral Visitation,
Intended for the Use of the Clergy in their Visitation of the Sick and Afflicted. By A PARISH PRIEST. Dedicated, by permission, to His Grace the Archbishop of Dublin. Second Edition, Crown 8vo., limp cloth, 3s. 6d.; roan, 4s.

The Cure of Souls.
By the Rev. G. ARDEN, M.A., Rector of Winterborne-Came, and Author of "Breviates from Holy Scripture," &c. Fcap. 8vo., cloth, 2s. 6d.

Questions on the Collects, Epistles, and Gospels,
Throughout the Year. Edited by the Rev. T. L. CLAUGHTON, Vicar of Kidderminster. For the Use of Teachers in Sunday Schools. Fifth Edition, 18mo., cl. In two Parts, *each* 2s. 6d.

Pleas for the Faith.
Especially designed for the use of Missionaries at Home and Abroad. By the Rev. W. SOMERVILLE LACH SZYRMA, M.A., St. Augustine's College, Canterbury. Fcap. 8vo., cl., 2s. 6d.

MEDITATIONS FOR THE FORTY DAYS OF LENT.
With a Prefatory Notice by the ARCHBISHOP OF DUBLIN. 18mo., cloth, 2s. 6d.

DAILY STEPS TOWARDS HEAVEN;
Or, PRACTICAL THOUGHTS on the GOSPEL HISTORY, and especially on the Life and Teaching of our Lord Jesus Christ, for Every Day in the Year, according to the Christian Seasons, with the Titles and Character of Christ, and a Harmony of the Four Gospels. Newly printed, with antique type. Fortieth thousand. 32mo., roan, gilt edges, 2s. 6d.; morocco, 5.
LARGE-TYPE EDITION. Square Crown 8vo., cloth antique, red edges, 5s.

ANNUS DOMINI.
A Prayer for each Day of the Year, founded on a Text of Holy Scripture. By CHRISTINA G. ROSSETTI. 32mo., cl., 3s. 6d.

LITURGIA DOMESTICA:
Services for every Morning and Evening in the Week. Third Edition. 18mo., 2s. Or in two Parts, 1s. each.

EARL NELSON'S FAMILY PRAYERS.
With Responsions and Variations for the different Seasons, for General Use. New and improved Edition, *large type*, cloth, 2s.

OF THE IMITATION OF CHRIST.
Four Books. By THOMAS A KEMPIS. Small 4to., printed on thick toned paper, with red border-lines, mediæval title-pages, ornamental initials, &c. Third Thousand. Cloth, 12s.

PRAYERS FOR MARRIED PERSONS.
From Various Sources, chiefly from the Ancient Liturgies. Selected and Edited by CHARLES WARD, M.A., Rector of Maulden. Second Edition, Revised. 24mo., cloth, 4s. 6d.

FOR THE LORD'S SUPPER.
DEVOTIONS BEFORE AND AFTER HOLY COMMUNION. With Preface by J. KEBLE. Sixth Edition. 32mo., cloth, 2s.
With the Office, cloth, 2s. 6d.
DEVOUT COMMUNION, from HORST. 18mo., cloth, 1s.
OFFICIUM EUCHARISTICUM. By EDWARD LAKE, D.D. New Edition. 32mo., cloth, 1s. 6d.
A SHORT AND PLAIN INSTRUCTION FOR THE BETTER UNDERSTANDING OF THE LORD'S SUPPER. By BISHOP WILSON. 32mo., with Rubrics, cloth, gilt edges, 2s.
——————— 32mo., limp cloth, 8d.; sewed, 6d.
——————— 24mo., limp cloth, 1s.

OXFORD, AND 377, STRAND, LONDON.

Oxford Editions of Devotional Works.

Fcap. 8vo., chiefly printed in Red and Black, on Toned Paper.

Andrewes' Devotions.
DEVOTIONS. By the Right Rev. LANCELOT ANDREWES. Translated from the Greek and Latin, and arranged anew. Cloth, 5s.

The Imitation of Christ.
FOUR BOOKS. By THOMAS A KEMPIS. A new Edition, revised. Cloth, 4s.

Laud's Devotions.
THE PRIVATE DEVOTIONS of Dr. WILLIAM LAUD, Archbishop of Canterbury, and Martyr. Antique cloth, 5s.

Spinckes' Devotions.
TRUE CHURCH OF ENGLAND MAN'S COMPANION IN THE CLOSET. By NATHANIEL SPINCKES. Floriated borders, antique cloth, 4s.

Sutton's Meditations.
GODLY MEDITATIONS UPON THE MOST HOLY SACRAMENT OF THE LORD'S SUPPER. By CHRISTOPHER SUTTON, D.D., late Prebend of Westminster. A new Edition. Antique cloth, 5s.

Taylor's Golden Grove.
THE GOLDEN GROVE: A Choice Manual, containing what is to be Believed, Practised, and Desired or Prayed for. By BISHOP JEREMY TAYLOR. Antique cloth, 3s. 6d.

Taylor's Holy Living.
THE RULE AND EXERCISES OF HOLY LIVING. By BISHOP JEREMY TAYLOR. Ant. cloth, 4s.

Taylor's Holy Dying.
THE RULE AND EXERCISES OF HOLY DYING. By BISHOP JEREMY TAYLOR. Ant. cloth, 4s.

Wilson's Sacra Privata.
THE PRIVATE MEDITATIONS, DEVOTIONS, and PRAYERS of the Right Rev. T. WILSON, D.D., Lord Bishop of Sodor and Man. Now first printed entire. Cloth, 4s.

Ancient Collects.
ANCIENT COLLECTS AND OTHER PRAYERS, Selected for Devotional Use from various Rituals, with an Appendix on the Collects in the Prayer-book. By WILLIAM BRIGHT, D.D. Fourth Edition. Antique cloth, 5s.

Devout Communicant.
THE DEVOUT COMMUNICANT, exemplified in his Behaviour before, at, and after the Sacrament of the Lord's Supper: Practically suited to all the Parts of that Solemn Ordinance. 7th Edition, revised. Edited by Rev. G. MOULTRIE. Fcap. 8vo., toned paper, red lines, ant.cl., 4s.

ΕΙΚΩΝ ΒΑΣΙΛΙΚΗ.
THE PORTRAITURE OF HIS SACRED MAJESTY KING CHARLES 1. in his Solitudes and Sufferings. Cloth, 5s.

THE AUTHORIZED EDITIONS OF
THE CHRISTIAN YEAR,
With the Author's latest Corrections and Additions,

NOTICE.—Messrs. PARKER are the sole Publishers of the Editions of the "Christian Year" issued with the sanction and under the direction of the Author's representatives. All Editions without their imprint are unauthorized.

SMALL 4to. EDITION.	s.	d.	32mo. EDITION.	s.	d.
Handsomely printed on toned paper, with red border lines and initial letters. Cl. extra	10	6	Cloth, limp	1	0
			Cloth boards, gilt edges	1	6
DEMY 8vo. EDITION.			48mo. EDITION.		
Cloth	6	0	Cloth, limp	0	6
			Roan	1	6
FOOLSCAP 8vo. EDITION.			FACSIMILE OF THE 1ST EDITION, with a list of the variations from the Original Text which the Author made in later Editions.		
Cloth	3	6			
24mo. EDITION.					
Cloth	2	0			
Ditto, with red lines	2	6	2 vols., 12mo., boards	7	6

The above Editions (except the Facsimile of the First Edition) are kept in a variety of bindings, the chief of which are Morocco plain, Morocco Antique, Calf Antique, and Vellum.

By the same Author.

LYRA INNOCENTIUM. Thoughts in Verse on Christian Children. *Thirteenth Edition.* Fcap. 8vo., cl., 5s.

———————— 48mo. edition, limp cloth, 6d.; cloth boards, 1s.

MISCELLANEOUS POEMS BY THE REV. JOHN KEBLE, M.A., Vicar of Hursley. *Third Edition.* Fcap., cloth, 6s.

THE PSALTER, OR PSALMS OF DAVID: In English Verse. *Fourth Edition.* Fcap., cloth, 6s.

The above may also be had in various bindings.

By the late Rev. ISAAC WILLIAMS.

THE CATHEDRAL; or, The Catholic and Apostolic Church in England. 32mo., cloth, 2s. 6d.

THE BAPTISTERY; or, The Way of Eternal Life, with Plates by BOETIUS A BOLSWEET. Fcap. 8vo., cloth, 7s. 6d.; 32mo., cloth, 2s. 6d.

HYMNS translated from the PARISIAN BREVIARY. 32mo., cloth, 2s. 6d.

THE CHRISTIAN SCHOLAR. Fcap. 8vo., cl., 5s.; 32mo., cloth, 2s. 6d.

THOUGHTS IN PAST YEARS. 32mo., cloth, 2s. 6d.

THE SEVEN DAYS; or, The Old and New Creation. Fcap. 8vo., cloth, 3s. 6d.

The Late Bishop Wilberforce.

Sermons preached before the University of Oxford: Second Series, from 1847 to 1862. By the late Samuel Wilberforce, Lord Bishop of Winchester. 8vo., cloth, 10s. 6d.
——— Third Series, from 1863 to 1870. 8vo., cloth, 7s. 6d.
Sermons preached on Various Occasions. With a Preface by the Lord Bishop of Ely. 8vo., cloth, 7s. 6d.

Rev. E. B. Pusey, D.D.

Parochial Sermons. Vol. I. From Advent to Whitsuntide. Seventh Edition. 8vo., cloth, 6s.
Parochial Sermons. Vol. II. Sixth Edition. 8vo., cloth, 6s.
Parochial Sermons. Vol. III. Reprinted from the "Plain Sermons by Contributors to the 'Tracts for the Times.'" Revised Edition, 8vo., cloth, 6s.
Parochial Sermons preached and printed on Various Occasions. 8vo., cloth, 6s.
Sermons preached before the University of Oxford, between A.D. 1859 and 1872. 8vo., cloth, 6s.
Lenten Sermons, preached chiefly to Young Men at the Universities, between A.D. 1858—1874. 8vo., cloth, 6s.
Eleven Short Addresses during a Retreat of the Companions of the Love of Jesus, engaged in Perpetual Intercession for the Conversion of Sinners. 8vo., cloth, 3s. 6d.

The Lord Bishop of Salisbury.

Sermons on the Beatitudes, with others mostly preached before the University of Oxford; to which is added a Preface relating to the volume of "Essays and Reviews." New Edition. Crown 8vo., cloth, 7s. 6d.

Rev. J. Keble.

Sermons for the Christian Year. By the Rev. John Keble, Author of "The Christian Year."

For Advent to Christmas Eve (46). 8vo., cloth, 6s.
For Christmas and Epiphany (48). 8vo., cloth, 6s.
For Septuagesima to Lent. 1 vol., *in preparation.*
For Lent to Passiontide (46). 8vo., cloth, 6s.
For Holy Week (57). 8vo., cloth, 6s.
For Easter to Ascension-Day (48). 8vo., cloth, 6s.
For Ascension-Day to Trinity Sunday (41). 8vo., cl., 6s.
For Saints' Days, (48). 8vo., cloth, 6s.

Village Sermons on the Baptismal Service. 8vo., cloth, 5s.
Sermons, Occasional and Parochial. 8vo., cloth, 12s.

The City of the Lost, and XIX. other Short Allegorical Sermons.
By Walter A. Gray, M.A. (Π.), Vicar of Arksey;—and B. Kerr Pearse, M.A. (Φ.), Rector of Ascot Heath. Fourth Edition. Fcap., cloth, 2s. 6d. *Cheap Edition*, sewed, 1s.

Characteristics of Christian Morality.
The Bampton Lectures for 1873. By the Rev. I. Gregory Smith, M.A., late Fellow of Brasenose College, Oxford; Vicar of Malvern, &c. Second Edition, Crown 8vo., cloth, 3s. 6d.

Rev. E. Monro.
Illustrations of Faith. Eight Plain Sermons. Fcap. 8vo., cloth, 2s. 6d.

Plain Sermons on the Book of Common Prayer. Fcap. 8vo., cloth, 5s.

Historical and Practical Sermons on the Sufferings and Resurrection of our Lord. 2 vols., Fcap. 8vo., cloth, 10s.

Sermons on New Testament Characters. Fcap. 8vo., 4s.

Lenten Sermons at Oxford.
Re-issue of the Series of Sermons preached at St. Mary's, &c.

The Series for 1857. 8vo., cloth, 5s.
For 1858. 8vo., cloth, 5s.
For 1859. 8vo., cloth, 5s.
For 1863. 8vo., cloth, 5s.
For 1865. 8vo., cloth, 5s.
For 1866. 8vo., cloth, 5s.
For 1867. 8vo., cloth, 5s.
For 1868. 8vo., cloth, 5s.
For 1869. 8vo., cloth, 5s.
For 1870-1. 8vo., cloth, 5s.

Short Sermons for Family Reading,
Following the Course of the Christian Seasons. By the Very Rev. J. W. Burgon, B.D., Dean of Chichester. First Series. 2 vols., Fcap. 8vo., cloth, 8s.

——— Second Series. 2 vols., Fcap. 8vo., cloth, 8s.

Rt. Rev. J. Armstrong, D.D.
Parochial Sermons. By the late Lord Bishop of Grahamstown. Fifth Edition. Fcap. 8vo., cloth, 5s.

Sermons on the Fasts and Festivals. Third Edition. Fcap. 8vo., cloth, 5s.

Sermons for the Christian Seasons.
Sermons for the Christian Seasons. First Series. Edited by John Armstrong, D.D., late Lord Bishop of Grahamstown. 4 vols., Fcap. 8vo., cloth, 10s.

——————————— Second Series. Edited by the Rev. John Barrow, D.D., late Principal of St. Edmund Hall, Oxford. 4 vols., Fcap. 8vo., cloth, 10s.

THE CLERGYMAN'S
DESK CALENDAR,
1878.

THE above consists of pages 2 to 14 and 63 of this CALENDAR, containing the DAILY AND PROPER LESSONS, &c., and is interleaved for Memoranda. It will be found convenient for use on READING DESKS in Churches.

Second Annual Issue, price 2d.

To be obtained of the Publishers of the
DIOCESAN CALENDAR.

Crown 8vo., in roan binding, 12s.; calf limp, or calf antique, 16s.; best morocco, or limp morocco, 18s.

The Service-Book of the Church of England,

Being a New Edition of "The Daily Services of the Church of England and Ireland,"

Arranged according to the new Table of Lessons.

The new "Prayer-book (Table of Lessons) Act, 1871," has necessitated reprinting nearly the whole book, and opportunity has been taken of still further adding to the improvements.

The Lessons appointed for the Immoveable festivals are printed entire in the course of the Daily Lessons where they occur. For the Sundays and Moveable Festivals, and for the days dependent on them, a table containing fuller references, with the initial words and ample directions where the Lesson may be found, is given. Where the Lesson for the Moveable Feast is not included entire amongst the Daily Lessons, it is printed in full in its proper place. Also in the part containing Daily Lessons, greater facilities have been provided for verifying the references.

There are also many modifications in the arrangement, wherein this Service-book differs from the Prayer-book: the Order for the Administration of the Holy Communion is printed as a distinct service, with the Collects, Epistles, and Gospels, which belong to the same: the Psalms immediately follow Daily Morning and Evening Prayer: the Morning and Evening Lessons also are by this arrangement brought nearer to the Service to which they belong, while the Occasional Offices are transferred to the end of the book.

JAMES PARKER AND CO., OXFORD AND LONDON.

www.ingramcontent.com/pod-product-compliance
Lightning Source LLC
Chambersburg PA
CBHW022018240426

43667CB00042B/938